BLACK PANTHER

THE INTERGALACTIC EMPIRE OF WAKANDA

PART ONE: MANY THOUSANDS GONE

Ta-Nehisi Coates
WRITER

◇◇◇◇◇◇◇◇◇◇◇◇◇◇ ISSUES #1-5 ◇◇◇◇◇◇◇◇◇◇◇◇◇◇

Daniel Acuña
ARTIST

SPECIAL THANKS TO **David Navarro**

◇◇◇◇◇◇◇◇◇◇◇◇◇◇ ISSUE #6 ◇◇◇◇◇◇◇◇◇◇◇◇◇◇

Jen Bartel
ARTIST

Paul Reinwand
LAYOUTS

Tríona Farrell
COLOR ARTIST

VC's Joe Sabino
LETTERER

Daniel Acuña (#1-2), **InHyuk Lee** (#3) and **Paolo Rivera** & **Daniel Acuña** (#4-6)
COVER ART

Sarah Brunstad
ASSOCIATE EDITOR

Wil Moss
EDITOR

BLACK PANTHER CREATED BY
Stan Lee & **Jack Kirby**

COLLECTION EDITOR **JENNIFER GRÜNWALD**
ASSISTANT EDITOR **CAITLIN O'CONNELL**
ASSOCIATE MANAGING EDITOR **KATERI WOODY**
EDITOR, SPECIAL PROJECTS **MARK D. BEAZLEY**
VP PRODUCTION & SPECIAL PROJECTS **JEFF YOUNGQUIST**
SVP PRINT, SALES & MARKETING **DAVID GABRIEL**

BOOK DESIGNER **ADAM DEL RE**

EDITOR IN CHIEF **C.B. CEBULSKI**
CHIEF CREATIVE OFFICER **JOE QUESADA**
PRESIDENT **DAN BUCKLEY**
EXECUTIVE PRODUCER **ALAN FINE**

BLACK PANTHER BOOK 6: INTERGALACTIC EMPIRE OF WAKANDA PART 1. Contains material originally published in magazine form as BLACK PANTHER #1-6. First printing 2018. ISBN 978-1-302-91293-2. Published by MARVEL WORLDWIDE, INC., a subsidiary of MARVEL ENTERTAINMENT, LLC. OFFICE OF PUBLICATION: 135 West 50th Street, New York, NY 10020. Copyright © 2018 MARVEL No similarity between any of the names, characters, persons, and/or institutions in this magazine with those of any living or dead person or institution is intended, and any such similarity which may exist is purely coincidental. Printed in the U.S.A. DAN BUCKLEY, President, Marvel Entertainment; JOHN NEE, Publisher; JOE QUESADA, Chief Creative Officer; TOM BREVOORT, SVP of Publishing; DAVID BOGART, SVP of Business Affairs & Operations, Publishing & Partnership; DAVID GABRIEL, SVP of Sales & Marketing, Publishing; JEFF YOUNGQUIST, VP of Production & Special Projects; DAN CARR, Executive Director of Publishing Technology; ALEX MORALES, Director of Publishing Operations; DAN EDINGTON, Managing Editor; SUSAN CRESPI, Production Manager; STAN LEE, Chairman Emeritus. For information regarding advertising in Marvel Comics or on Marvel.com, please contact Vit DeBellis, Custom Solutions & Integrated Advertising Manager, at vdebellis@marvel.com. For Marvel subscription inquiries, please call 888-511-5480. Manufactured between 11/30/2018 and 1/1/2019 by LSC COMMUNICATIONS INC., KENDALLVILLE, IN, USA.

10 9 8 7 6 5 4 3 2 1

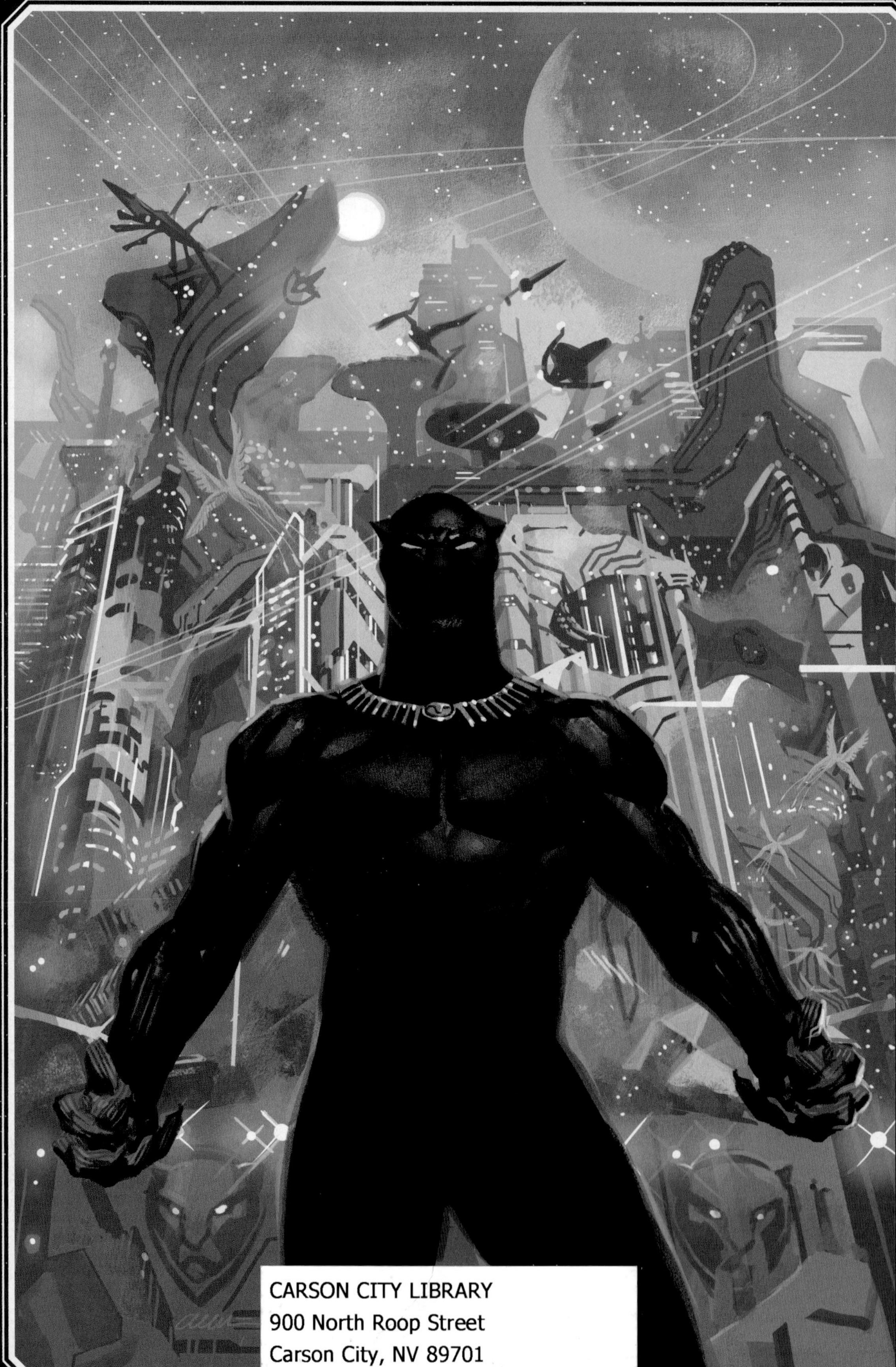

THE INTERGALACTIC EMPIRE OF WAKANDA

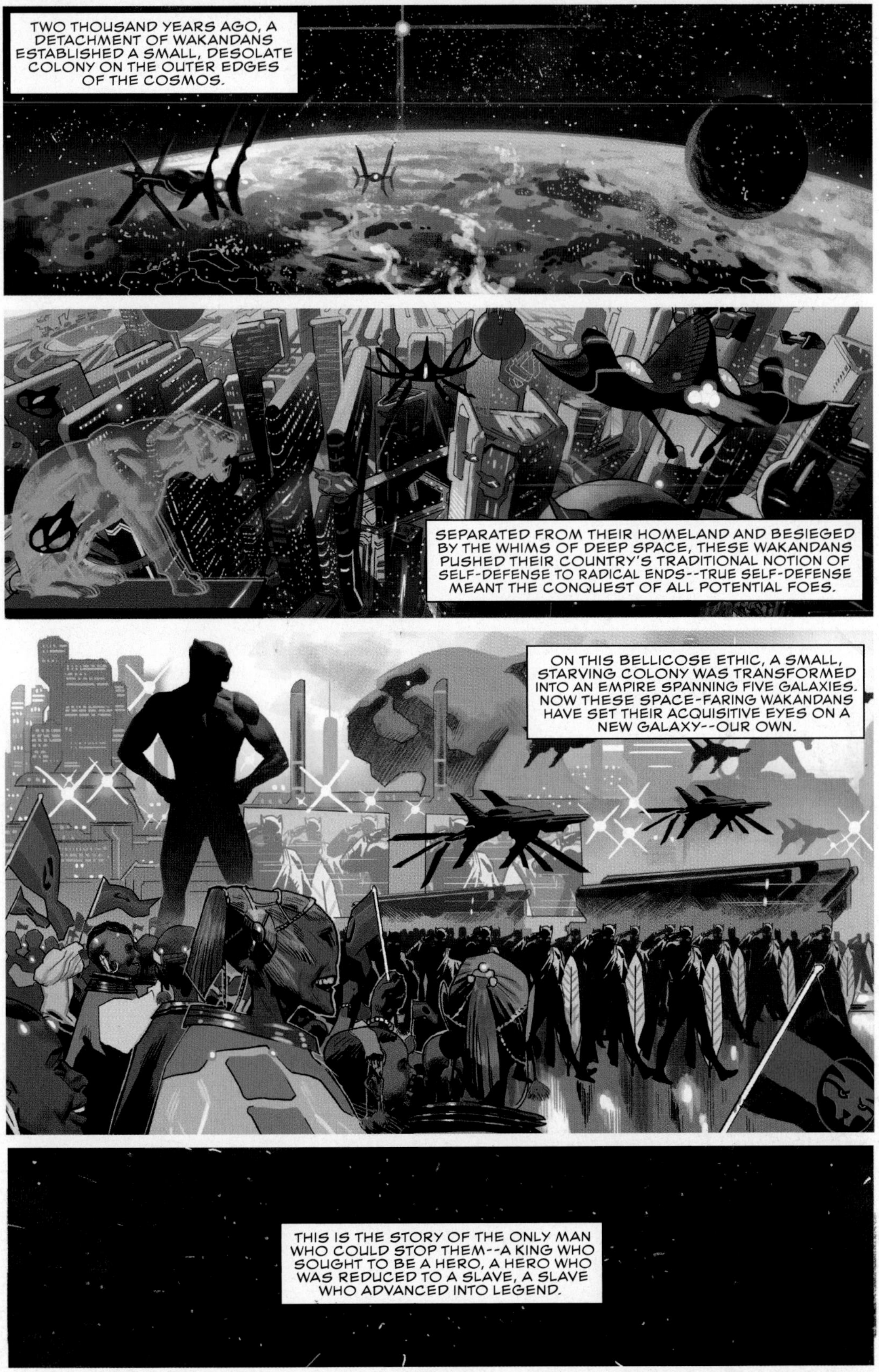
TWO THOUSAND YEARS AGO, A DETACHMENT OF WAKANDANS ESTABLISHED A SMALL, DESOLATE COLONY ON THE OUTER EDGES OF THE COSMOS.
SEPARATED FROM THEIR HOMELAND AND BESIEGED BY THE WHIMS OF DEEP SPACE, THESE WAKANDANS PUSHED THEIR COUNTRY'S TRADITIONAL NOTION OF SELF-DEFENSE TO RADICAL ENDS--TRUE SELF-DEFENSE MEANT THE CONQUEST OF ALL POTENTIAL FOES.
ON THIS BELLICOSE ETHIC, A SMALL, STARVING COLONY WAS TRANSFORMED INTO AN EMPIRE SPANNING FIVE GALAXIES. NOW THESE SPACE-FARING WAKANDANS HAVE SET THEIR ACQUISITIVE EYES ON A NEW GALAXY--OUR OWN.
THIS IS THE STORY OF THE ONLY MAN WHO COULD STOP THEM--A KING WHO SOUGHT TO BE A HERO, A HERO WHO WAS REDUCED TO A SLAVE, A SLAVE WHO ADVANCED INTO LEGEND.

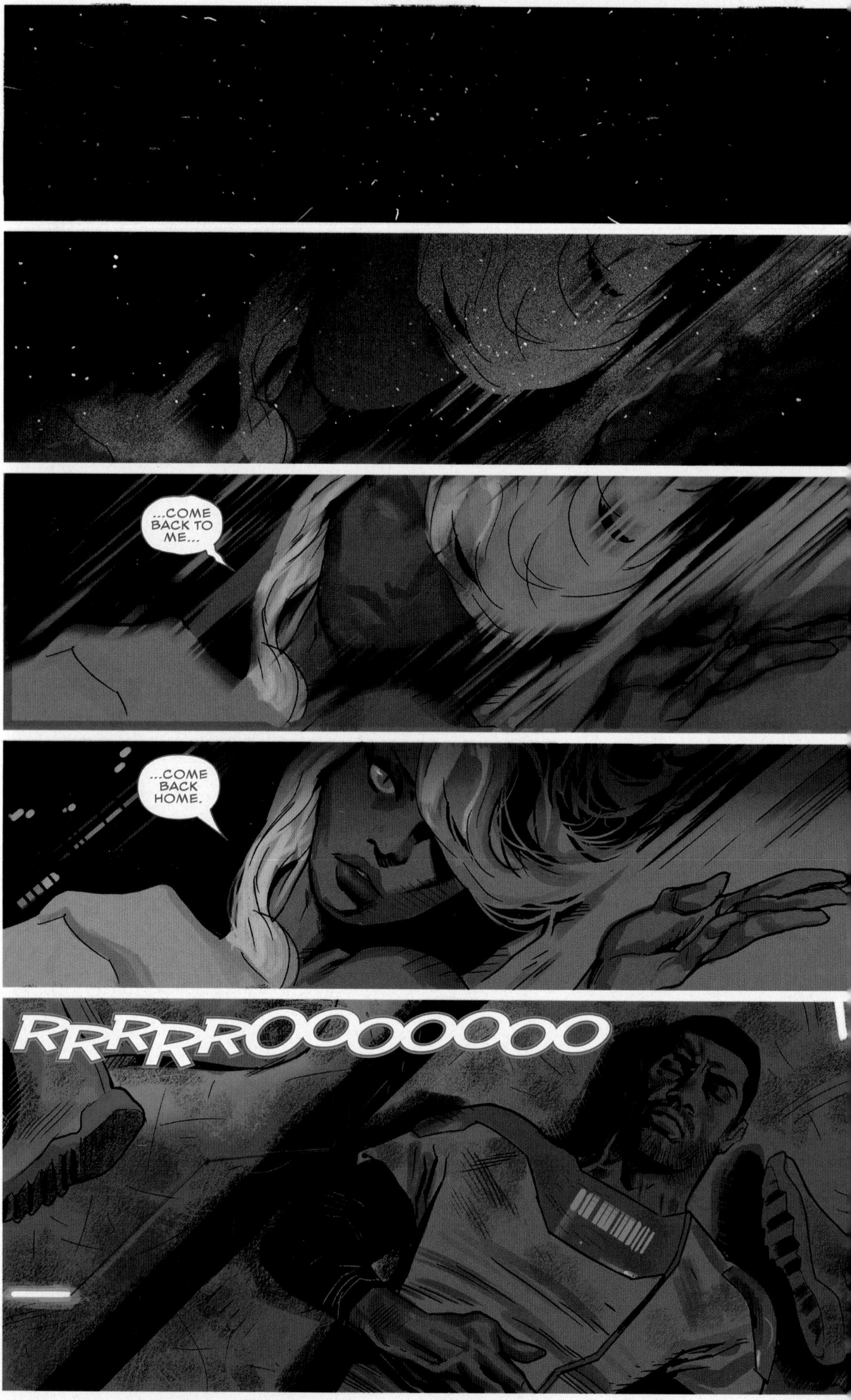
...COME BACK TO ME...
...COME BACK HOME.
RRRRROOOOOOOO

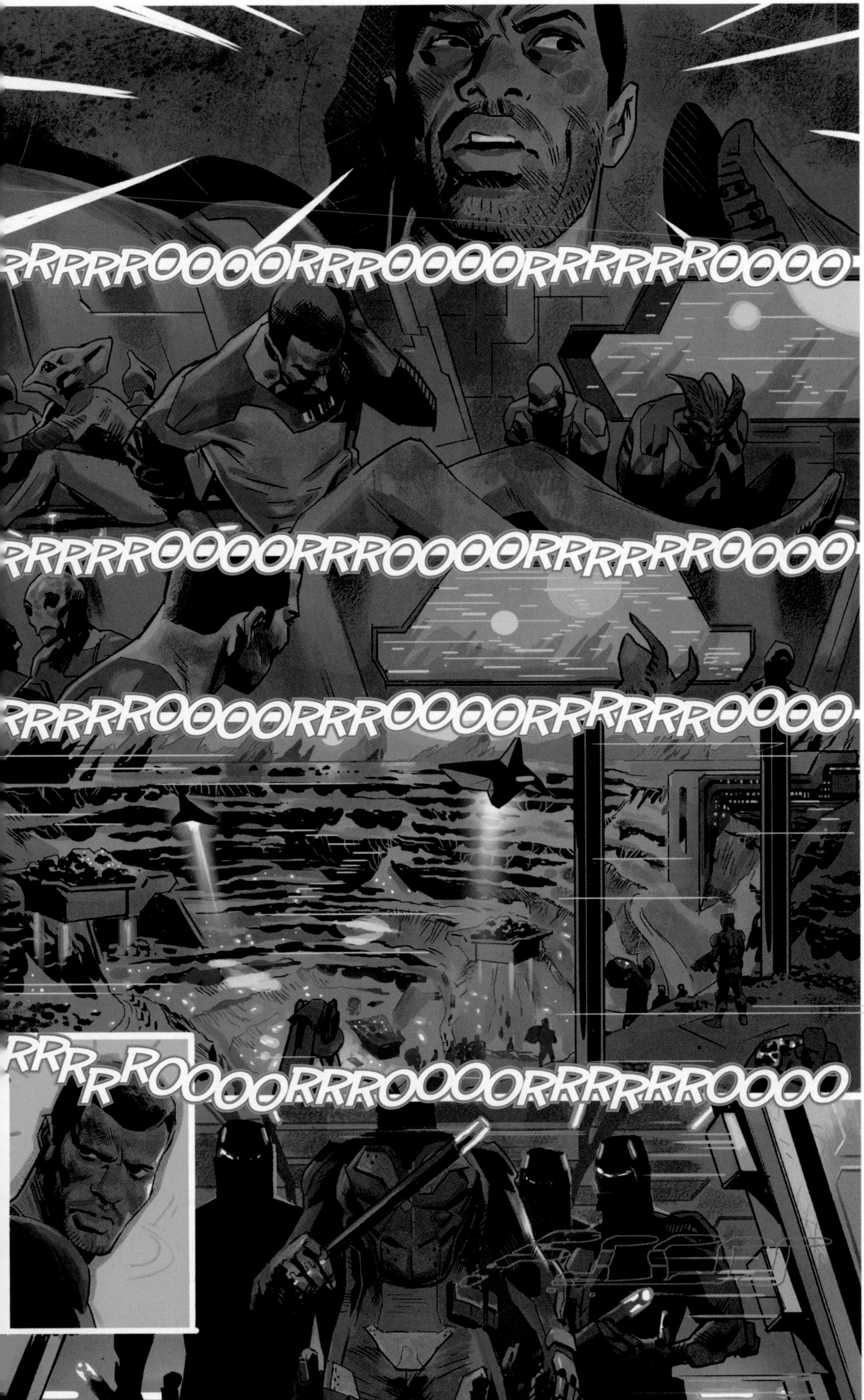
RRRRROOOORRROOOOORRRRRROOOO
RRRRROOOORRROOOOORRRRRROOOO
RRRRROOOORRROOOOORRRRRROOOO
RRRRROOOORRROOOOORRRRRROOOO

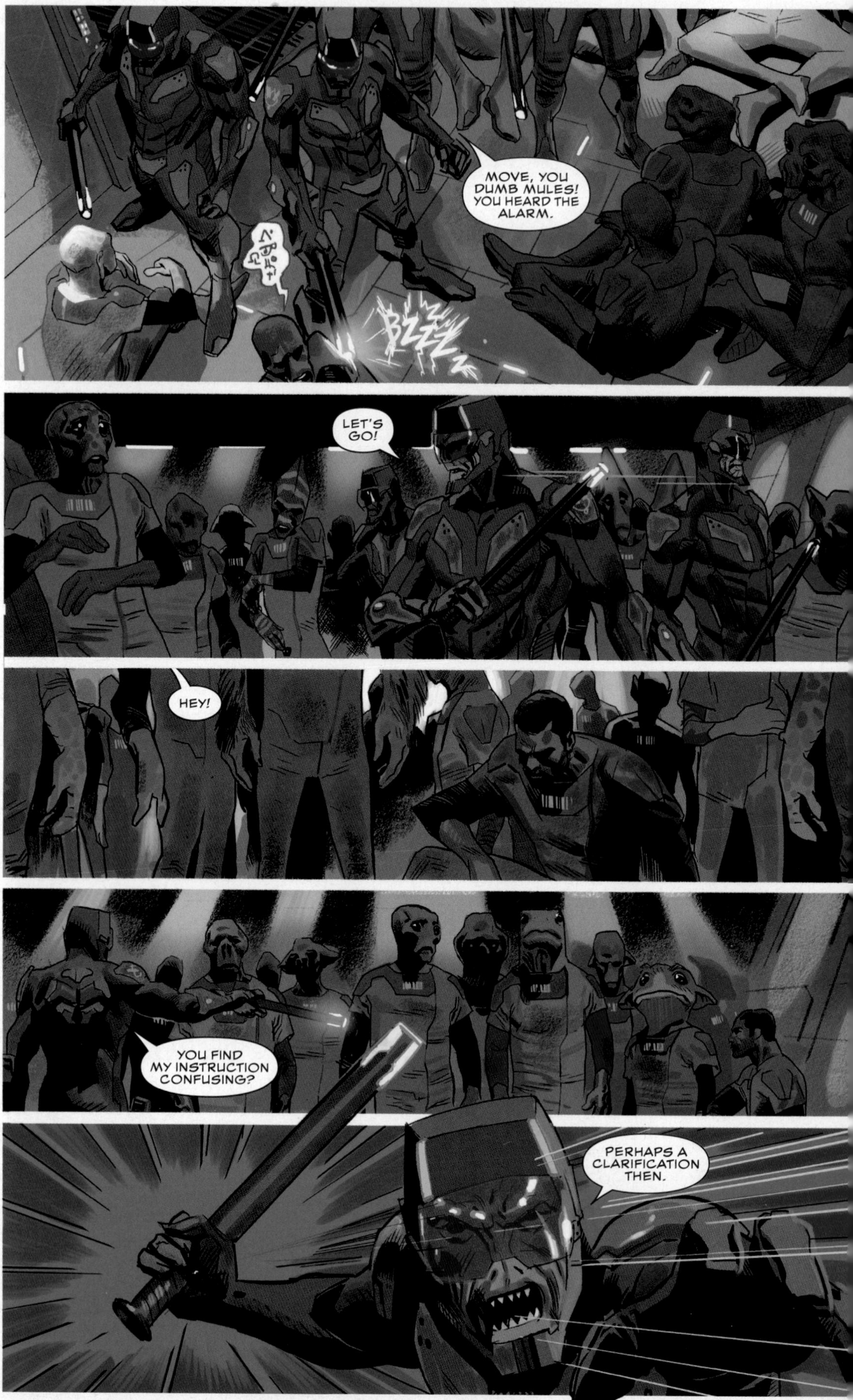
MOVE, YOU DUMB MULES! YOU HEARD THE ALARM.
BZZZZ
LET'S GO!
HEY!
YOU FIND MY INSTRUCTION CONFUSING?
PERHAPS A CLARIFICATION THEN.

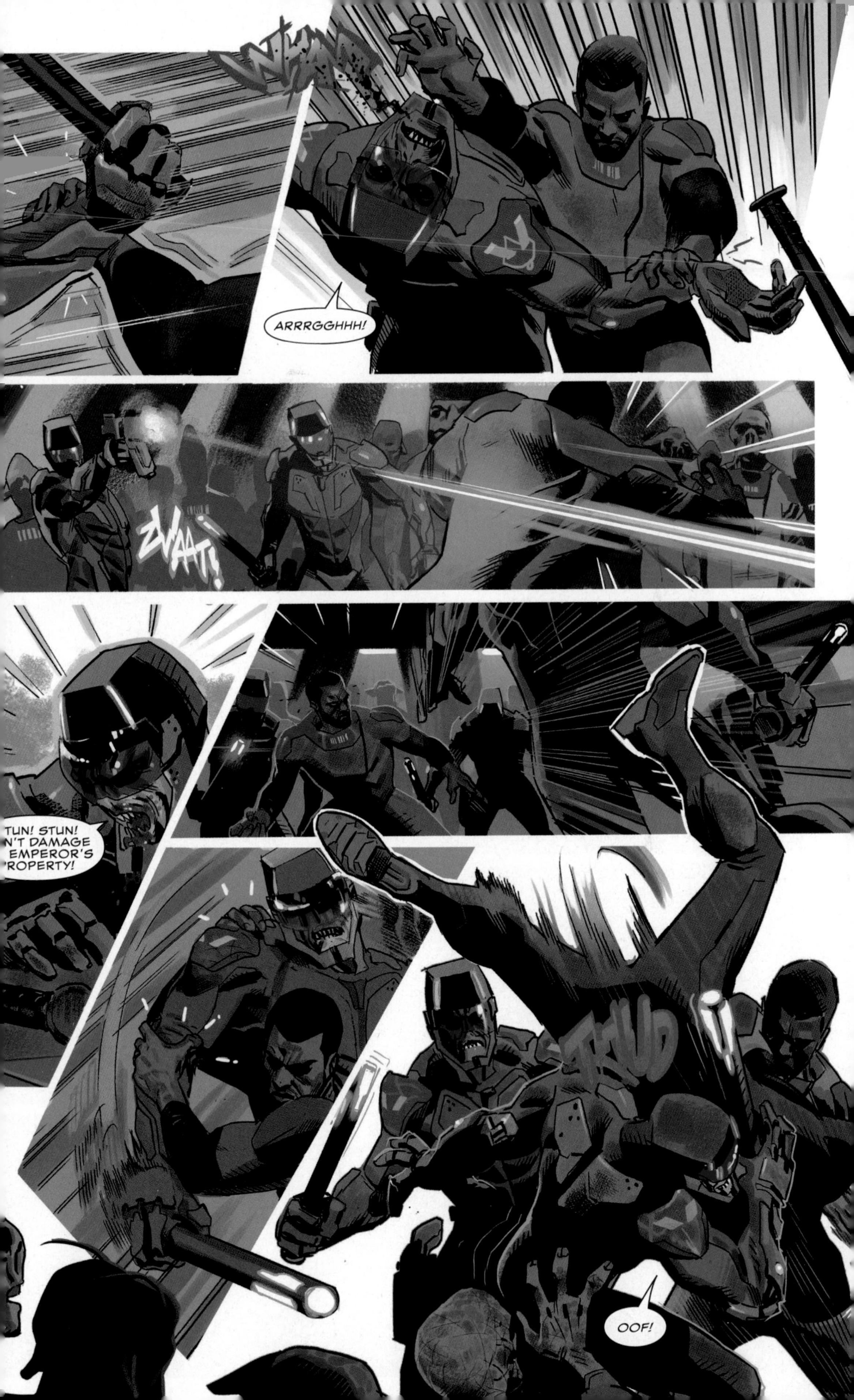
WHUMP
ARRRGGHHH!
ZVAAT!
TUN! STUN!
N'T DAMAGE
EMPEROR'S
ROPERTY!
THUD
OOF!

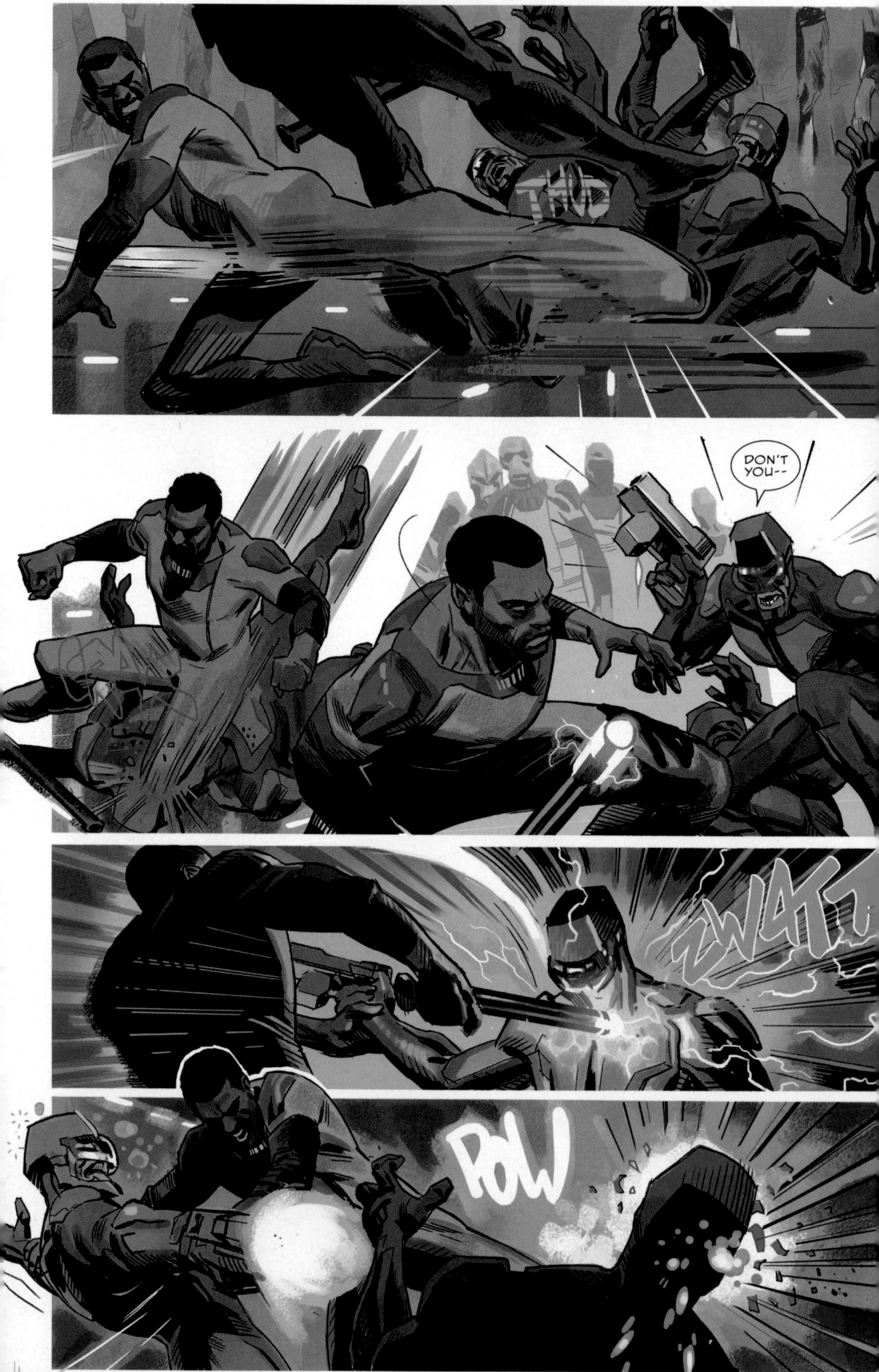
THUD
DON'T YOU--
ZWATT
POW

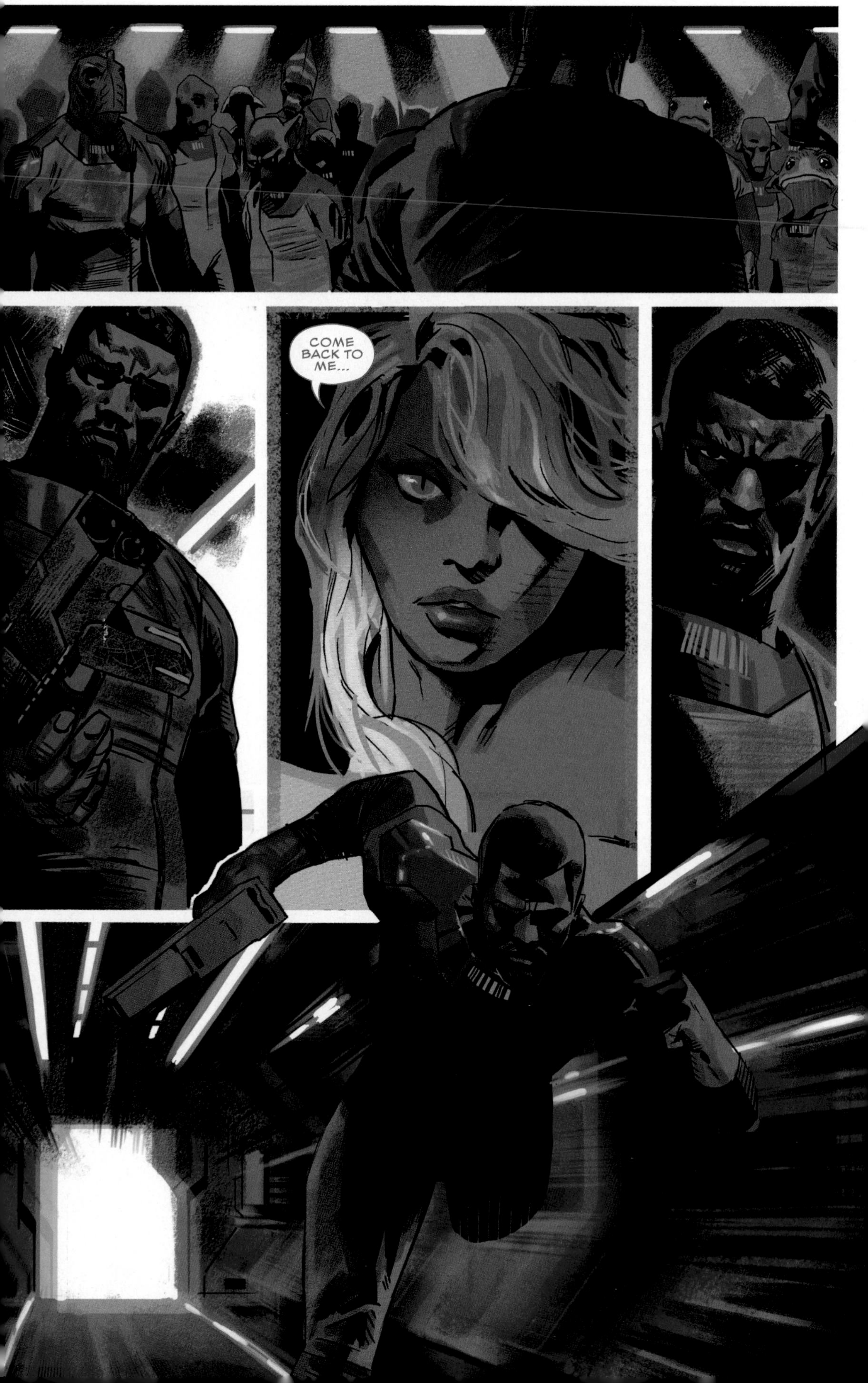
COME BACK TO ME...

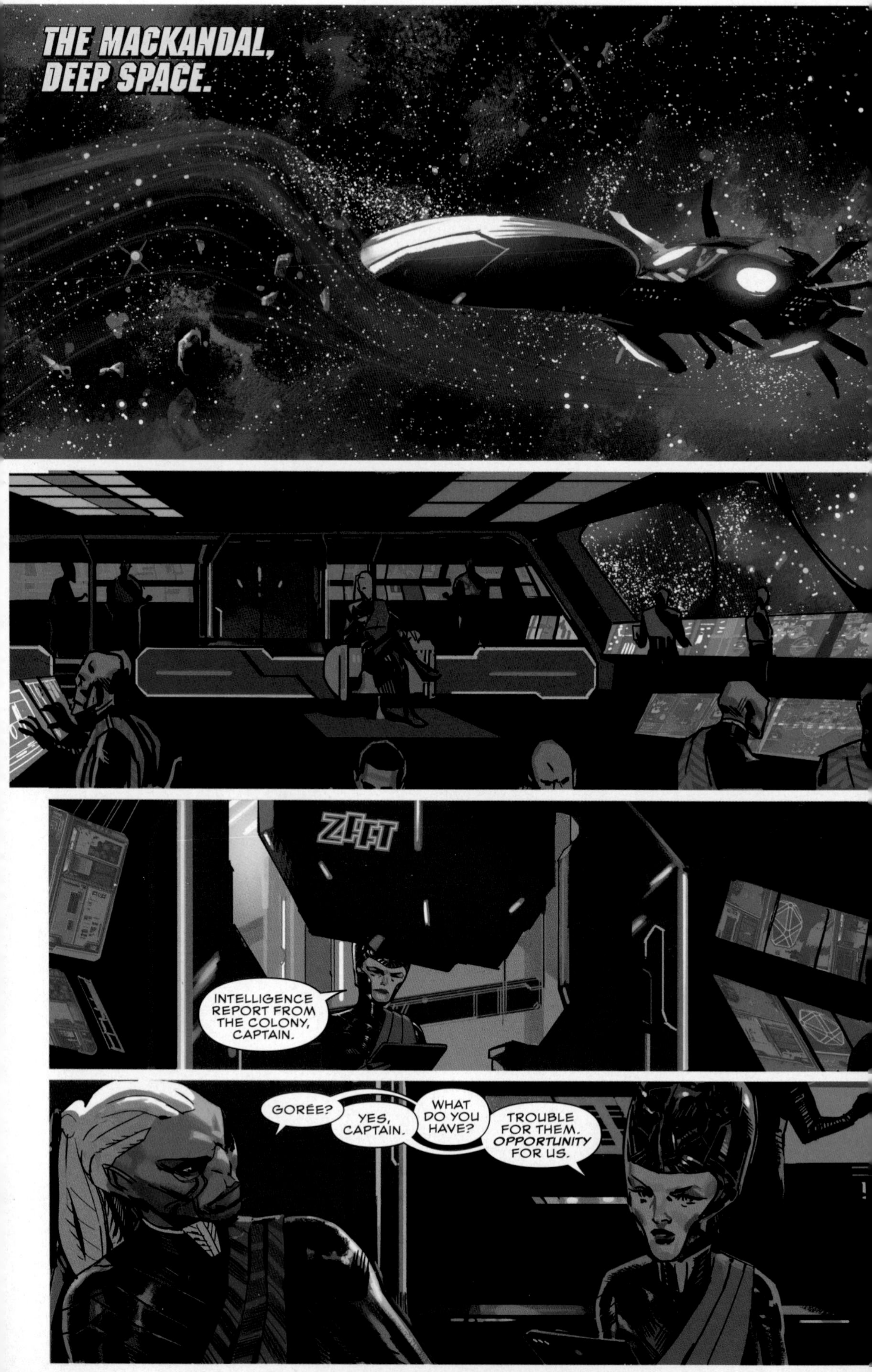
THE MACKANDAL, DEEP SPACE.
ZFFT
INTELLIGENCE REPORT FROM THE COLONY, CAPTAIN.
GORÉE?
YES, CAPTAIN.
WHAT DO YOU HAVE?
TROUBLE FOR THEM. OPPORTUNITY FOR US.

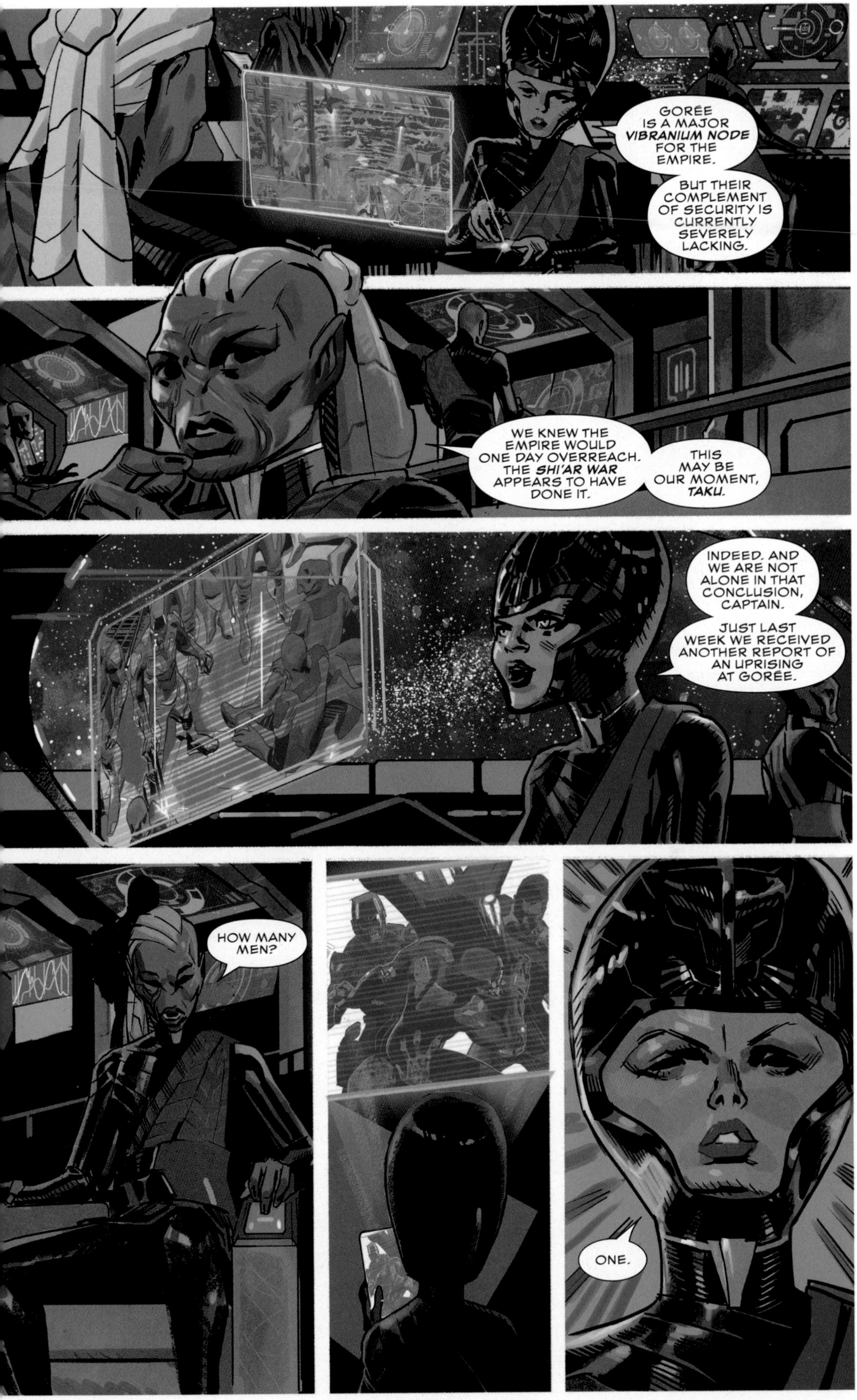
GORÉE IS A MAJOR VIBRANIUM NODE FOR THE EMPIRE.
BUT THEIR COMPLEMENT OF SECURITY IS CURRENTLY SEVERELY LACKING.
WE KNEW THE EMPIRE WOULD ONE DAY OVERREACH. THE SHI'AR WAR APPEARS TO HAVE DONE IT.
THIS MAY BE OUR MOMENT, TAKU.
INDEED. AND WE ARE NOT ALONE IN THAT CONCLUSION, CAPTAIN.
JUST LAST WEEK WE RECEIVED ANOTHER REPORT OF AN UPRISING AT GORÉE.
HOW MANY MEN?
ONE.

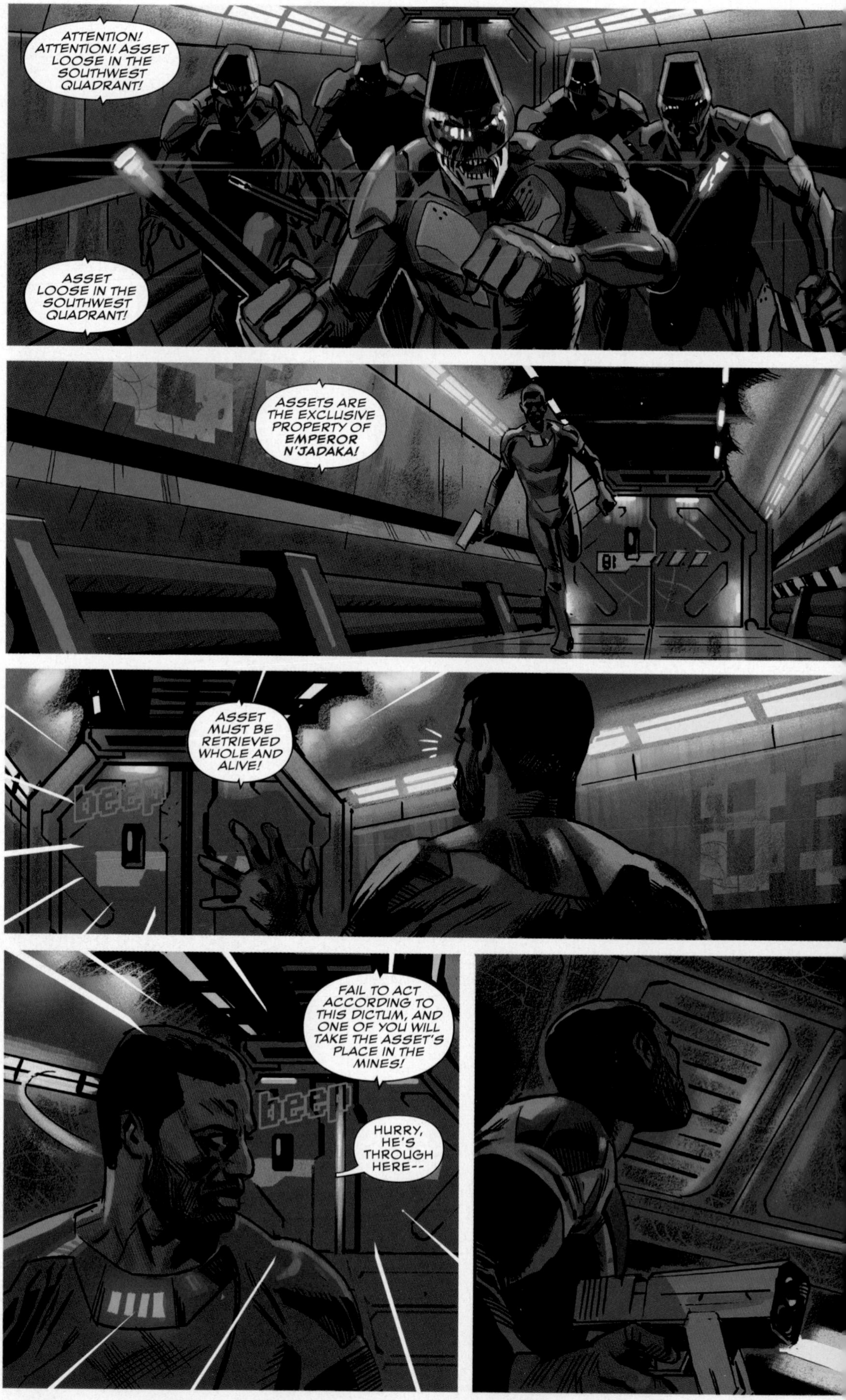
ATTENTION! ATTENTION! ASSET LOOSE IN THE SOUTHWEST QUADRANT!
ASSET LOOSE IN THE SOUTHWEST QUADRANT!
ASSETS ARE THE EXCLUSIVE PROPERTY OF EMPEROR N'JADAKA!
ASSET MUST BE RETRIEVED WHOLE AND ALIVE!
beep
FAIL TO ACT ACCORDING TO THIS DICTUM, AND ONE OF YOU WILL TAKE THE ASSET'S PLACE IN THE MINES!
beep
HURRY, HE'S THROUGH HERE--

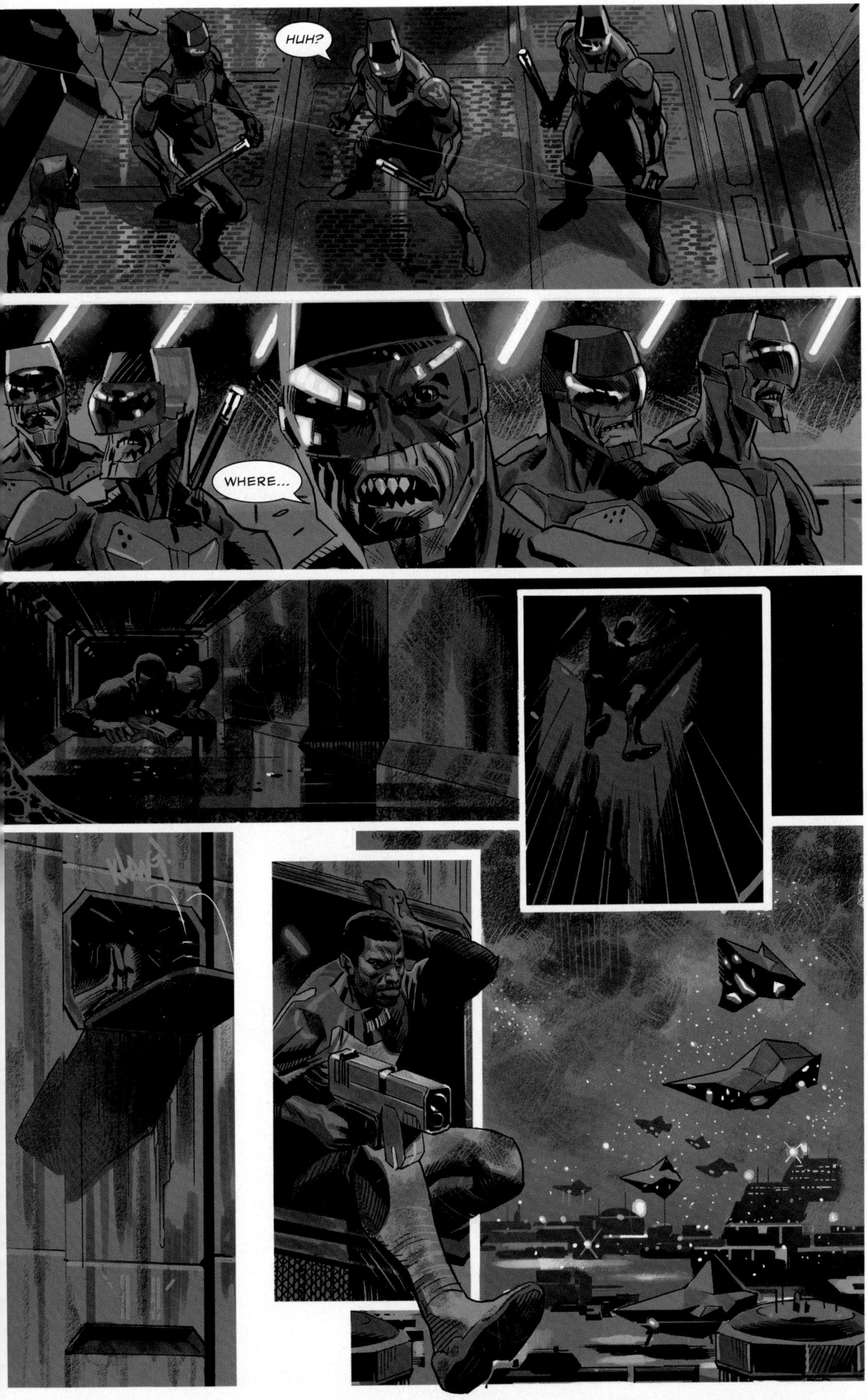
HUH?
WHERE...

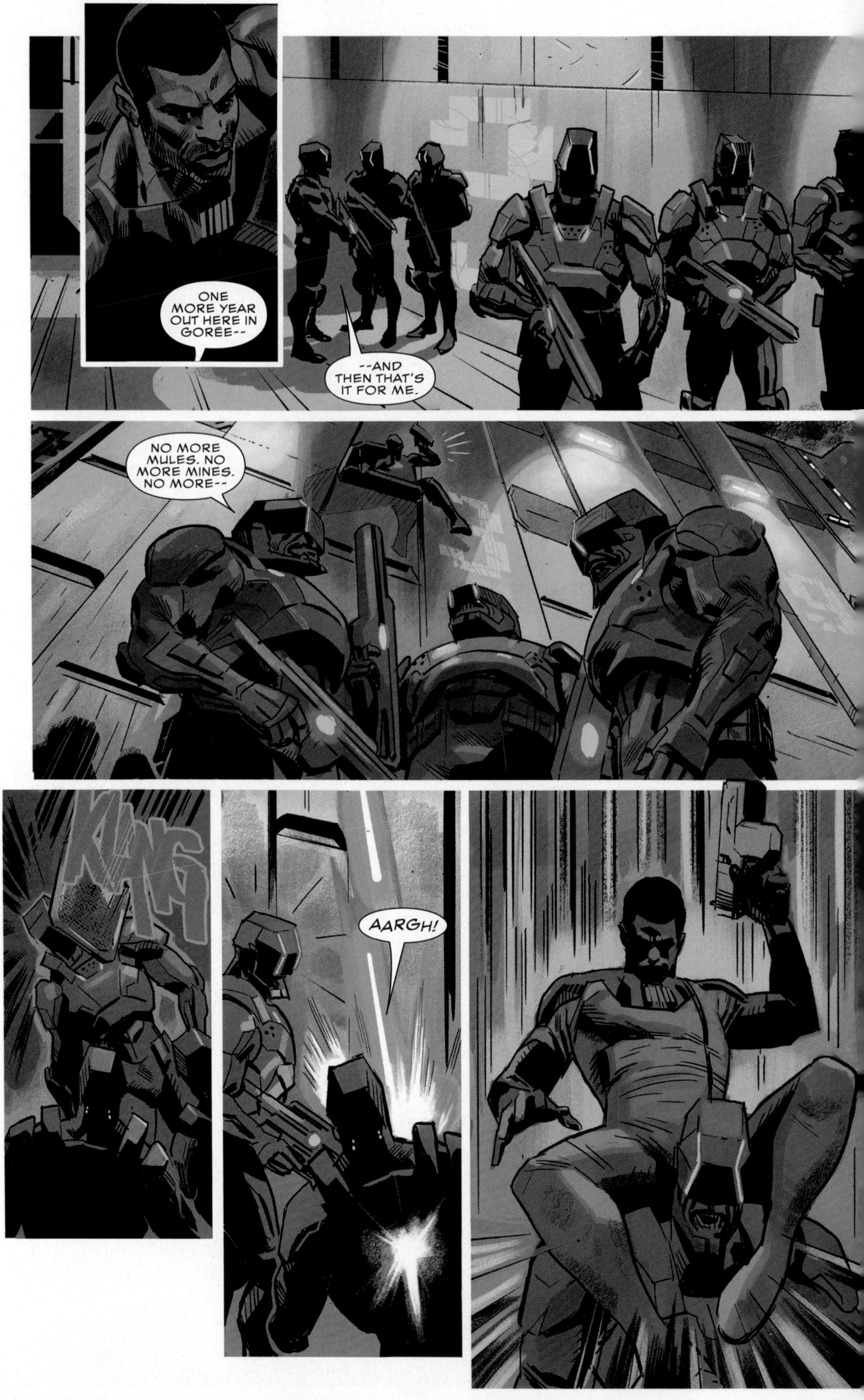
ONE MORE YEAR OUT HERE IN GORÉE--
--AND THEN THAT'S IT FOR ME.
NO MORE MULES. NO MORE MINES. NO MORE--
KLANG
AARGH!

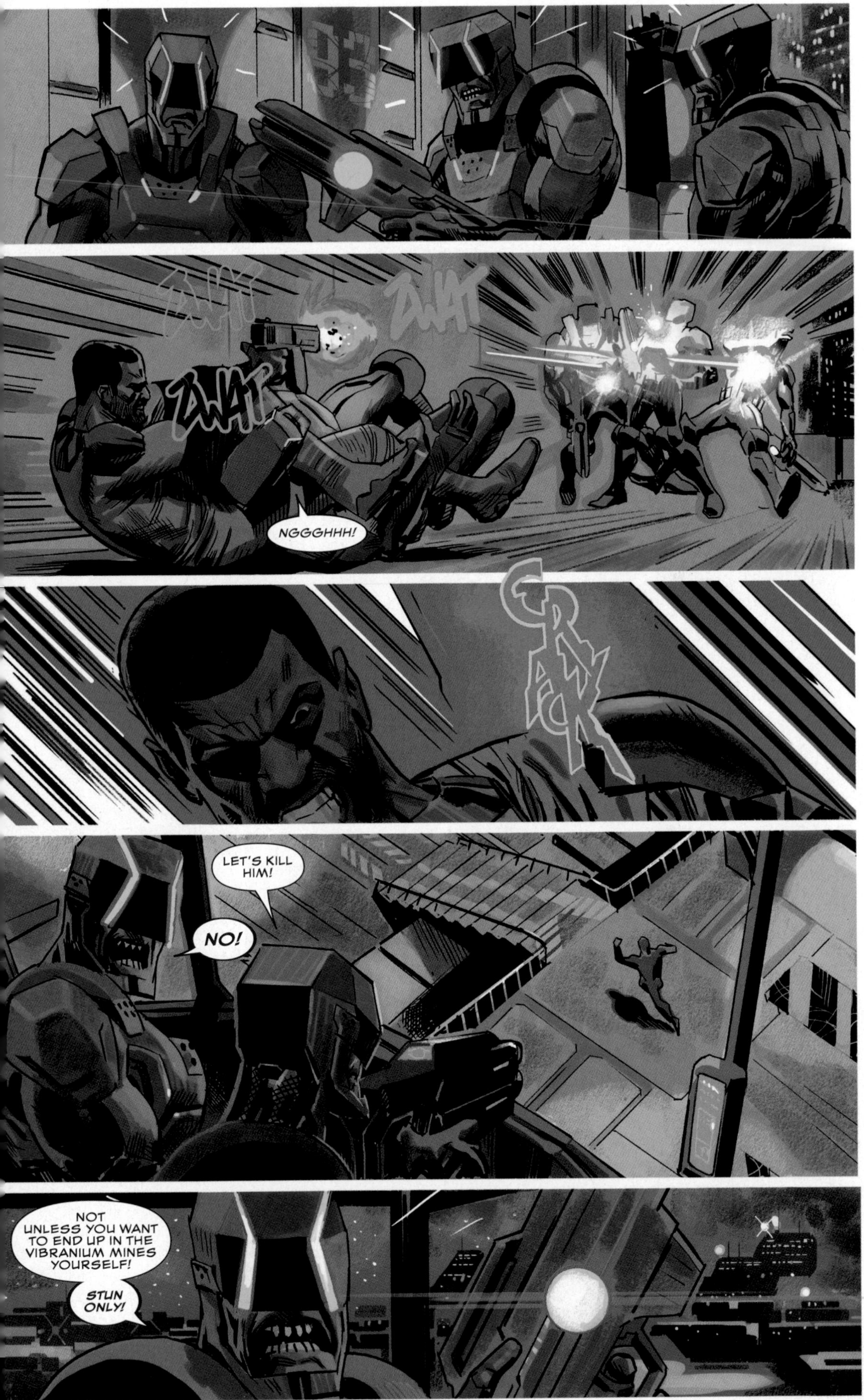
ZWAT
ZWAT
ZWAT
NGGGHHH!
CRAACK
LET'S KILL HIM!
NO!
NOT UNLESS YOU WANT TO END UP IN THE VIBRANIUM MINES YOURSELF!
STUN ONLY!

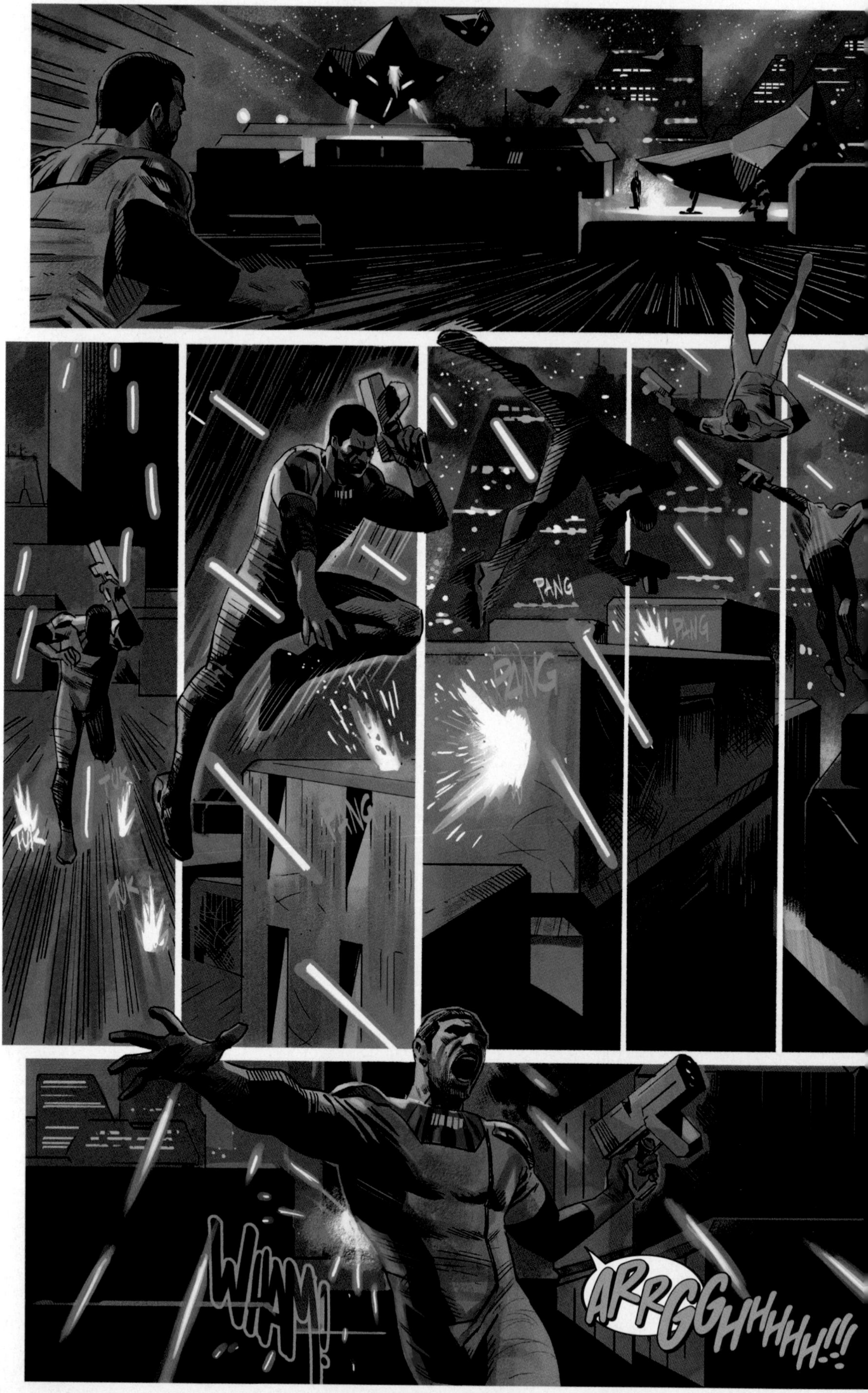

TUK
TUK
TUK
PANG
PANG
PANG
PANG
WHAM!
ARRGGHHHHH!!!

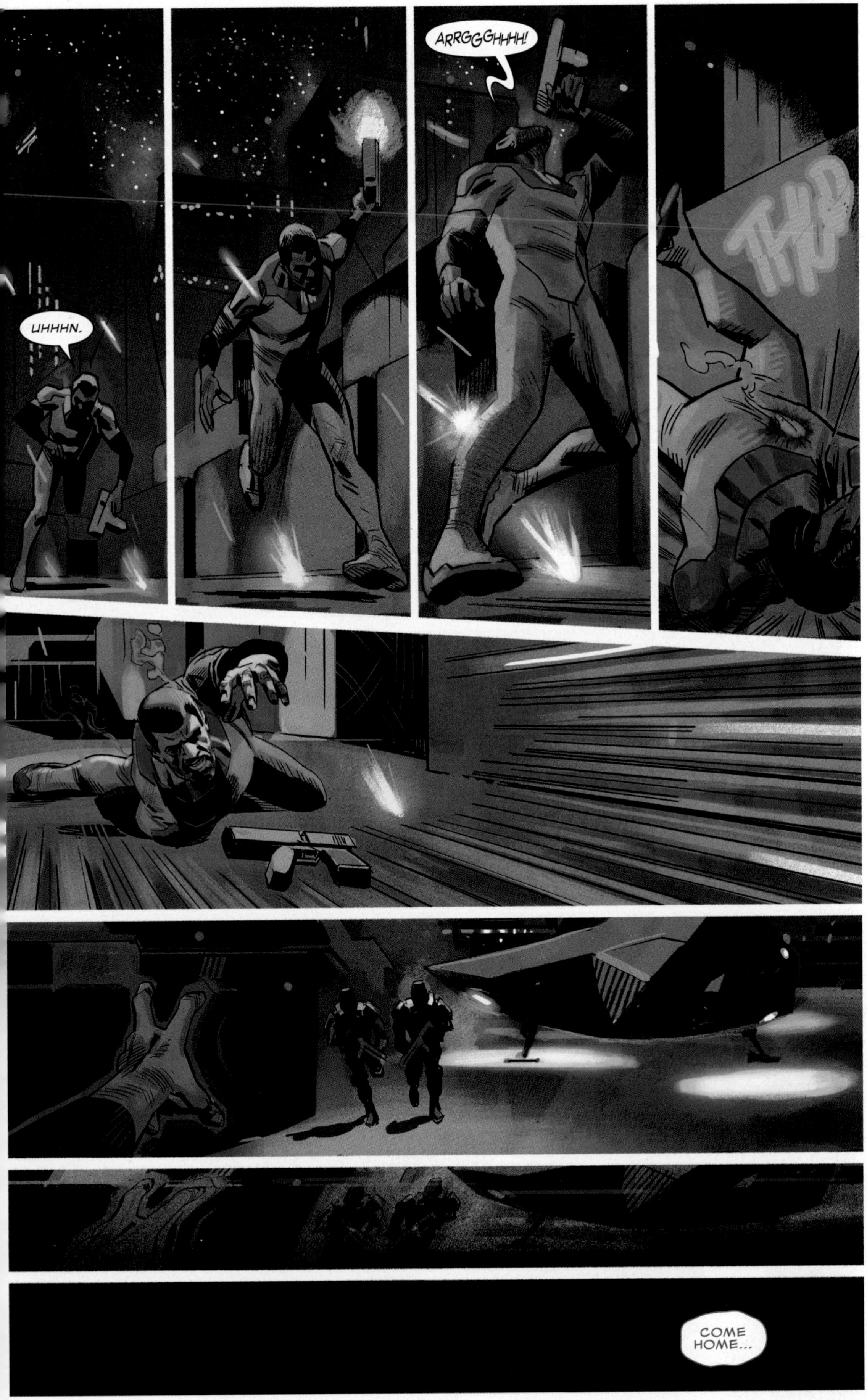
UHHHN.
ARRGGGHHHH!
THUD
COME HOME...

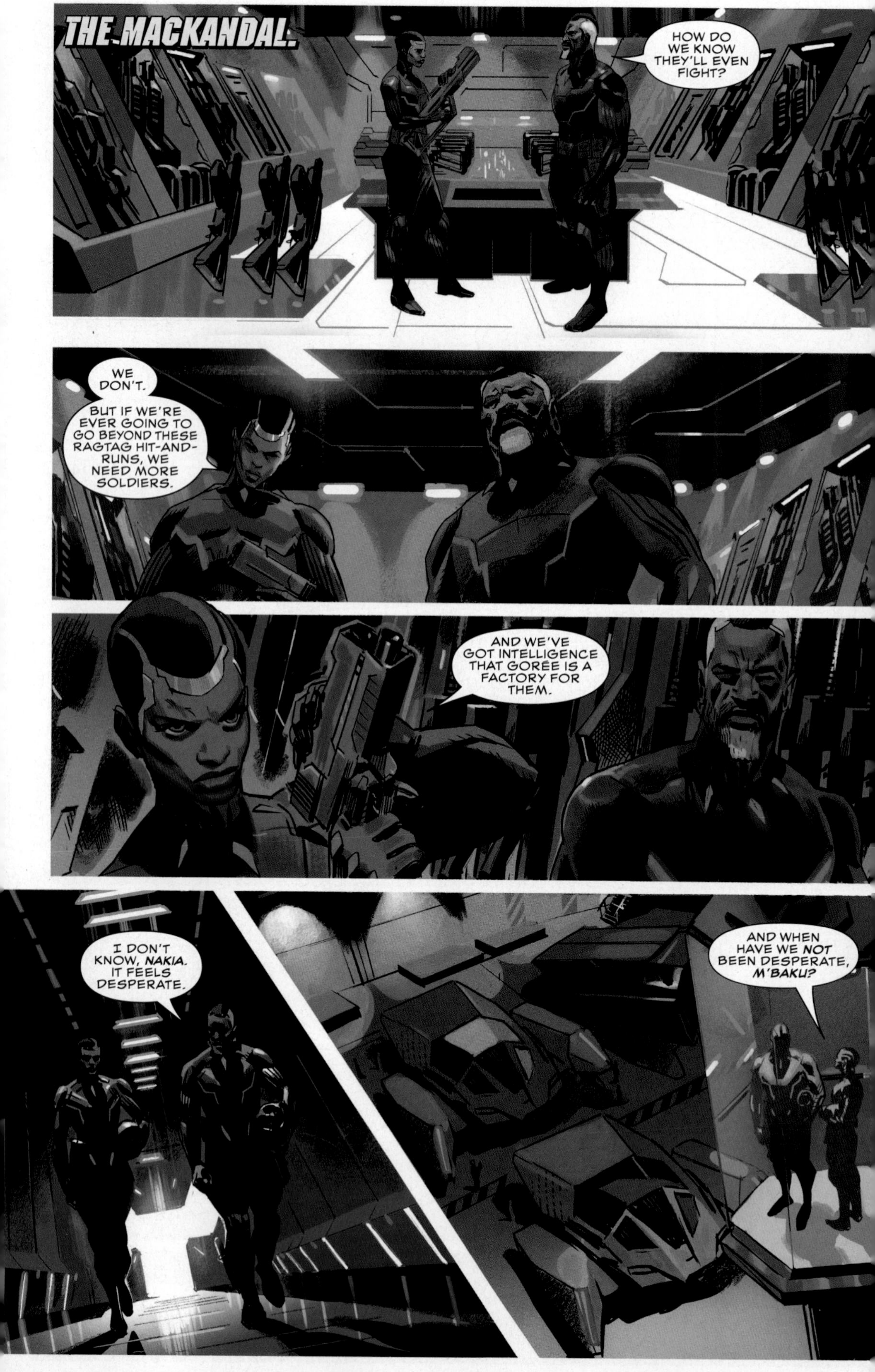
THE MACKANDAL.
HOW DO WE KNOW THEY'LL EVEN FIGHT?
WE DON'T.
BUT IF WE'RE EVER GOING TO GO BEYOND THESE RAGTAG HIT-AND-RUNS, WE NEED MORE SOLDIERS.
AND WE'VE GOT INTELLIGENCE THAT GORÉE IS A FACTORY FOR THEM.
I DON'T KNOW, NAKIA. IT FEELS DESPERATE.
AND WHEN HAVE WE NOT BEEN DESPERATE, M'BAKU?

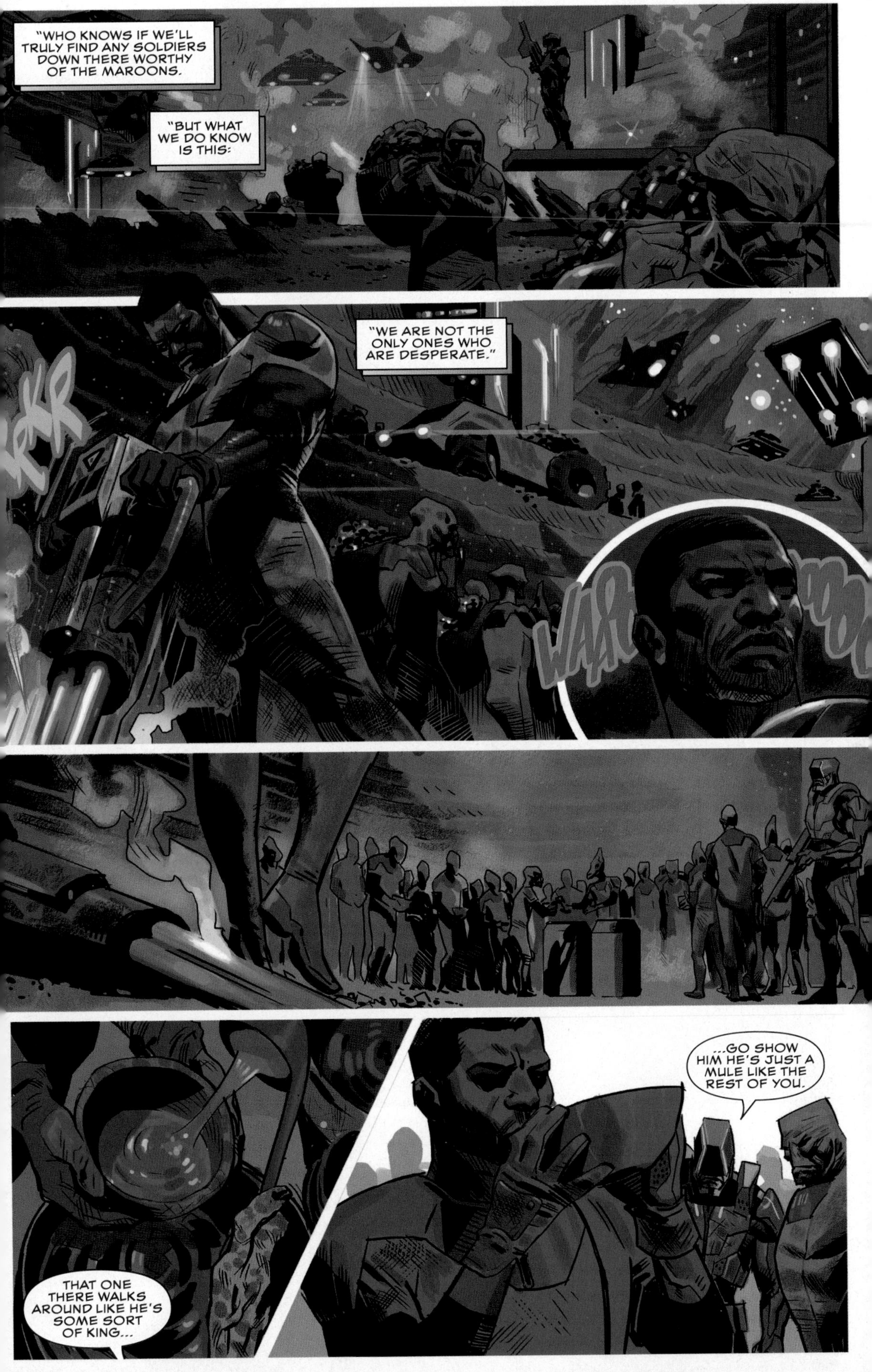
"WHO KNOWS IF WE'LL TRULY FIND ANY SOLDIERS DOWN THERE WORTHY OF THE MAROONS.
"BUT WHAT WE DO KNOW IS THIS:
"WE ARE NOT THE ONLY ONES WHO ARE DESPERATE."
THAT ONE THERE WALKS AROUND LIKE HE'S SOME SORT OF KING...
...GO SHOW HIM HE'S JUST A MULE LIKE THE REST OF YOU.

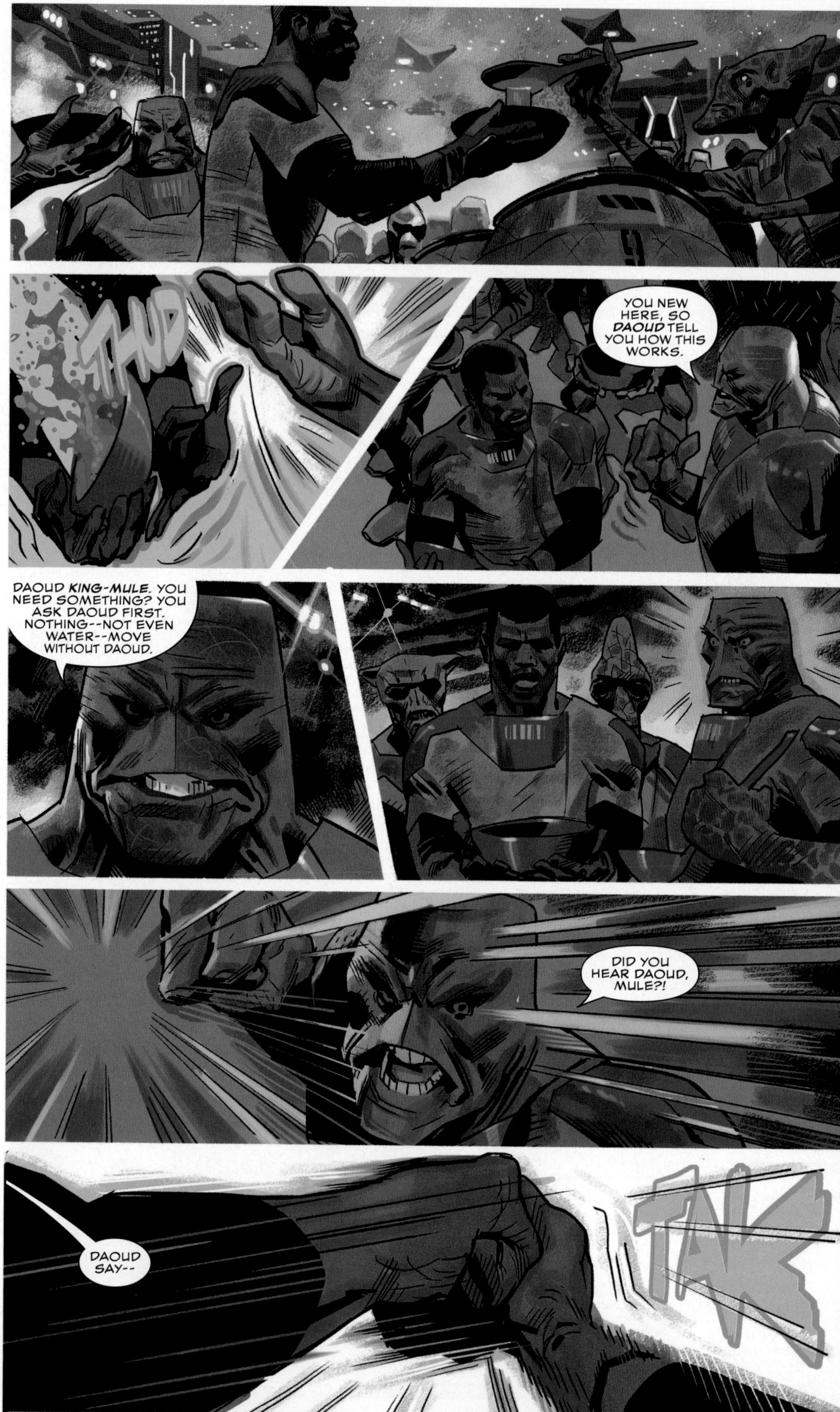
THUD
YOU NEW HERE, SO DAOUD TELL YOU HOW THIS WORKS.
DAOUD KING-MULE. YOU NEED SOMETHING? YOU ASK DAOUD FIRST. NOTHING--NOT EVEN WATER--MOVE WITHOUT DAOUD.
DID YOU HEAR DAOUD, MULE?!
DAOUD SAY--
TAK

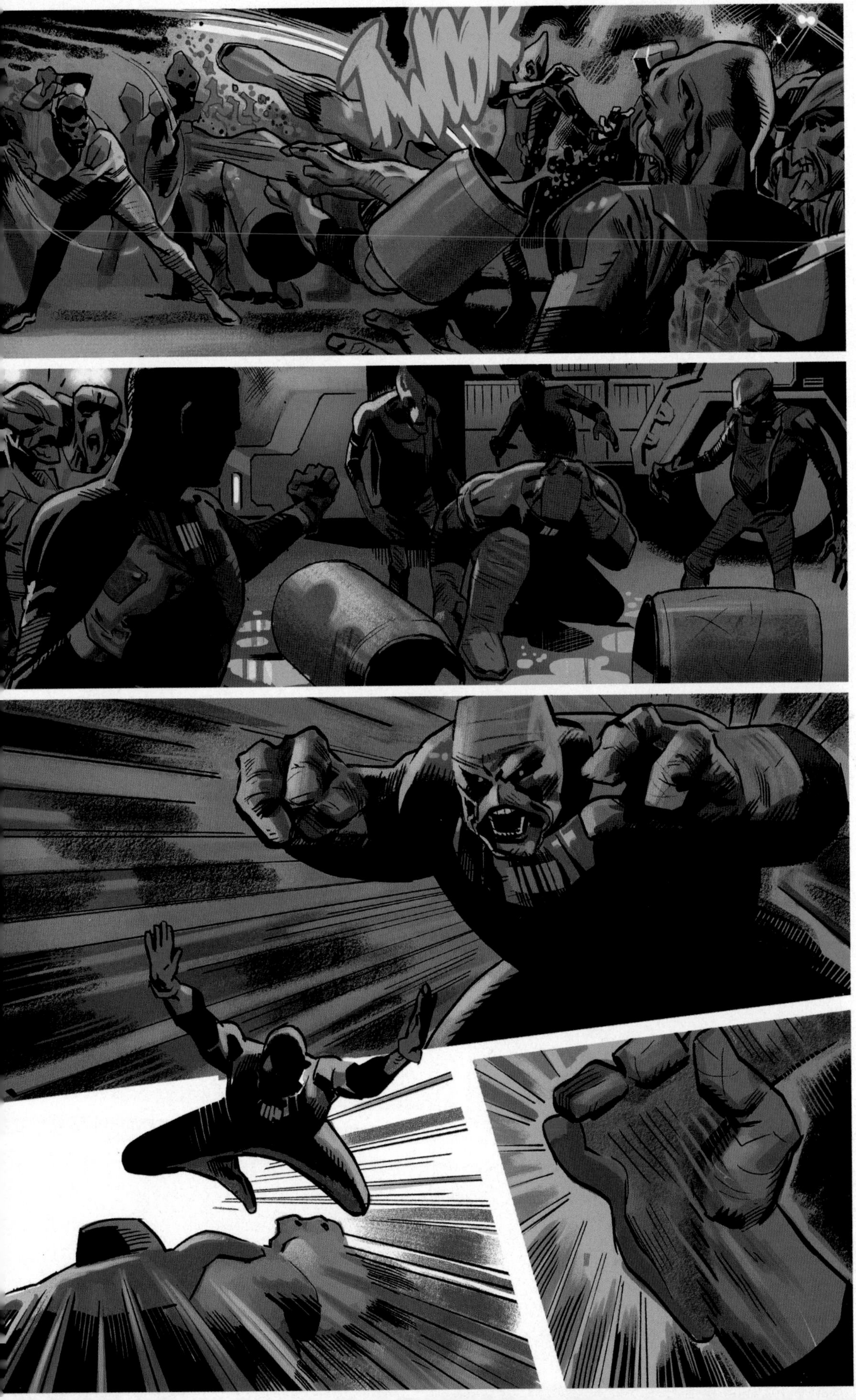

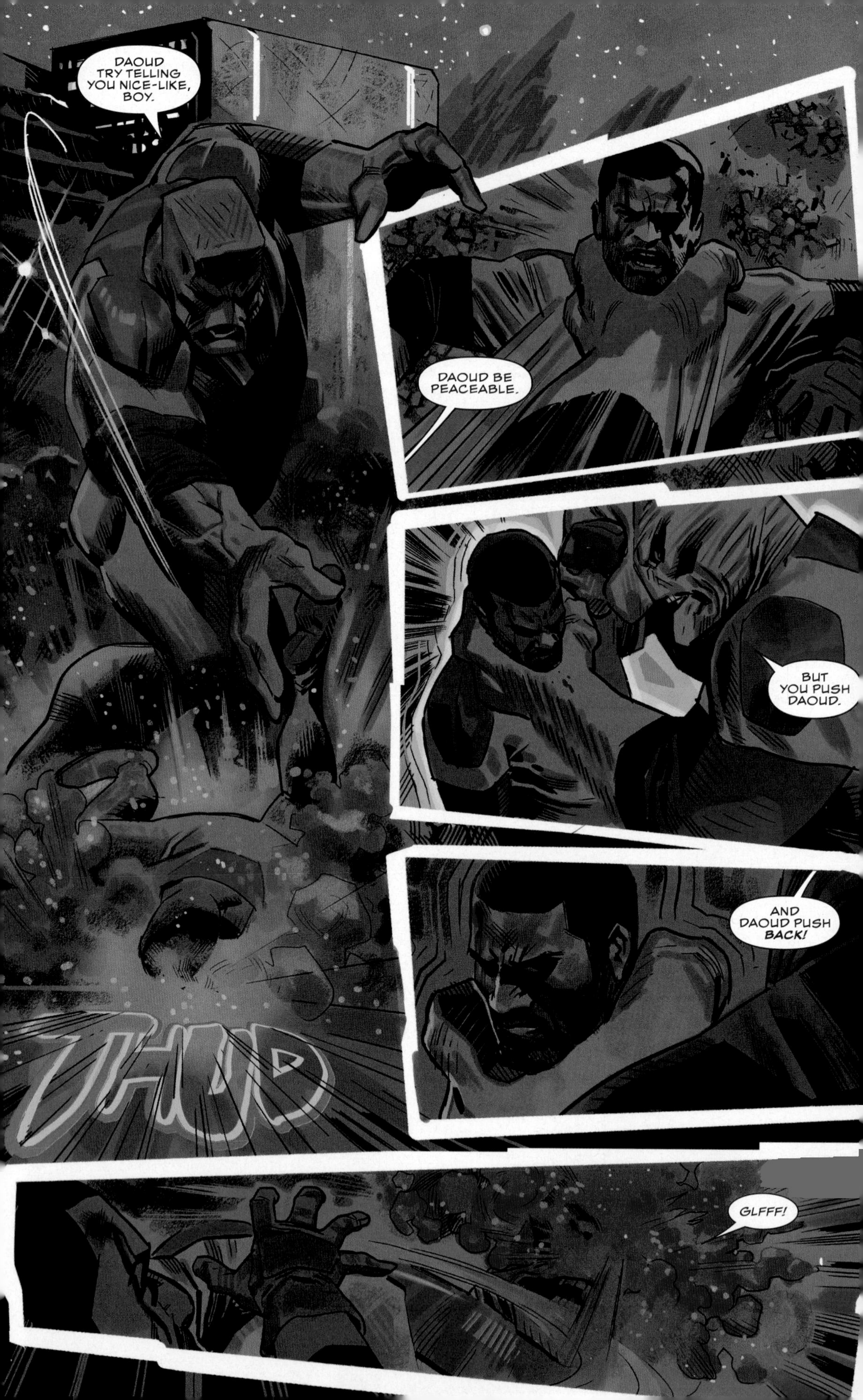
DAOUD TRY TELLING YOU NICE-LIKE, BOY.
DAOUD BE PEACEABLE.
BUT YOU PUSH DAOUD.
AND DAOUD PUSH BACK!
THUD
GLFFF!

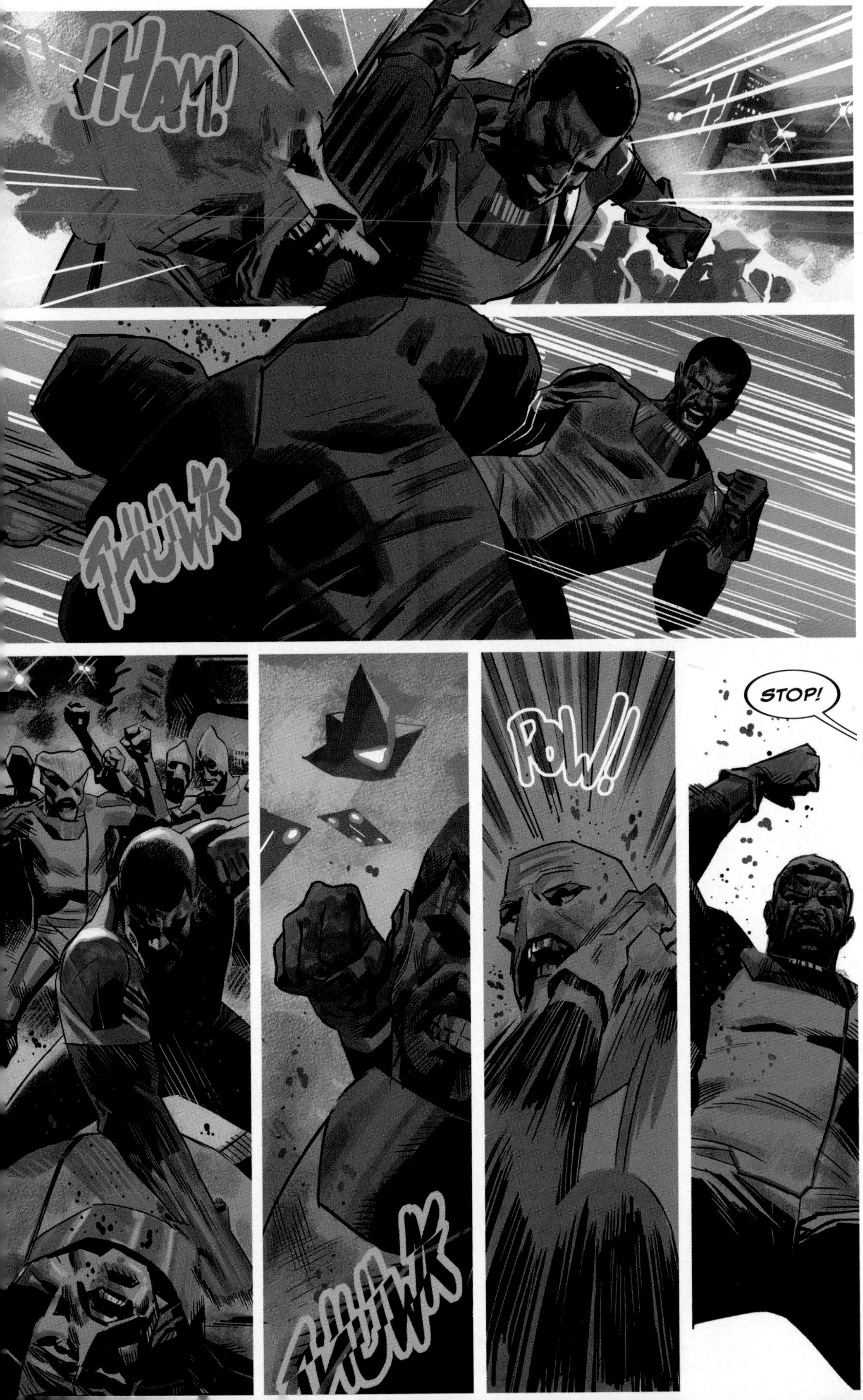
WHAM!
THUNK
THUNK
POW!!
STOP!

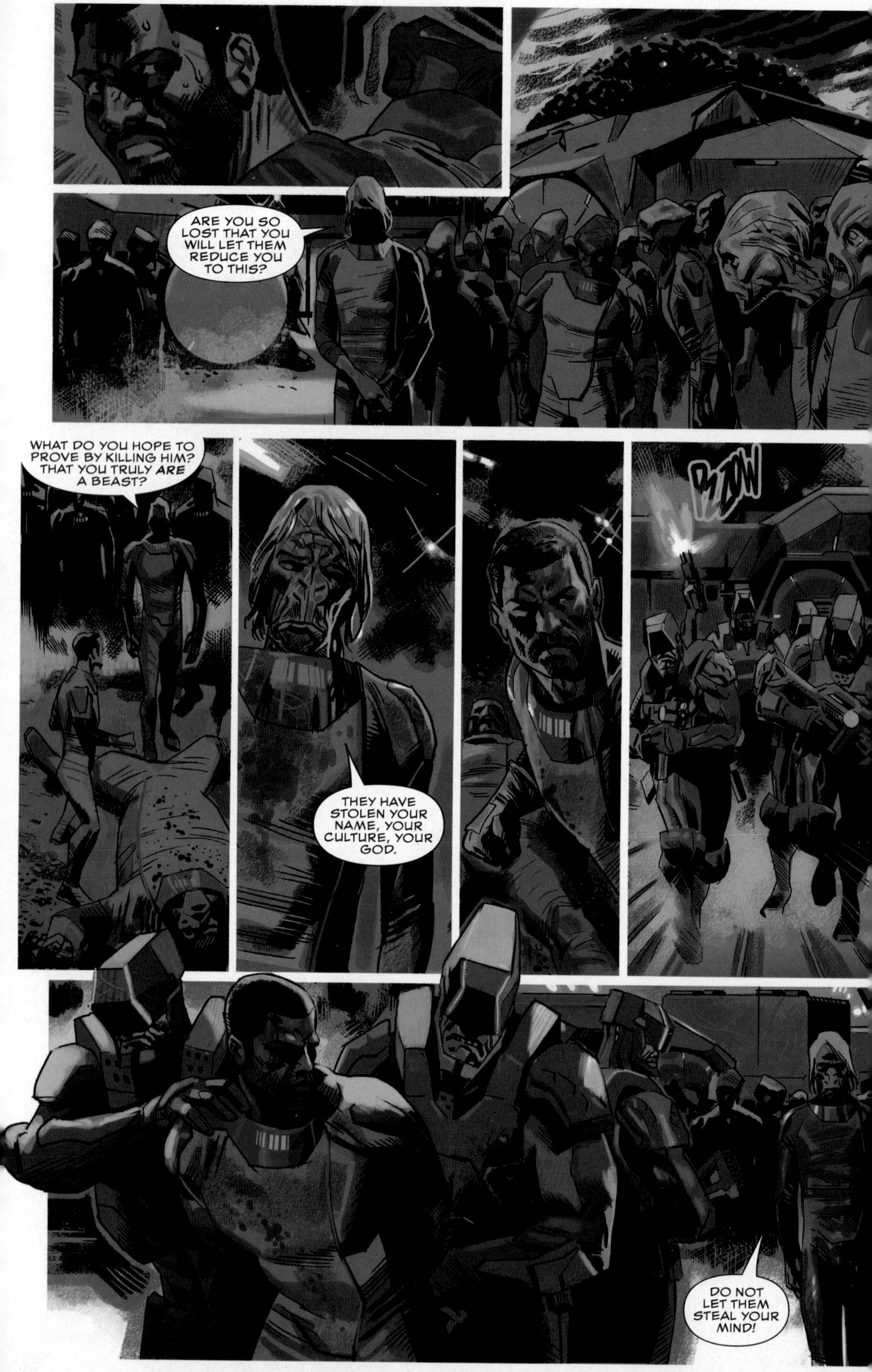
ARE YOU SO LOST THAT YOU WILL LET THEM REDUCE YOU TO THIS?
WHAT DO YOU HOPE TO PROVE BY KILLING HIM? THAT YOU TRULY ARE A BEAST?
THEY HAVE STOLEN YOUR NAME, YOUR CULTURE, YOUR GOD.
BZZOW
DO NOT LET THEM STEAL YOUR MIND!

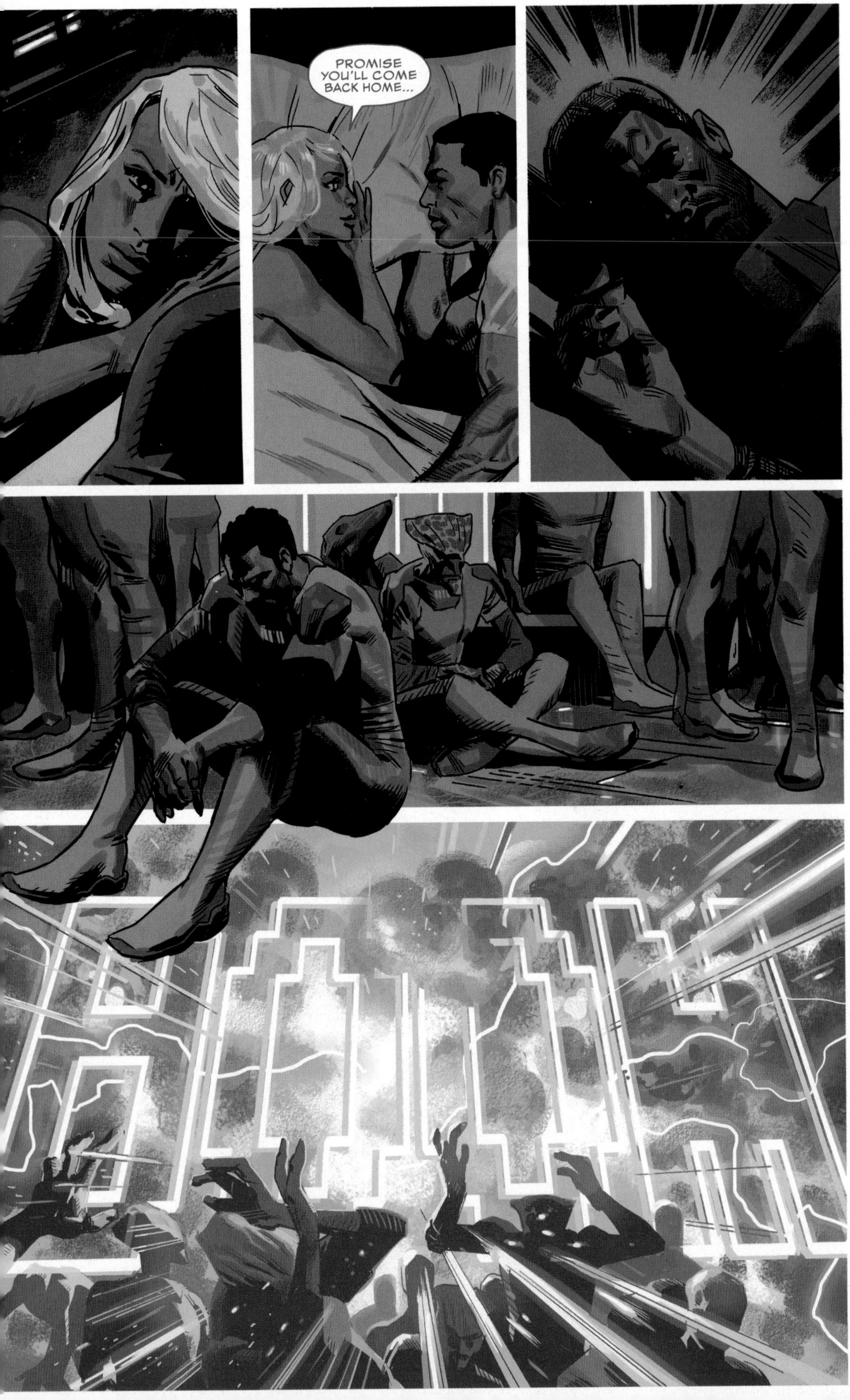
PROMISE YOU'LL COME BACK HOME...

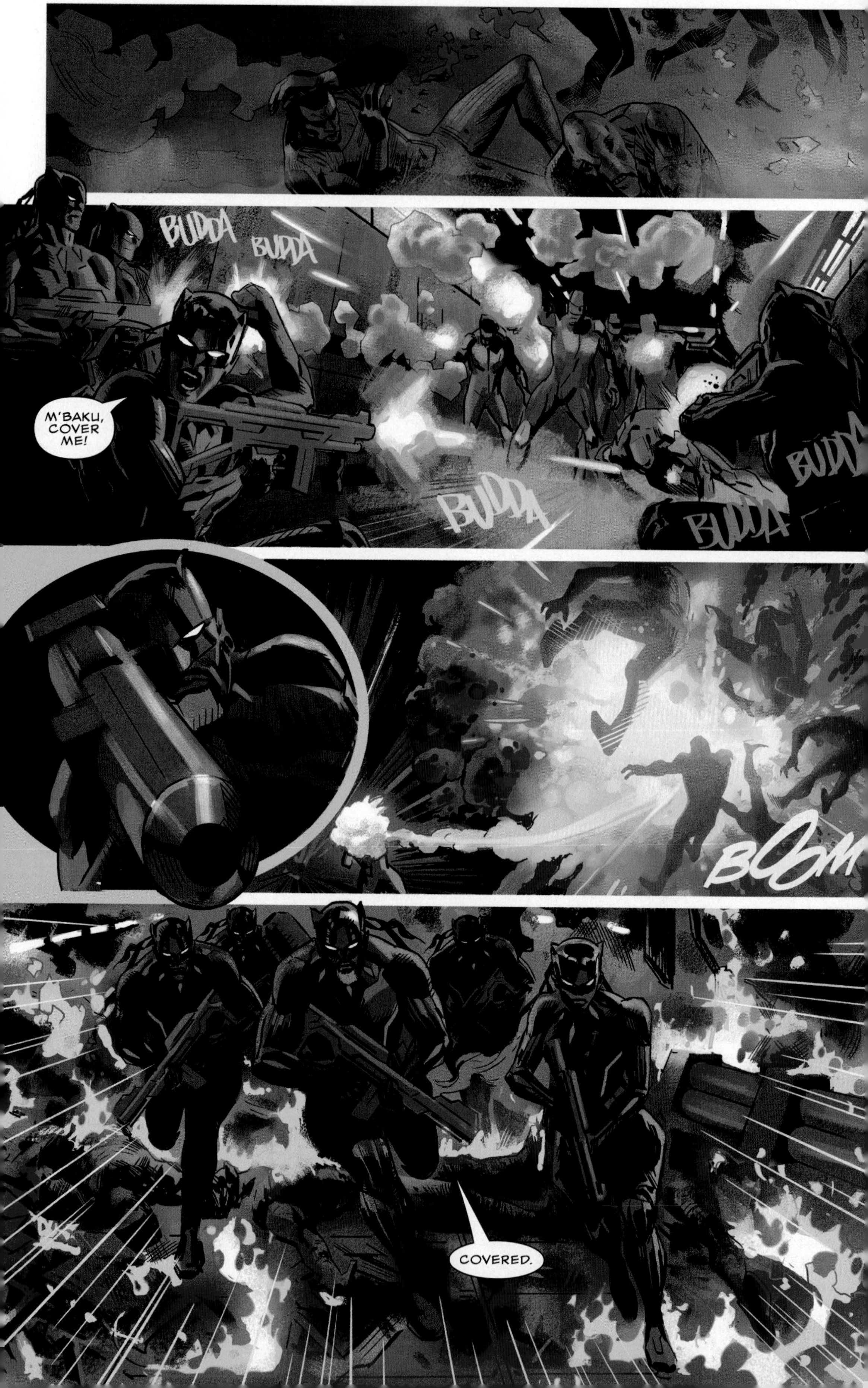
BUDDA
BUDDA
M'BAKU, COVER ME!
BUDDA
BUDDA
BUDDA
BUDDA
BOOM
COVERED.

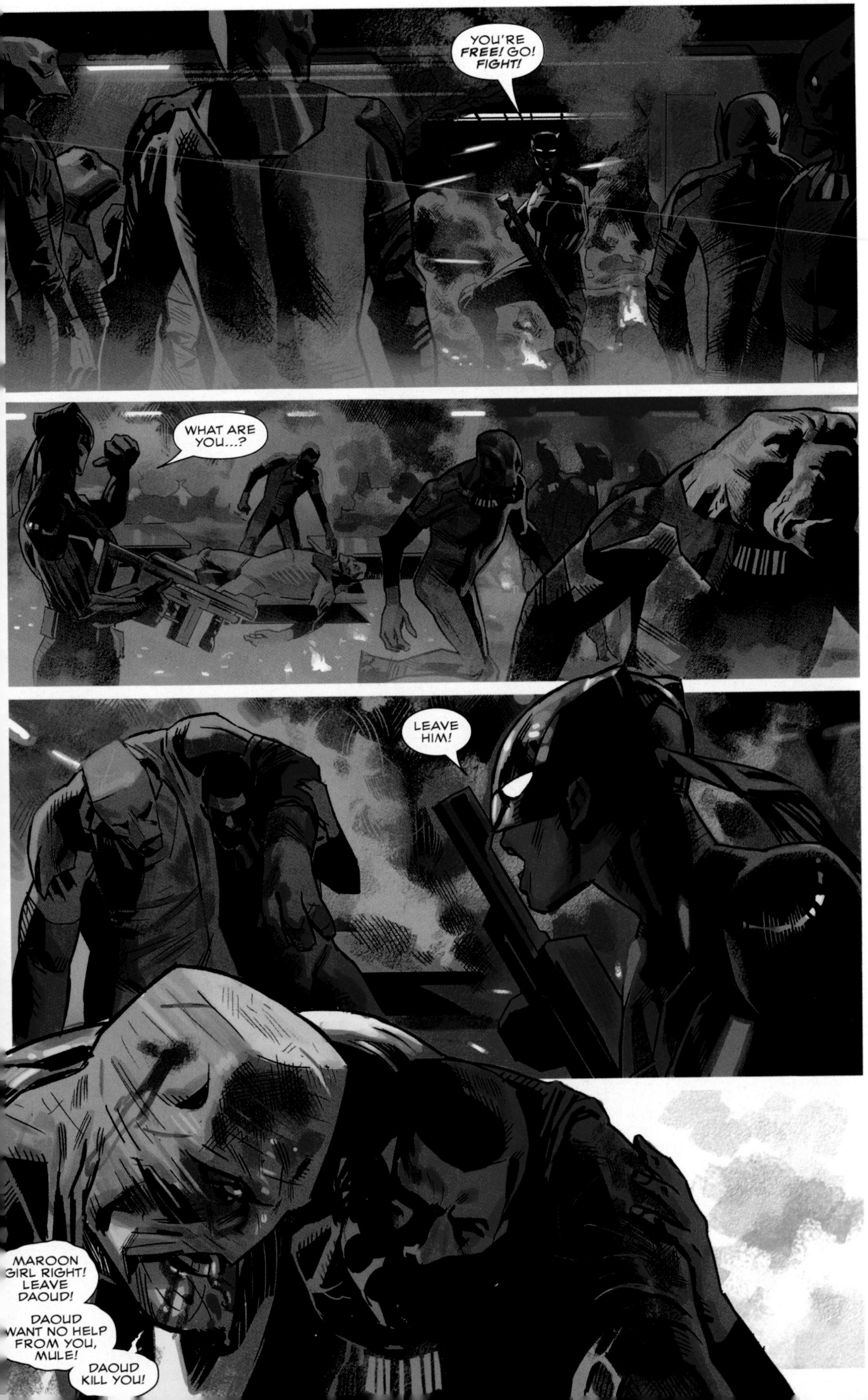
YOU'RE FREE! GO! FIGHT!
WHAT ARE YOU...?
LEAVE HIM!
MAROON GIRL RIGHT! LEAVE DAOUD!
DAOUD WANT NO HELP FROM YOU, MULE!
DAOUD KILL YOU!

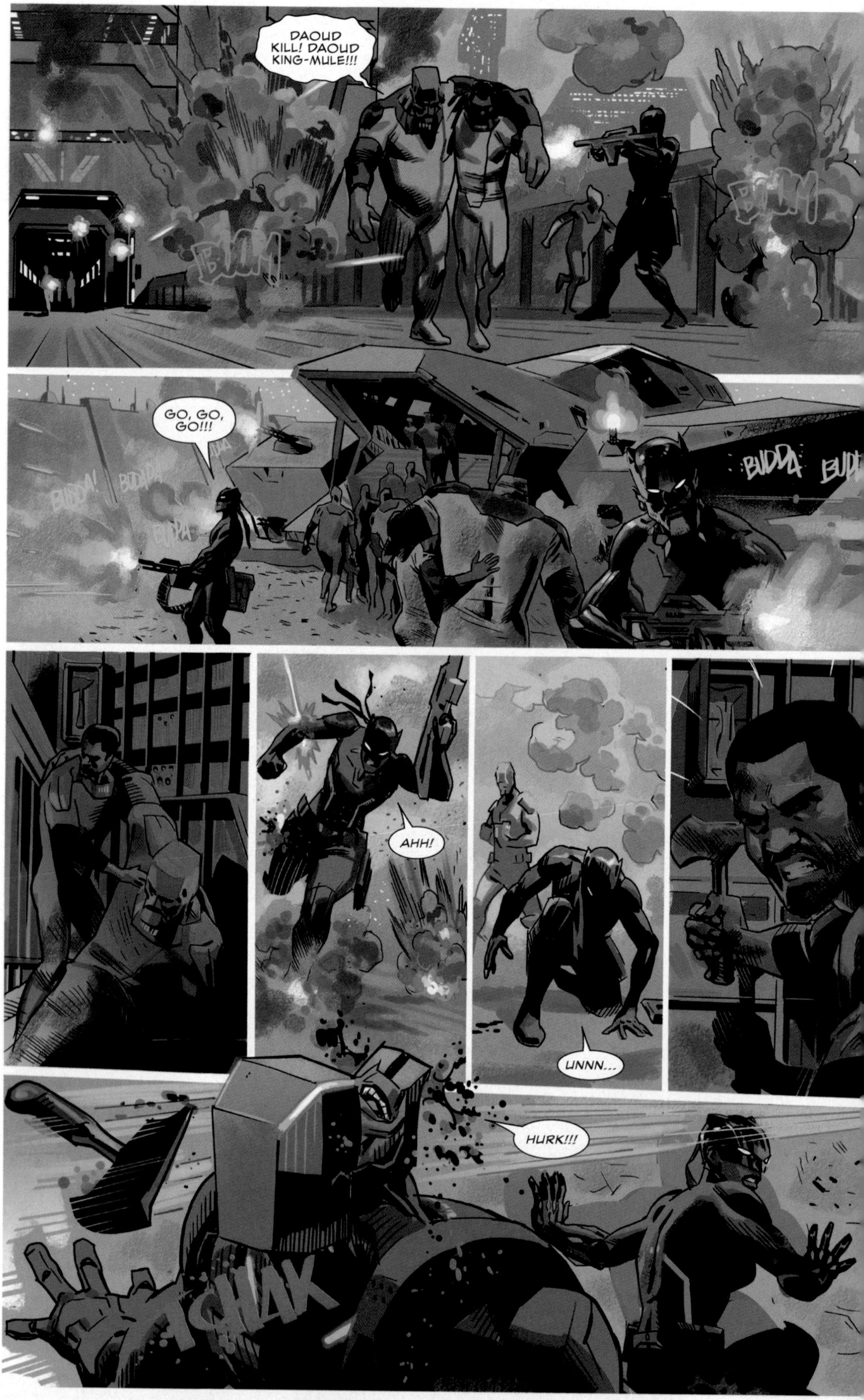
DAOUD KILL! DAOUD KING-MULE!!!
BOOM
BOOM
GO, GO, GO!!!
BUDDA!
BUDDA
AHH!
UNNN...
HURK!!!
TCHAK

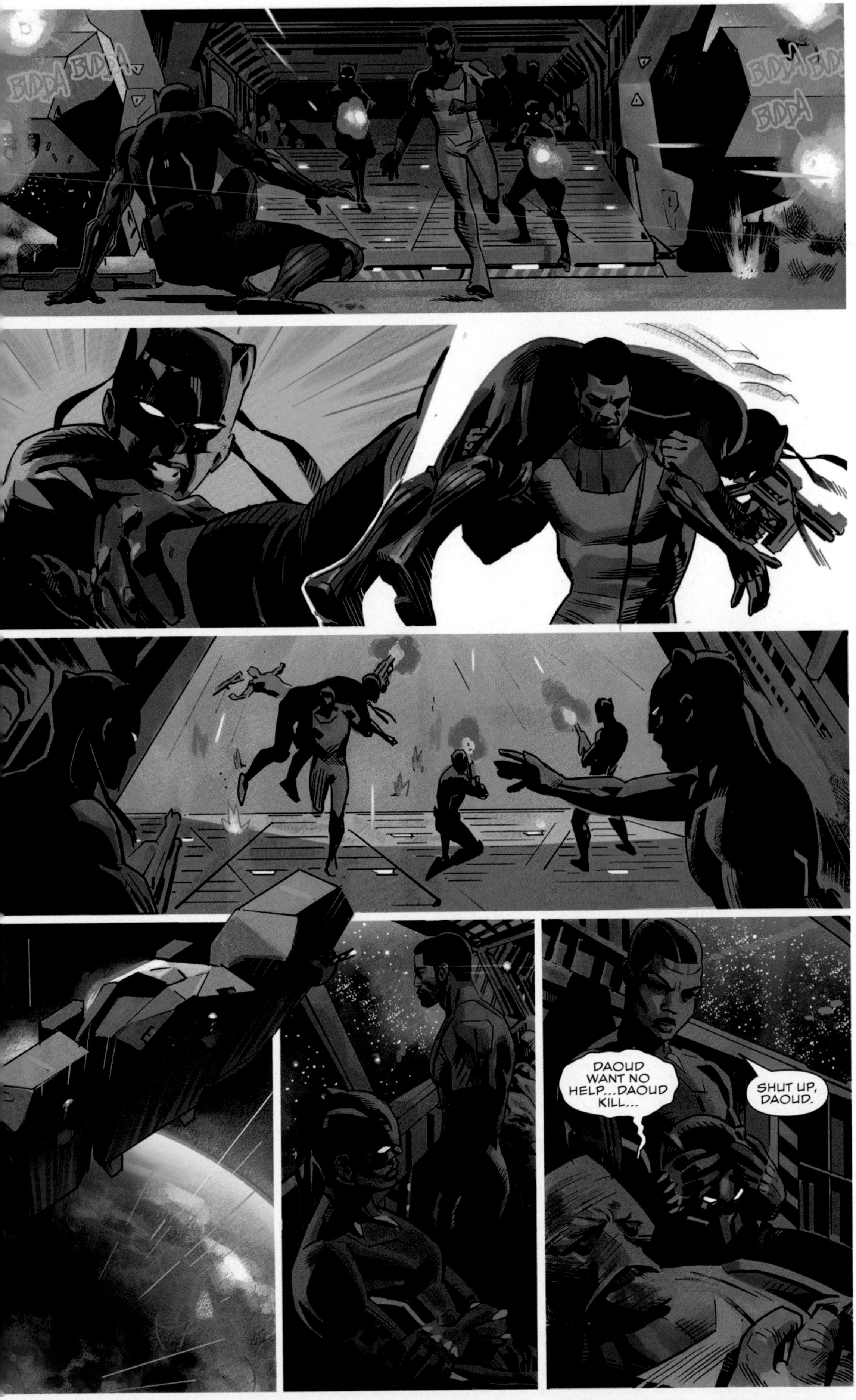
BUDDA BUDDA
BUDDA BUDDA
BUDDA
DAOUD WANT NO HELP...DAOUD KILL...
SHUT UP, DAOUD.

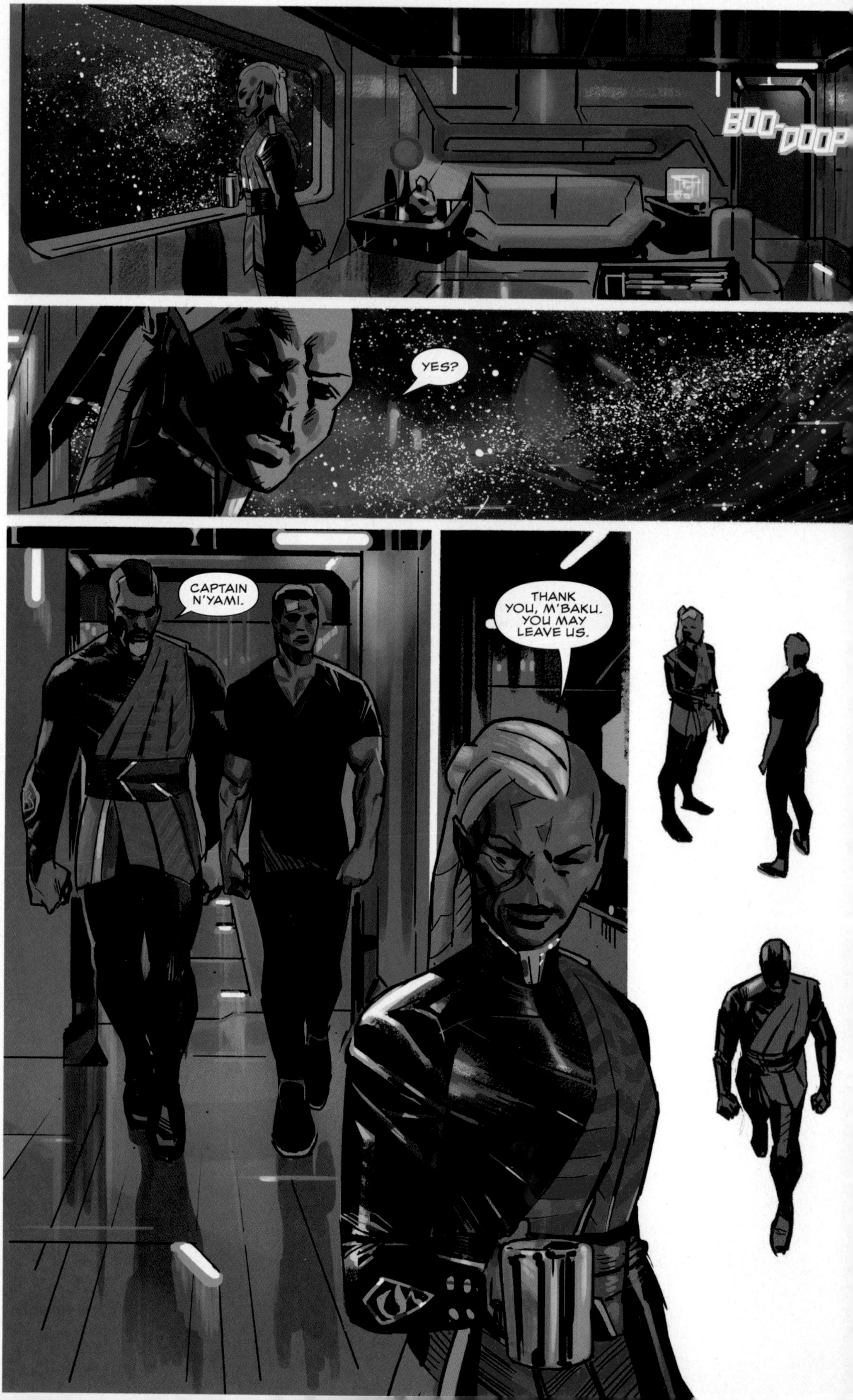
BOO-DOOP
YES?
CAPTAIN N'YAMI.
THANK YOU, M'BAKU. YOU MAY LEAVE US.

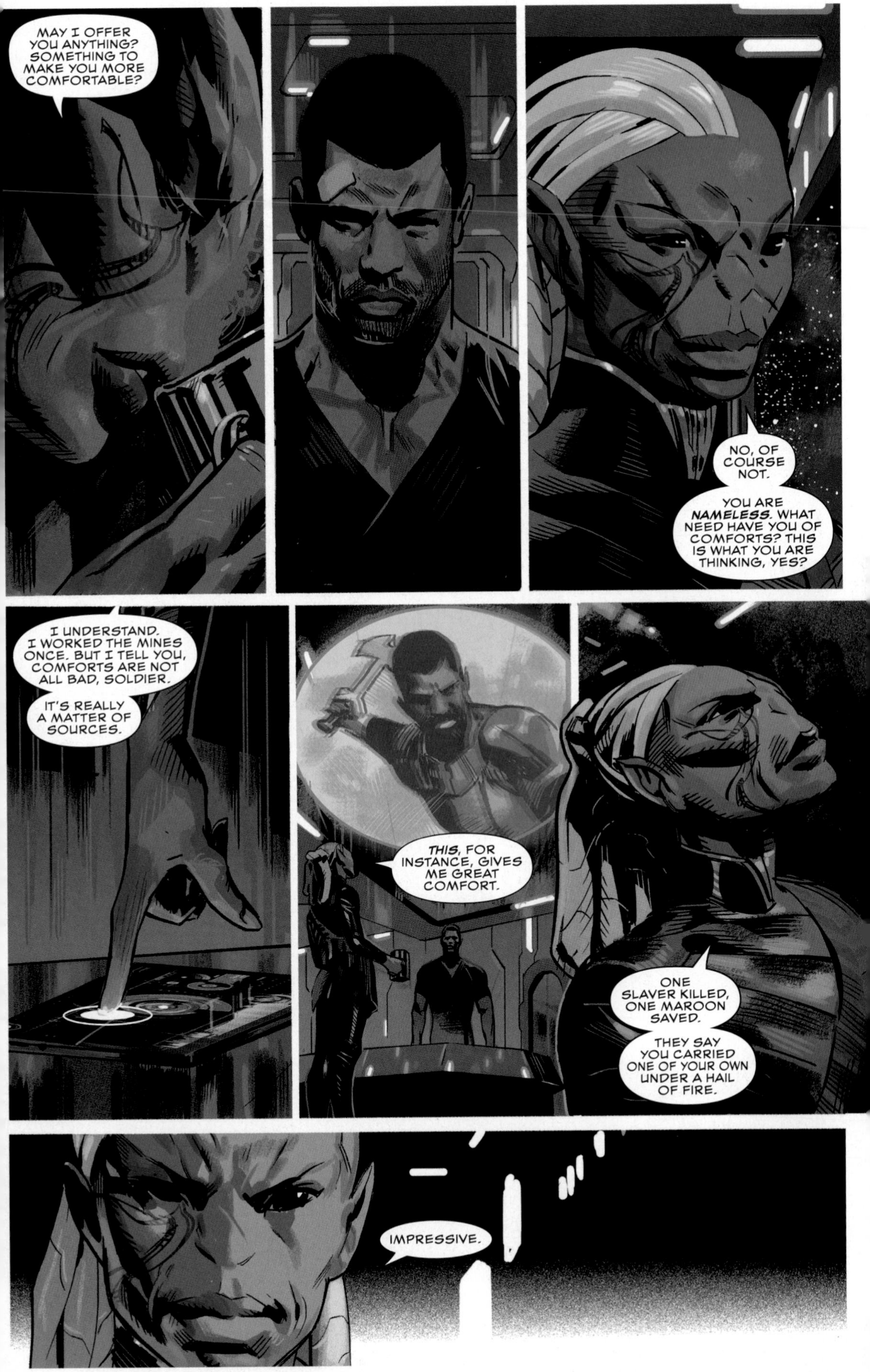
MAY I OFFER YOU ANYTHING? SOMETHING TO MAKE YOU MORE COMFORTABLE?
NO, OF COURSE NOT.
YOU ARE *NAMELESS*. WHAT NEED HAVE YOU OF COMFORTS? THIS IS WHAT YOU ARE THINKING, YES?
I UNDERSTAND. I WORKED THE MINES ONCE. BUT I TELL YOU, COMFORTS ARE NOT ALL BAD, SOLDIER.
IT'S REALLY A MATTER OF SOURCES.
THIS, FOR INSTANCE, GIVES ME GREAT COMFORT.
ONE SLAVER KILLED, ONE MAROON SAVED.
THEY SAY YOU CARRIED ONE OF YOUR OWN UNDER A HAIL OF FIRE.
IMPRESSIVE.

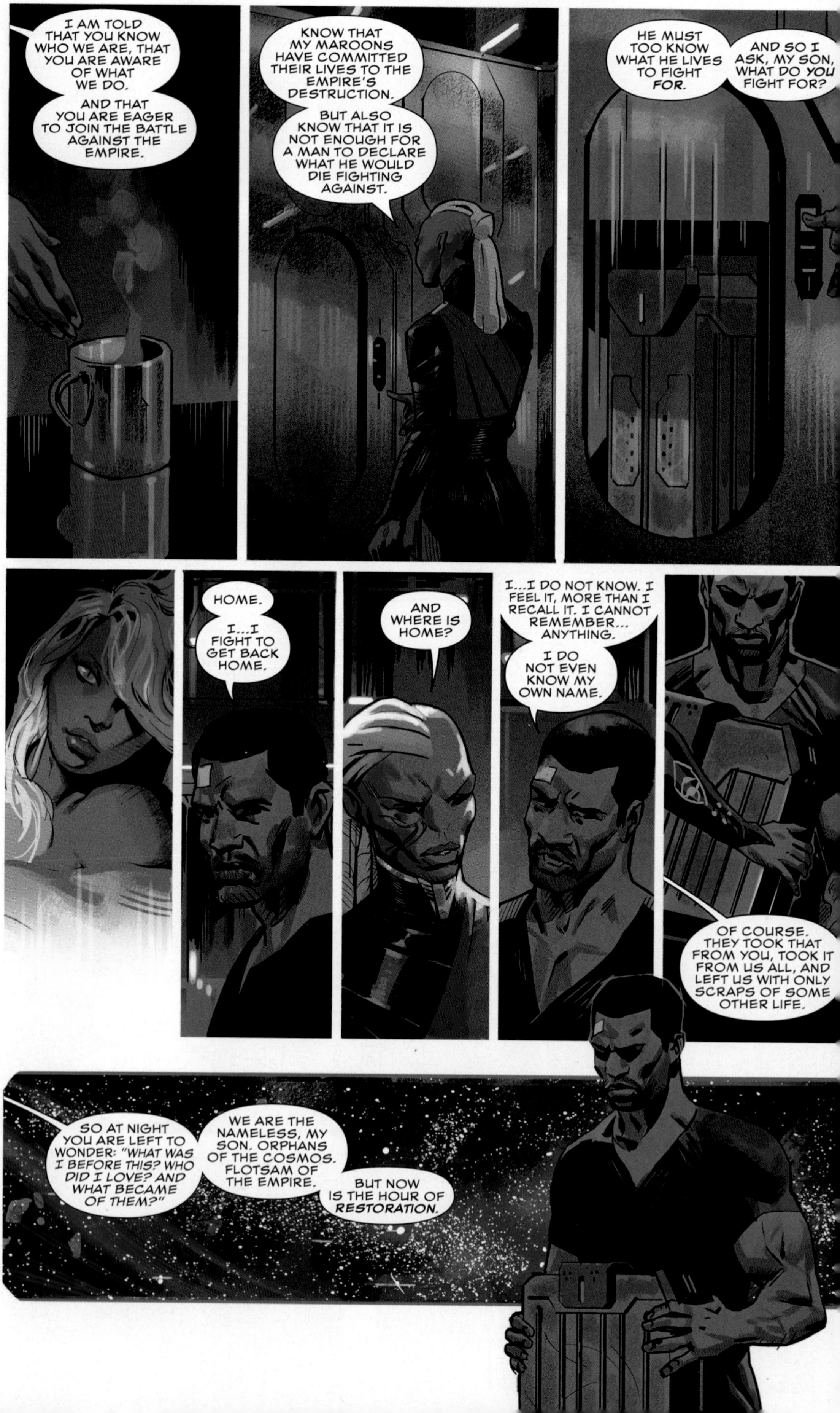
I AM TOLD THAT YOU KNOW WHO WE ARE, THAT YOU ARE AWARE OF WHAT WE DO.
AND THAT YOU ARE EAGER TO JOIN THE BATTLE AGAINST THE EMPIRE.
KNOW THAT MY MAROONS HAVE COMMITTED THEIR LIVES TO THE EMPIRE'S DESTRUCTION.
BUT ALSO KNOW THAT IT IS NOT ENOUGH FOR A MAN TO DECLARE WHAT HE WOULD DIE FIGHTING AGAINST.
HE MUST TOO KNOW WHAT HE LIVES TO FIGHT *FOR*.
AND SO I ASK, MY SON, WHAT DO *YOU* FIGHT FOR?
HOME.
I...I FIGHT TO GET BACK HOME.
AND WHERE IS HOME?
I...I DO NOT KNOW. I FEEL IT, MORE THAN I RECALL IT. I CANNOT REMEMBER... ANYTHING.
I DO NOT EVEN KNOW MY OWN NAME.
OF COURSE. THEY TOOK THAT FROM YOU, TOOK IT FROM US ALL, AND LEFT US WITH ONLY SCRAPS OF SOME OTHER LIFE.
SO AT NIGHT YOU ARE LEFT TO WONDER: *"WHAT WAS I BEFORE THIS? WHO DID I LOVE? AND WHAT BECAME OF THEM?"*
WE ARE THE NAMELESS, MY SON. ORPHANS OF THE COSMOS. FLOTSAM OF THE EMPIRE.
BUT NOW IS THE HOUR OF *RESTORATION*.

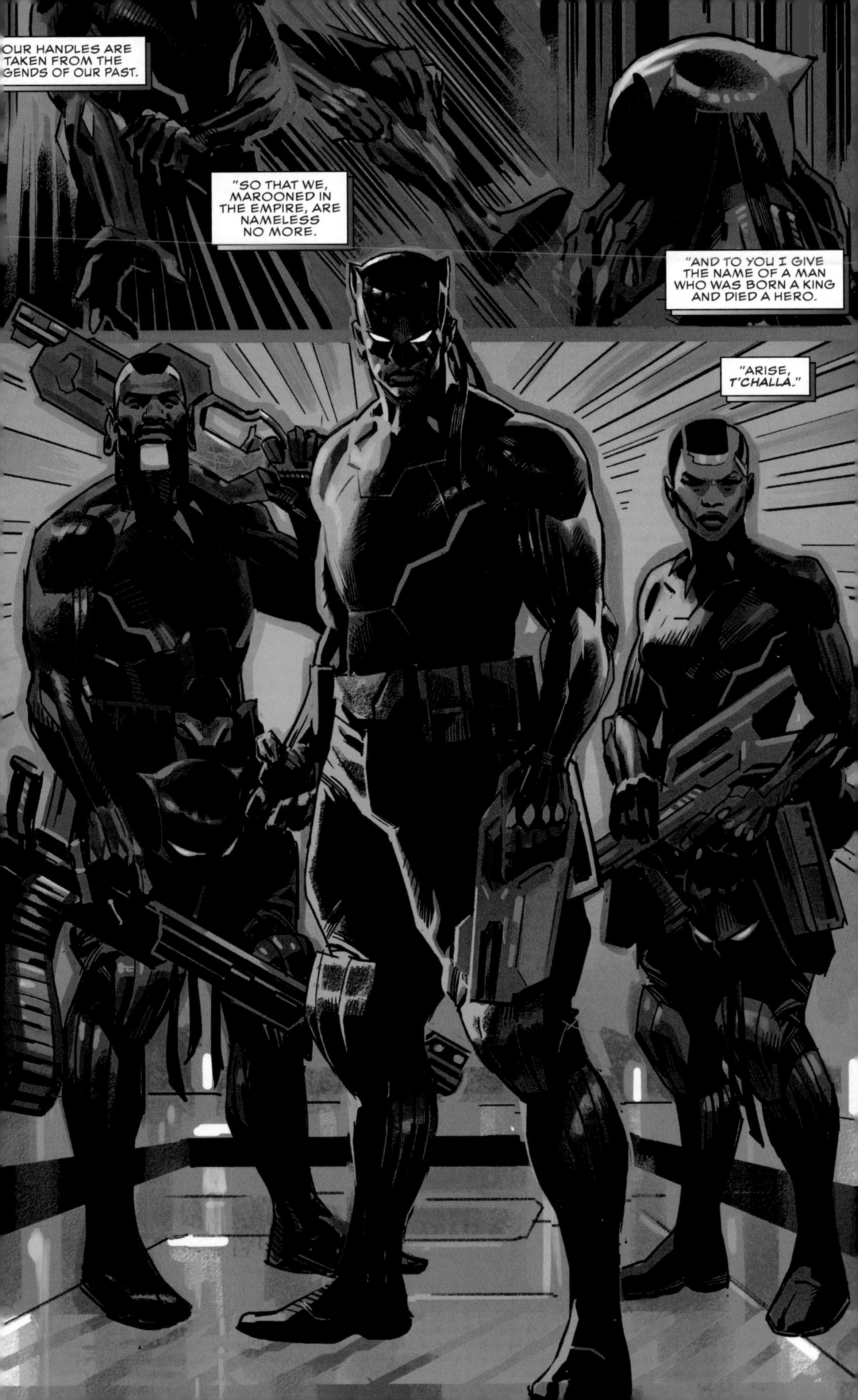

OUR HANDLES ARE TAKEN FROM THE GENDS OF OUR PAST.
"SO THAT WE, MAROONED IN THE EMPIRE, ARE NAMELESS NO MORE.
"AND TO YOU I GIVE THE NAME OF A MAN WHO WAS BORN A KING AND DIED A HERO.
"ARISE, T'CHALLA."

WELCOME TO THE INTERGALACTIC EMPIRE OF WAKANDA! WE'RE SURE YOU HAVE LOTS O
QUESTIONS — HOW DID T'CHALLA GET HERE? IS THAT REALLY NAKIA AND M'BAKU? HOW
HAS NO ONE HEARD OF THIS EMPIRE BEFORE? — BUT HANG TIGHT, IT'S ALL PART OF THE
JOURNEY! HERE'S A LITTLE INTRODUCTION BY TA-NEHISI COATES TO SOME OF THE FACTIO
AND RACES WHO APPEAR IN THIS ISSUE, ALONG WITH DANIEL ACUÑA'S GORGEOUS DESIG

THE IMPERIALS:

THE HIGHEST CASTE OF ALL WAKANDANS, THE IMPERIALS CLAIM TO BE THE BLOOD DESCENDANTS OF THE FOUNDERS OF THE INTERGALACTIC EMPIRE OF WAKANDA — THOUGH THAT CLAIM IS HARD TO VALIDATE OR REFUTE.

THE MINERS, A.K.A. THE NAMELESS:

SUBJECTS OF THE EMPIRE CONDEMNED TO SLAVERY IN THE VIBRANIUM MINES, THE NAMELESS HAVE BEEN MIND-WIPED. THEY KNOW NOTHING OF THEIR ORIGINAL HISTORY.

THE ASKARI:

THE ASKARI ARE BOTH THE POLICE FORCE OF THE EMPIRE AND THE ARM OF THE WAKANDAN SLAVE TRADE. AS A CASTE, THEY ARE HATED BY THE NAMELESS AND DENIGRATED BY THE IMPERIALS. THE ASKARI HAIL FROM MANY RACES — INCLUDING MANY THAT WERE THEMSELVES CONQUERED BY THE WAKANDAN EMPIRE.

THE REBELS, A.K.A. THE MAROONS:

THOUGH THE EMPIRE'S POWERS ARE VAST, THERE ARE THOSE WHO FIGHT BACK. THEY ARE THE MAROONS, COMPRISED OF FREED NAMELESS AND LED BY CAPTAIN N'YAMI OF THE STARSHIP MAKANDAL.

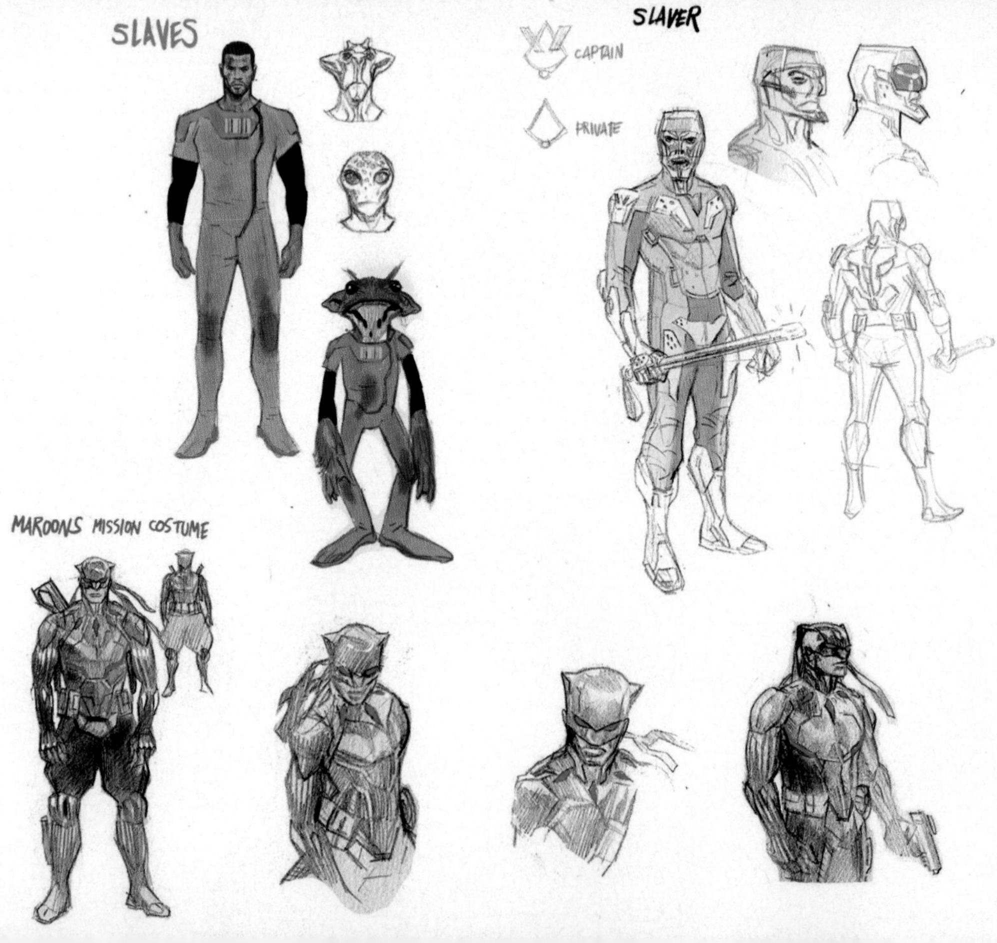
SLAVES
SLAVER
CAPTAIN
PRIVATE
MAROONS MISSION COSTUME

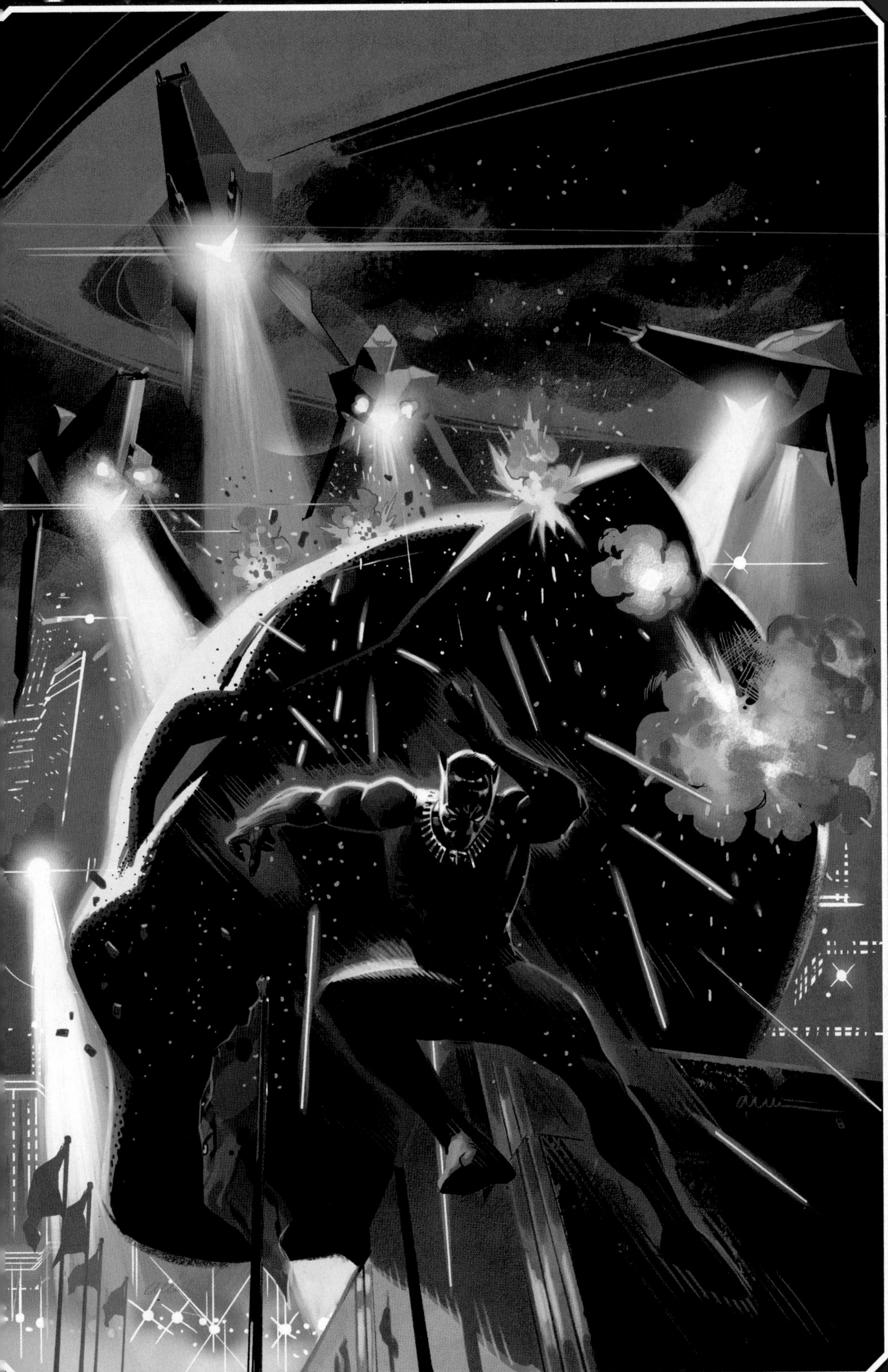

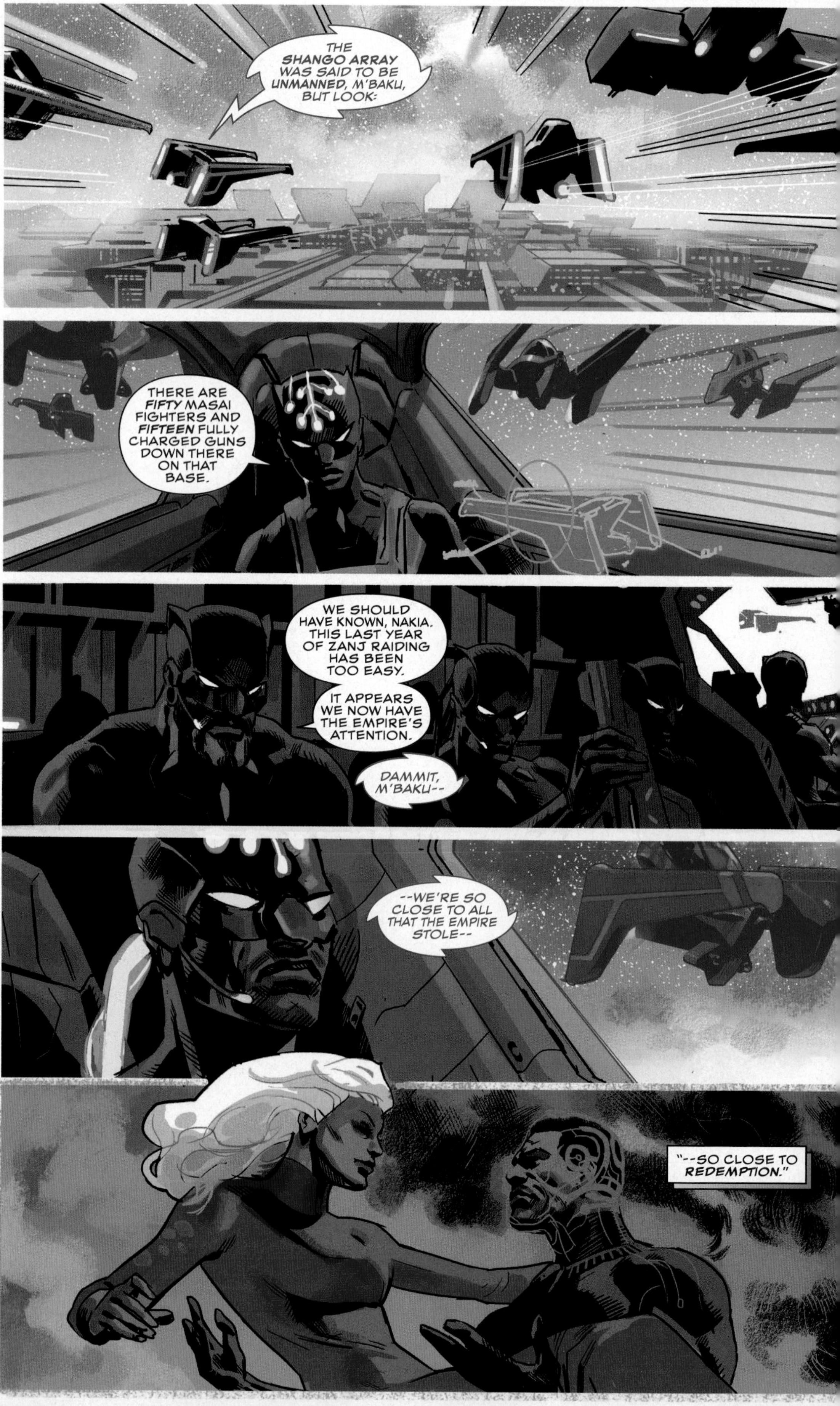
THE SHANGO ARRAY WAS SAID TO BE UNMANNED, M'BAKU, BUT LOOK:
THERE ARE FIFTY MASAI FIGHTERS AND FIFTEEN FULLY CHARGED GUNS DOWN THERE ON THAT BASE.
WE SHOULD HAVE KNOWN, NAKIA. THIS LAST YEAR OF ZANJ RAIDING HAS BEEN TOO EASY.
IT APPEARS WE NOW HAVE THE EMPIRE'S ATTENTION.
DAMMIT, M'BAKU--
--WE'RE SO CLOSE TO ALL THAT THE EMPIRE STOLE--
"--SO CLOSE TO REDEMPTION."

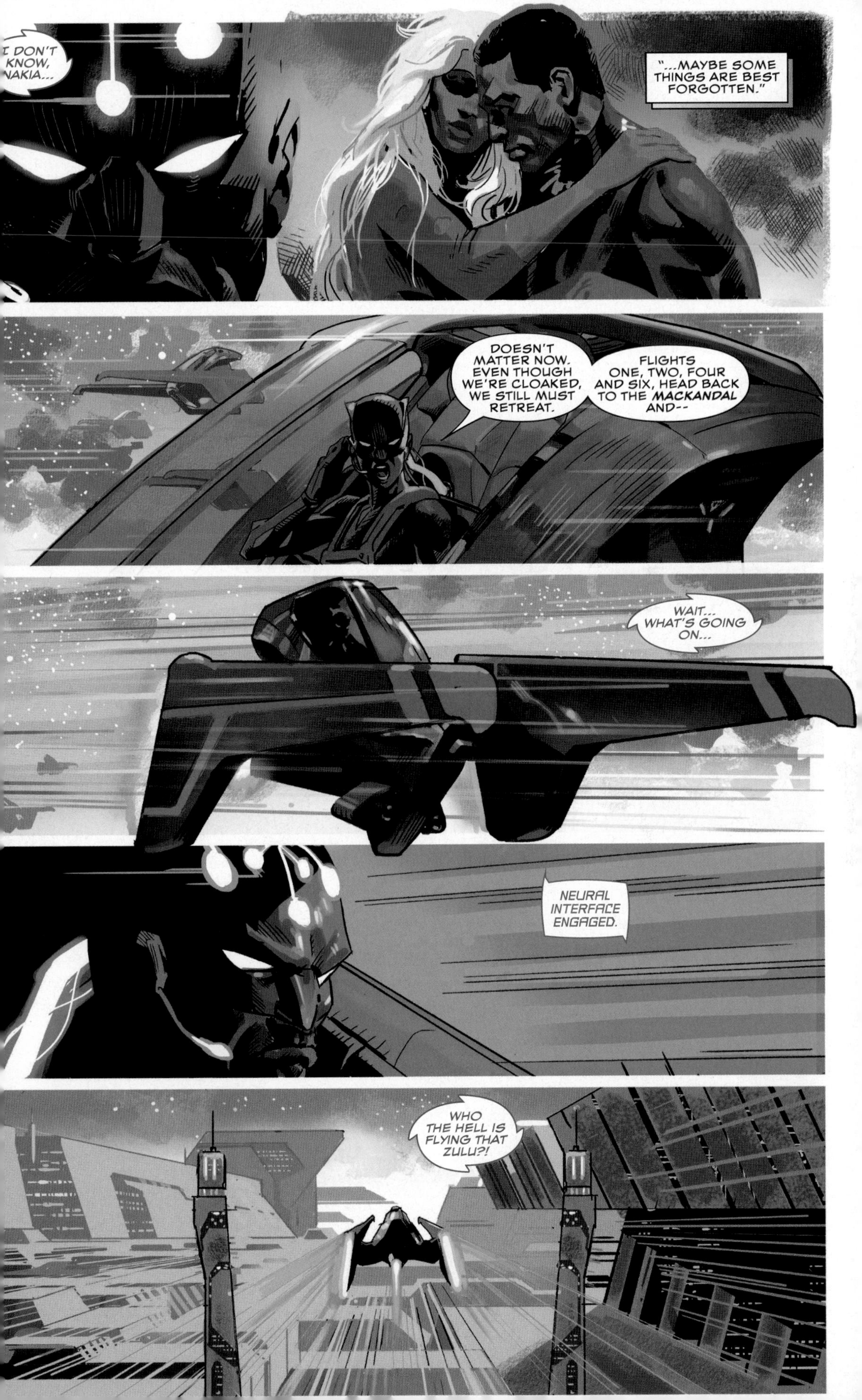
I DON'T KNOW, NAKIA...
"...MAYBE SOME THINGS ARE BEST FORGOTTEN."
DOESN'T MATTER NOW. EVEN THOUGH WE'RE CLOAKED, WE STILL MUST RETREAT.
FLIGHTS ONE, TWO, FOUR AND SIX, HEAD BACK TO THE MACKANDAL AND--
WAIT... WHAT'S GOING ON...
NEURAL INTERFACE ENGAGED.
WHO THE HELL IS FLYING THAT ZULU?!

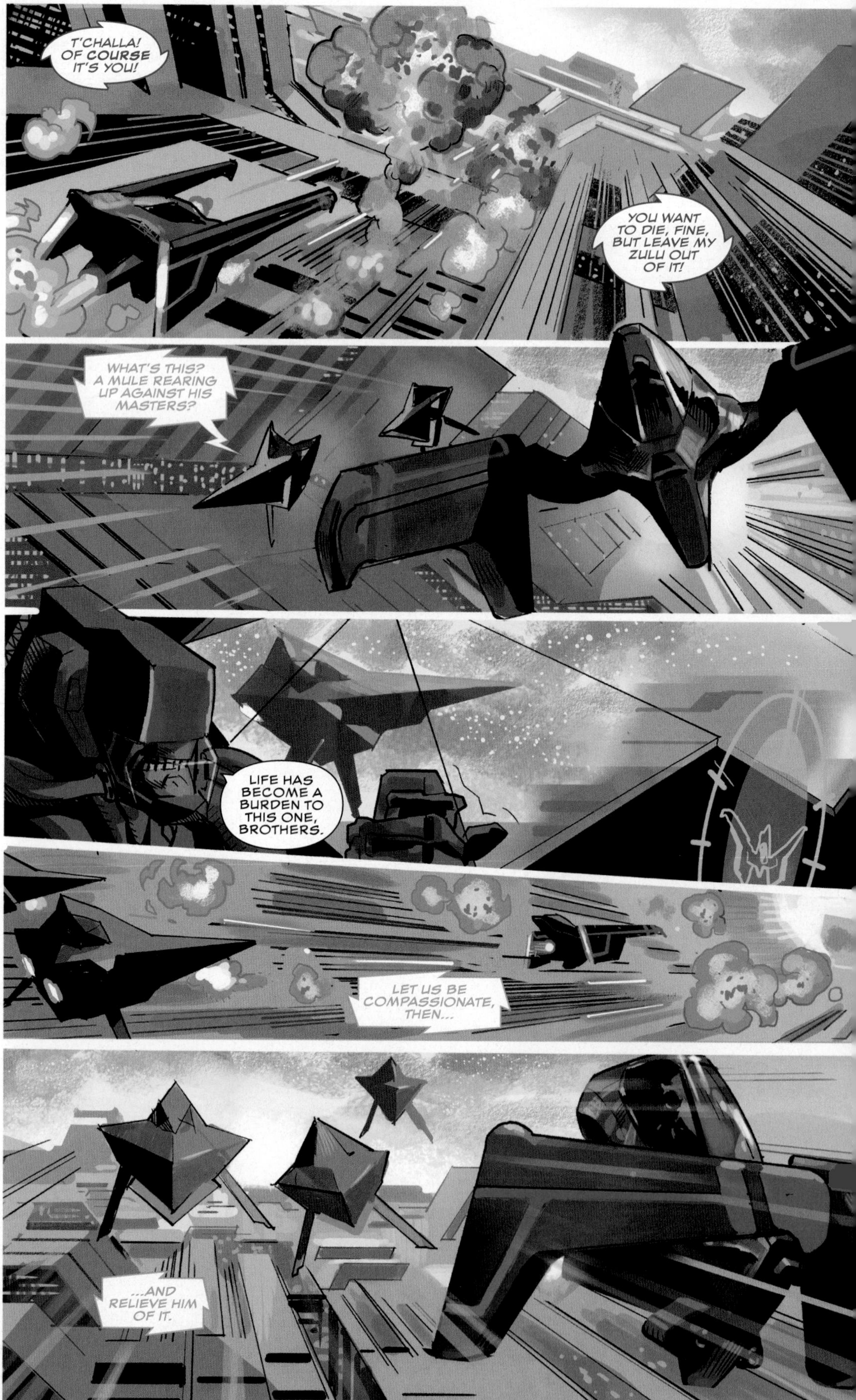
T'CHALLA! OF COURSE IT'S YOU!
YOU WANT TO DIE, FINE, BUT LEAVE MY ZULU OUT OF IT!
WHAT'S THIS? A MULE REARING UP AGAINST HIS MASTERS?
LIFE HAS BECOME A BURDEN TO THIS ONE, BROTHERS.
LET US BE COMPASSIONATE, THEN...
...AND RELIEVE HIM OF IT.

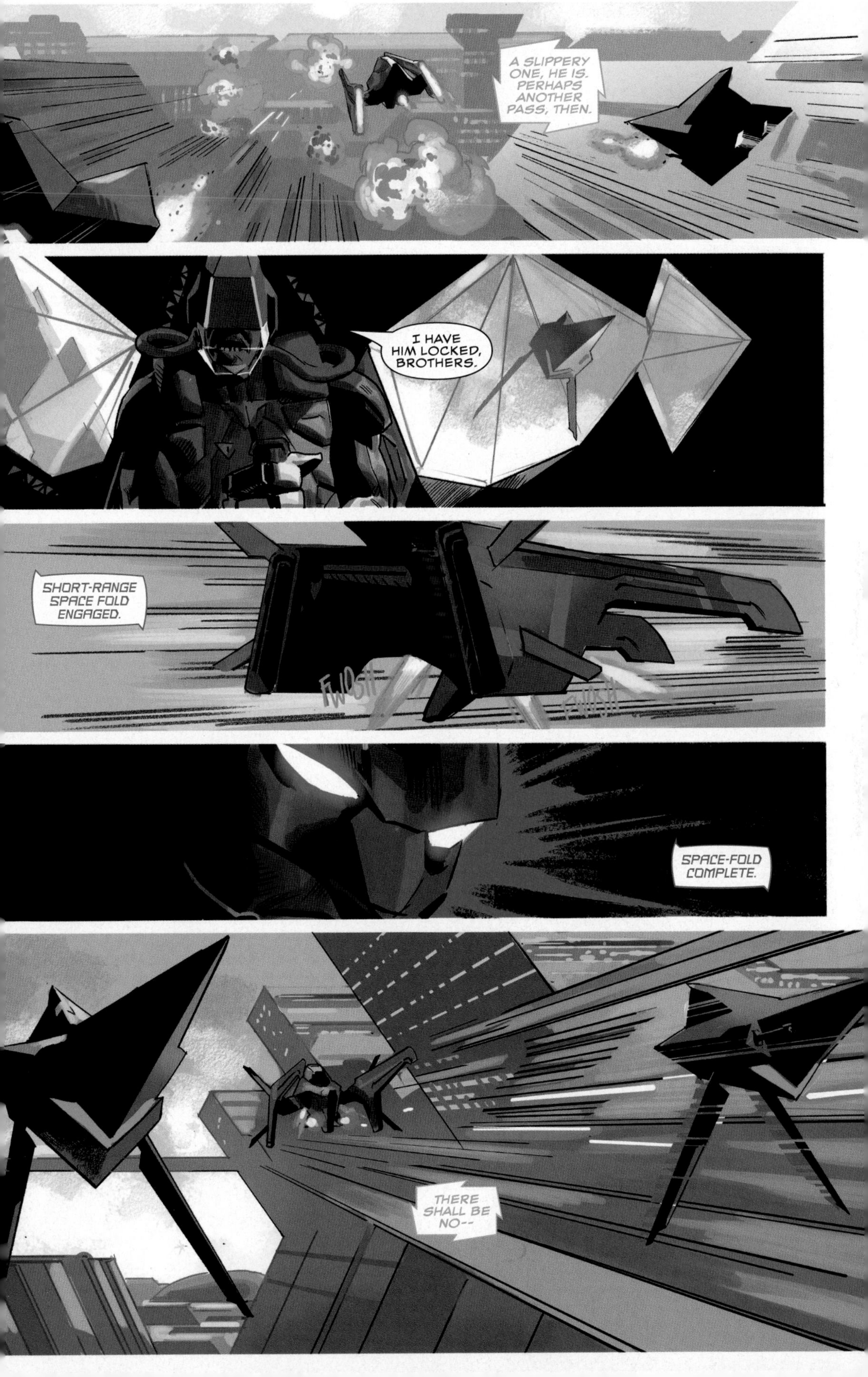
A SLIPPERY ONE, HE IS. PERHAPS ANOTHER PASS, THEN.
I HAVE HIM LOCKED, BROTHERS.
SHORT-RANGE SPACE FOLD ENGAGED.
SPACE-FOLD COMPLETE.
THERE SHALL BE NO--

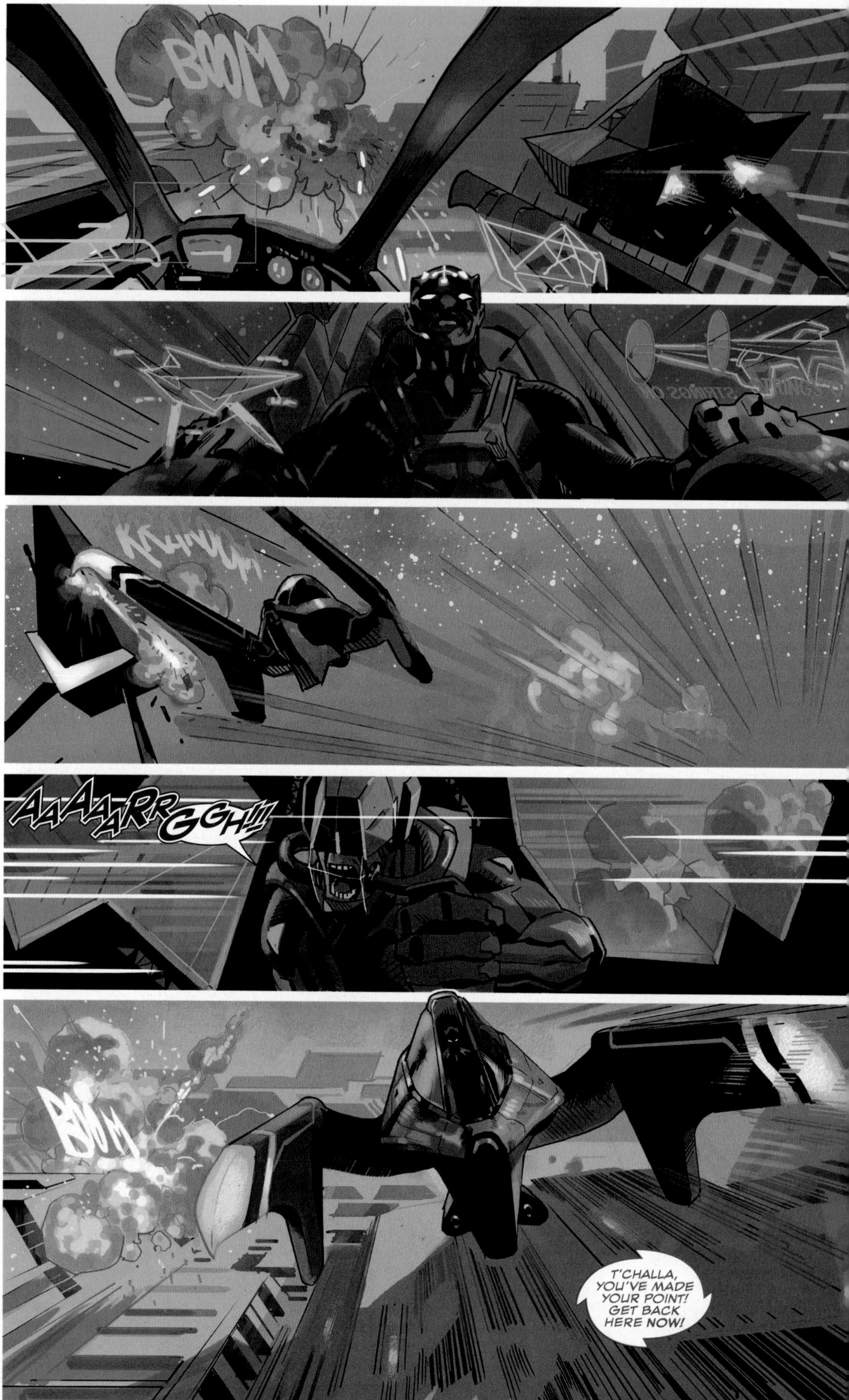
BOOM
AAAAARRGGH!!!
BOOM
T'CHALLA, YOU'VE MADE YOUR POINT! GET BACK HERE NOW!

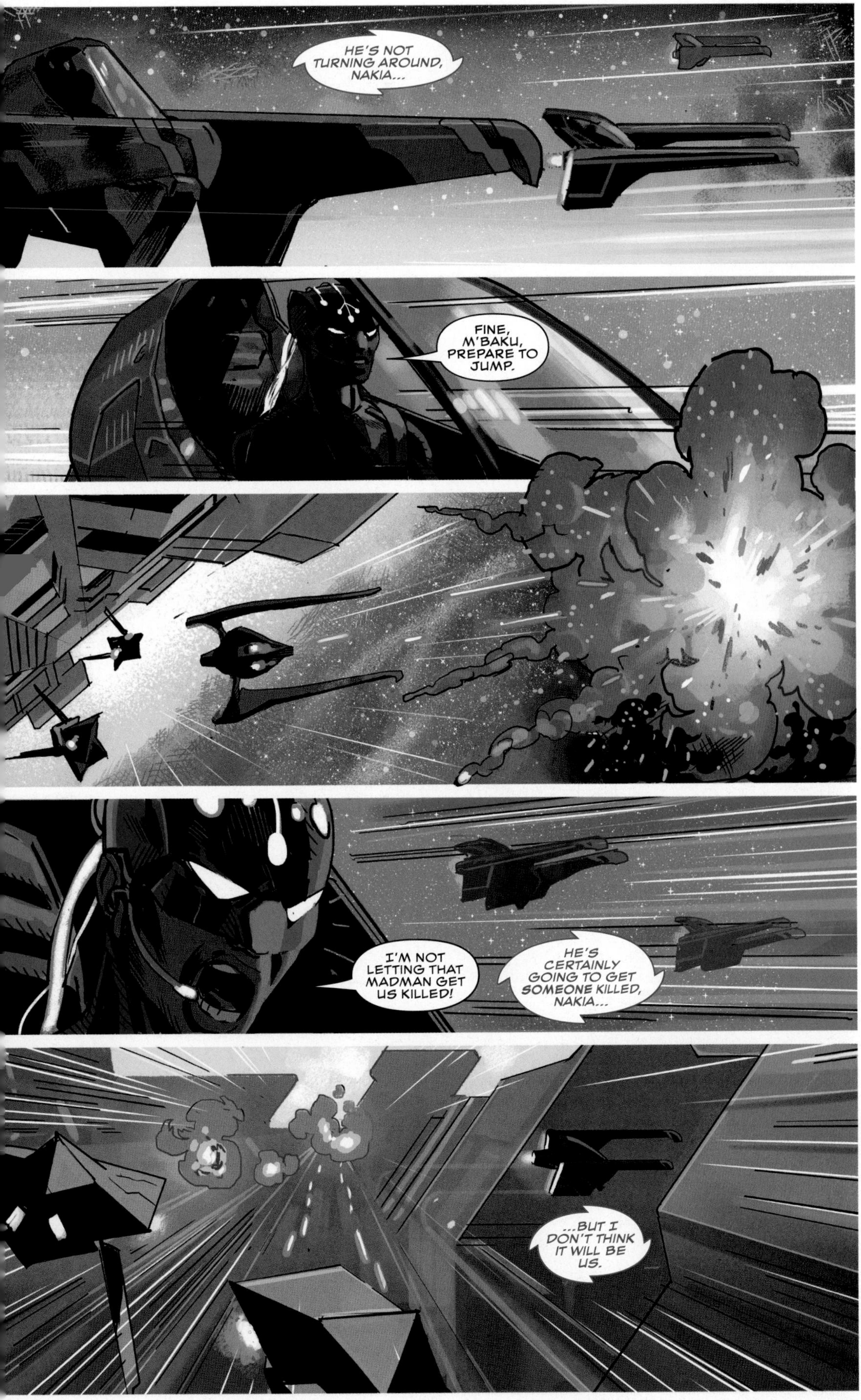
HE'S NOT TURNING AROUND, NAKIA...
FINE, M'BAKU, PREPARE TO JUMP.
I'M NOT LETTING THAT MADMAN GET US KILLED!
HE'S CERTAINLY GOING TO GET SOMEONE KILLED, NAKIA...
...BUT I DON'T THINK IT WILL BE US.

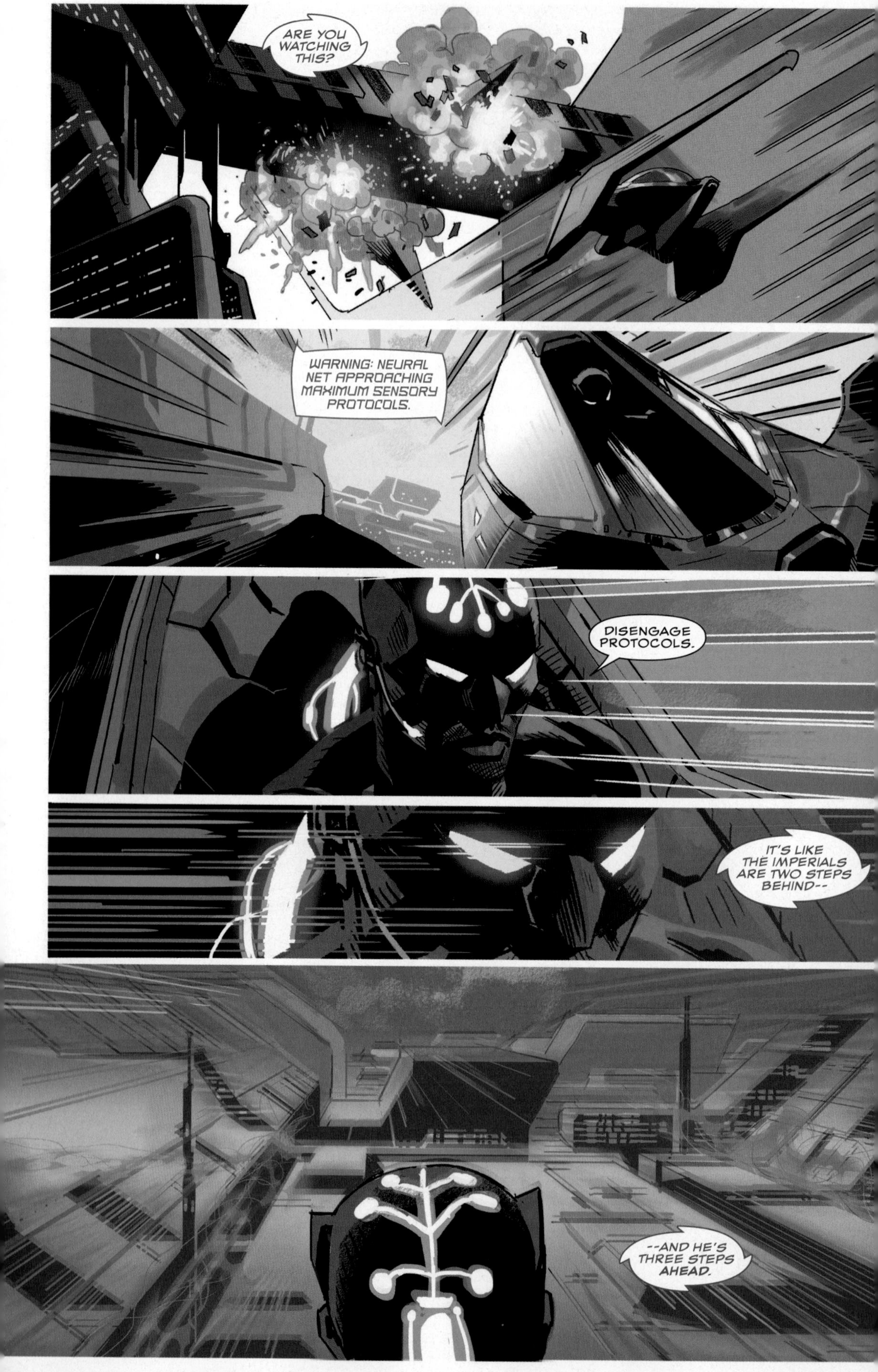
ARE YOU WATCHING THIS?
WARNING: NEURAL NET APPROACHING MAXIMUM SENSORY PROTOCOLS.
DISENGAGE PROTOCOLS.
IT'S LIKE THE IMPERIALS ARE TWO STEPS BEHIND--
--AND HE'S THREE STEPS AHEAD.

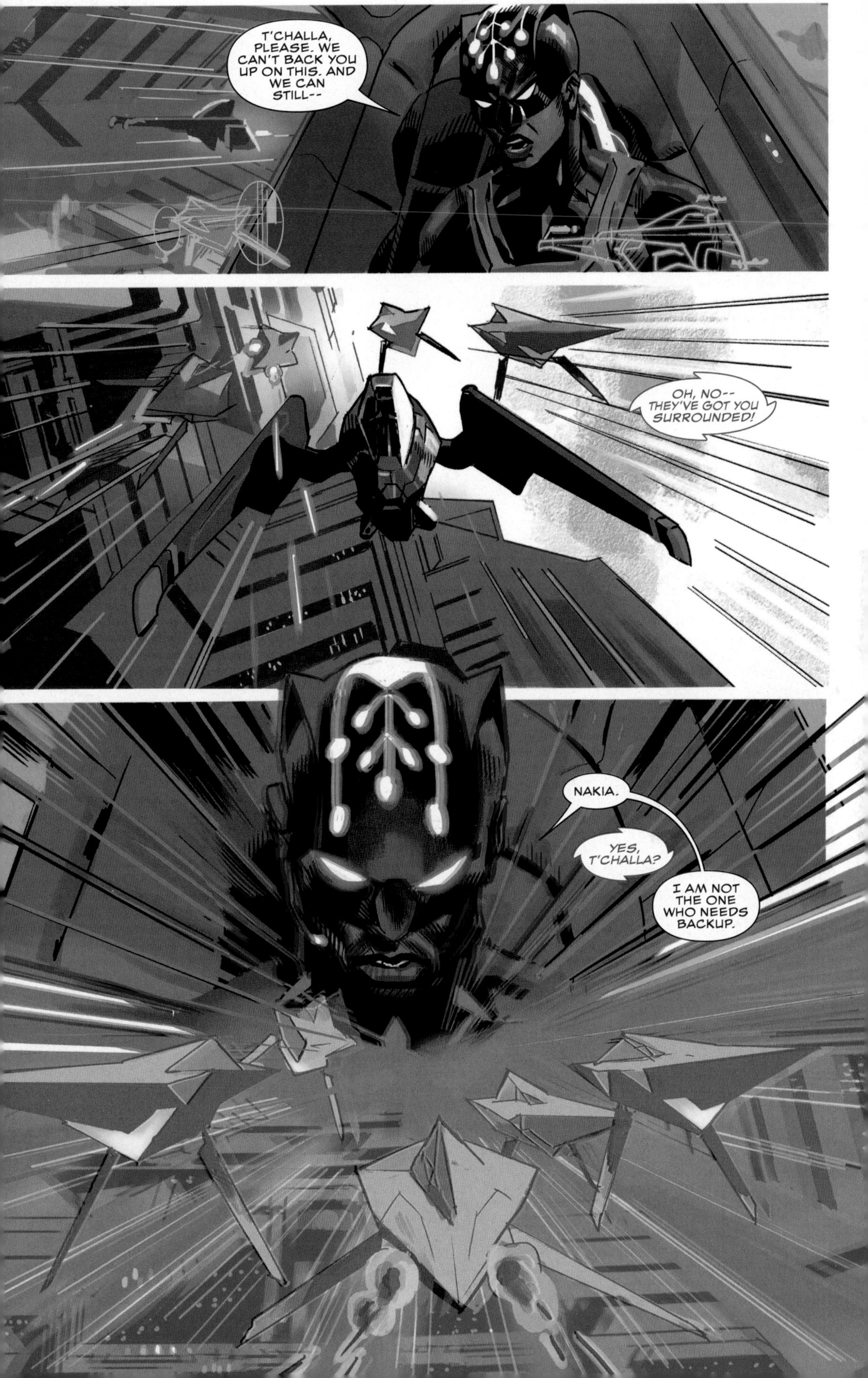
T'CHALLA, PLEASE. WE CAN'T BACK YOU UP ON THIS. AND WE CAN STILL--
OH, NO-- THEY'VE GOT YOU SURROUNDED!
NAKIA.
YES, T'CHALLA?
I AM NOT THE ONE WHO NEEDS BACKUP.

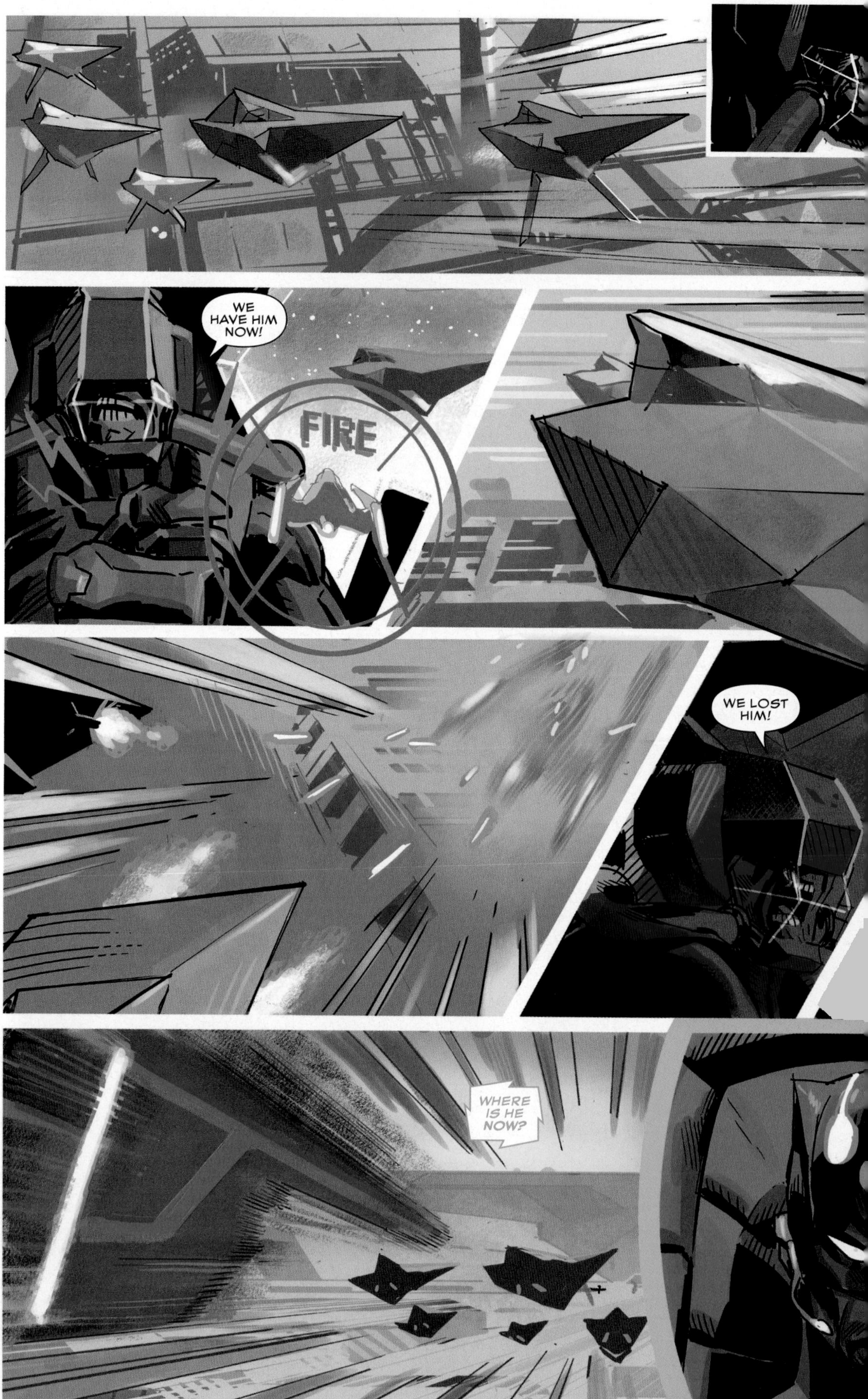
WE HAVE HIM NOW!
FIRE
WE LOST HIM!
WHERE IS HE NOW?

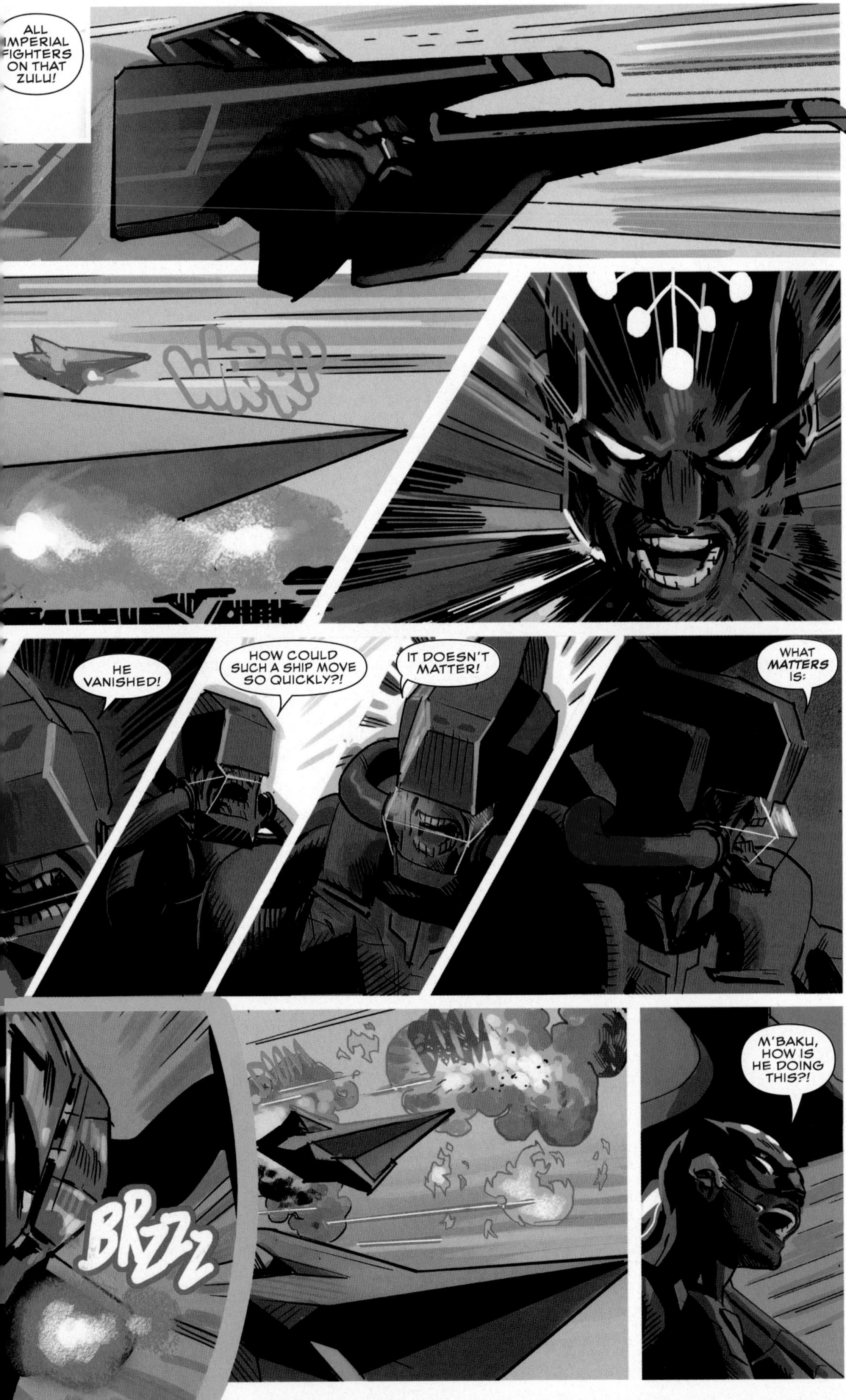
ALL IMPERIAL FIGHTERS ON THAT ZULU!
HE VANISHED!
HOW COULD SUCH A SHIP MOVE SO QUICKLY?!
IT DOESN'T MATTER!
WHAT MATTERS IS:
BRZZZ
M'BAKU, HOW IS HE DOING THIS?!

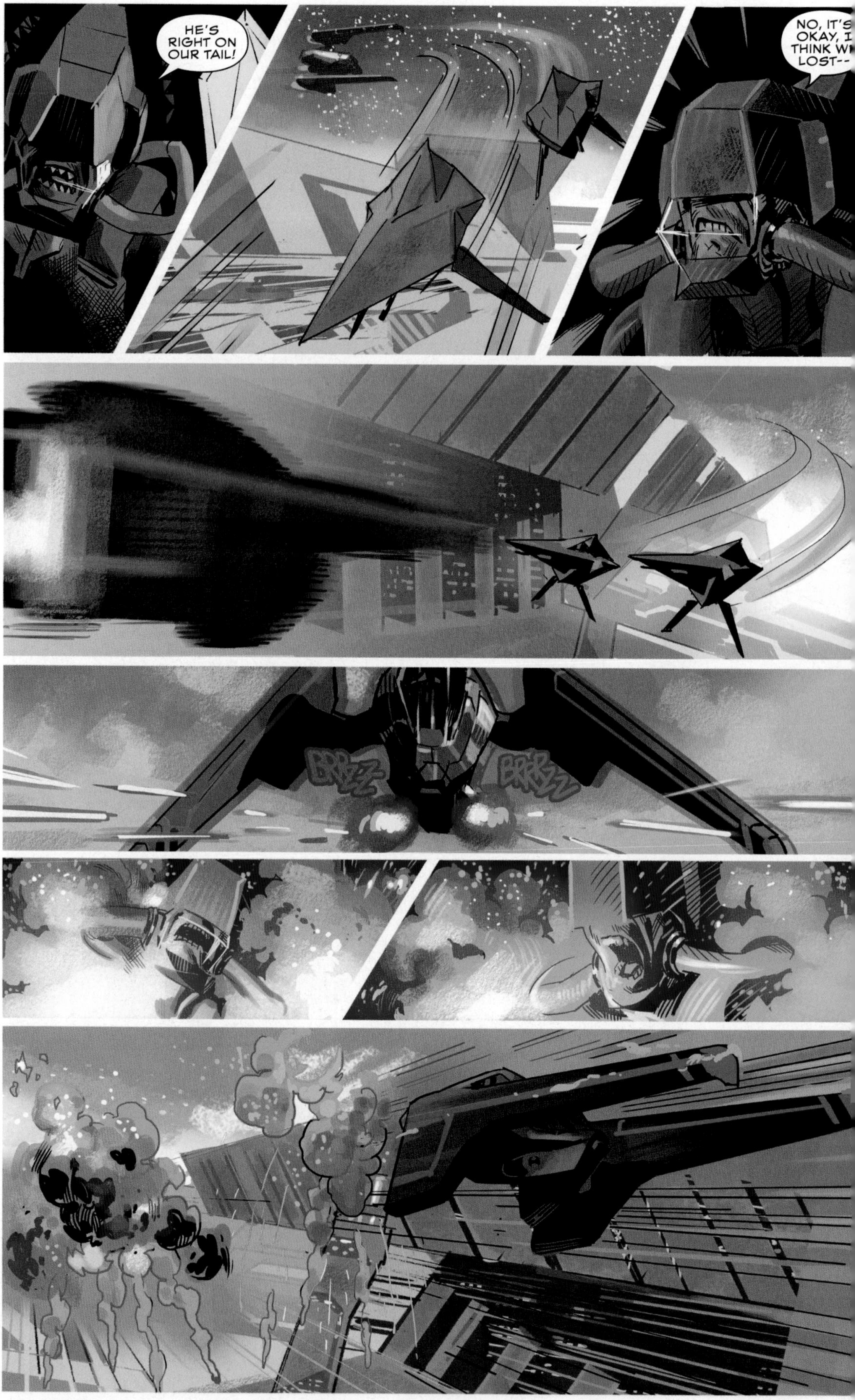
HE'S RIGHT ON OUR TAIL!
NO, IT'S OKAY, I THINK W-- LOST--
BRRRZZ
BRRRZZ

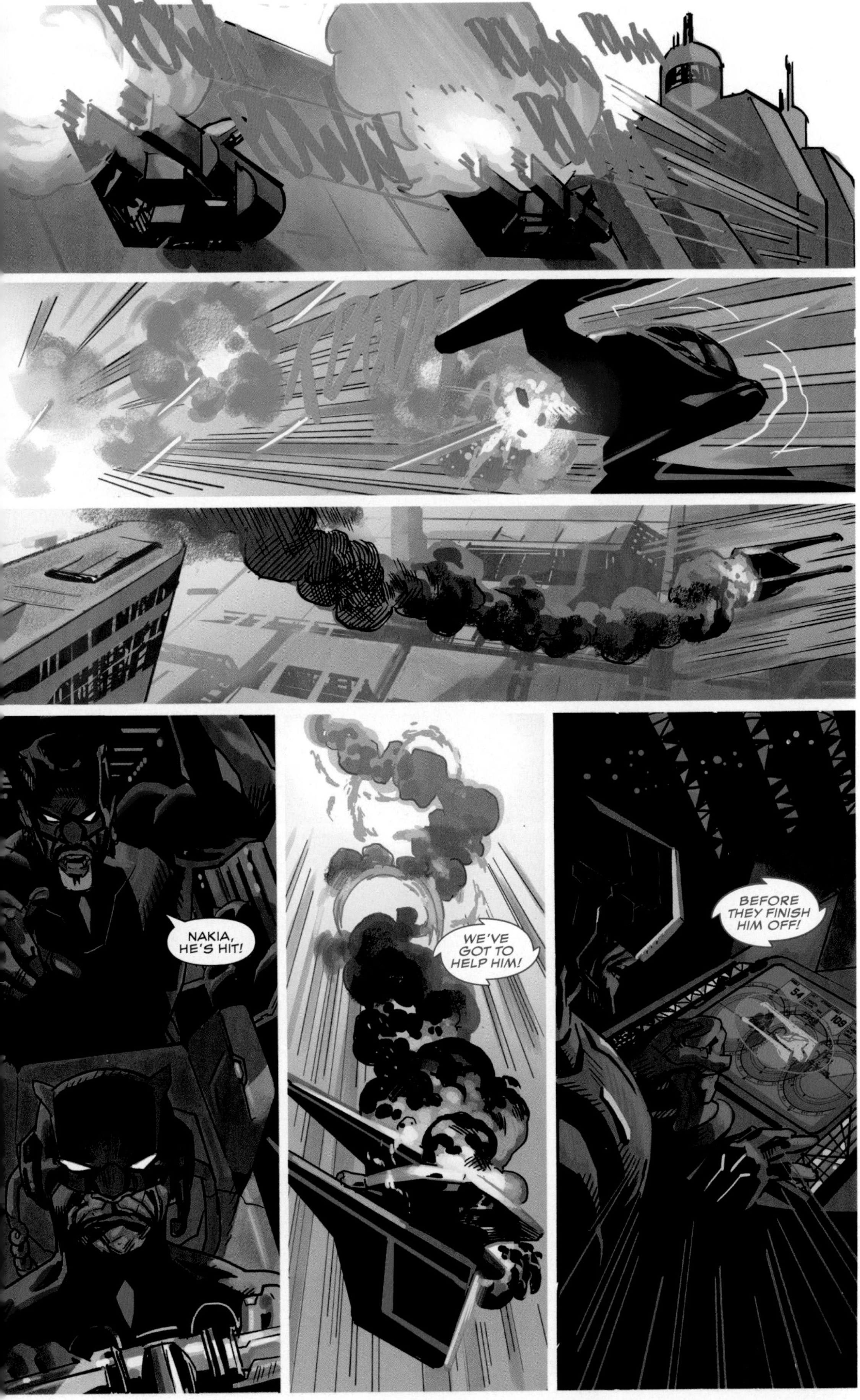
NAKIA, HE'S HIT!
WE'VE GOT TO HELP HIM!
BEFORE THEY FINISH HIM OFF!

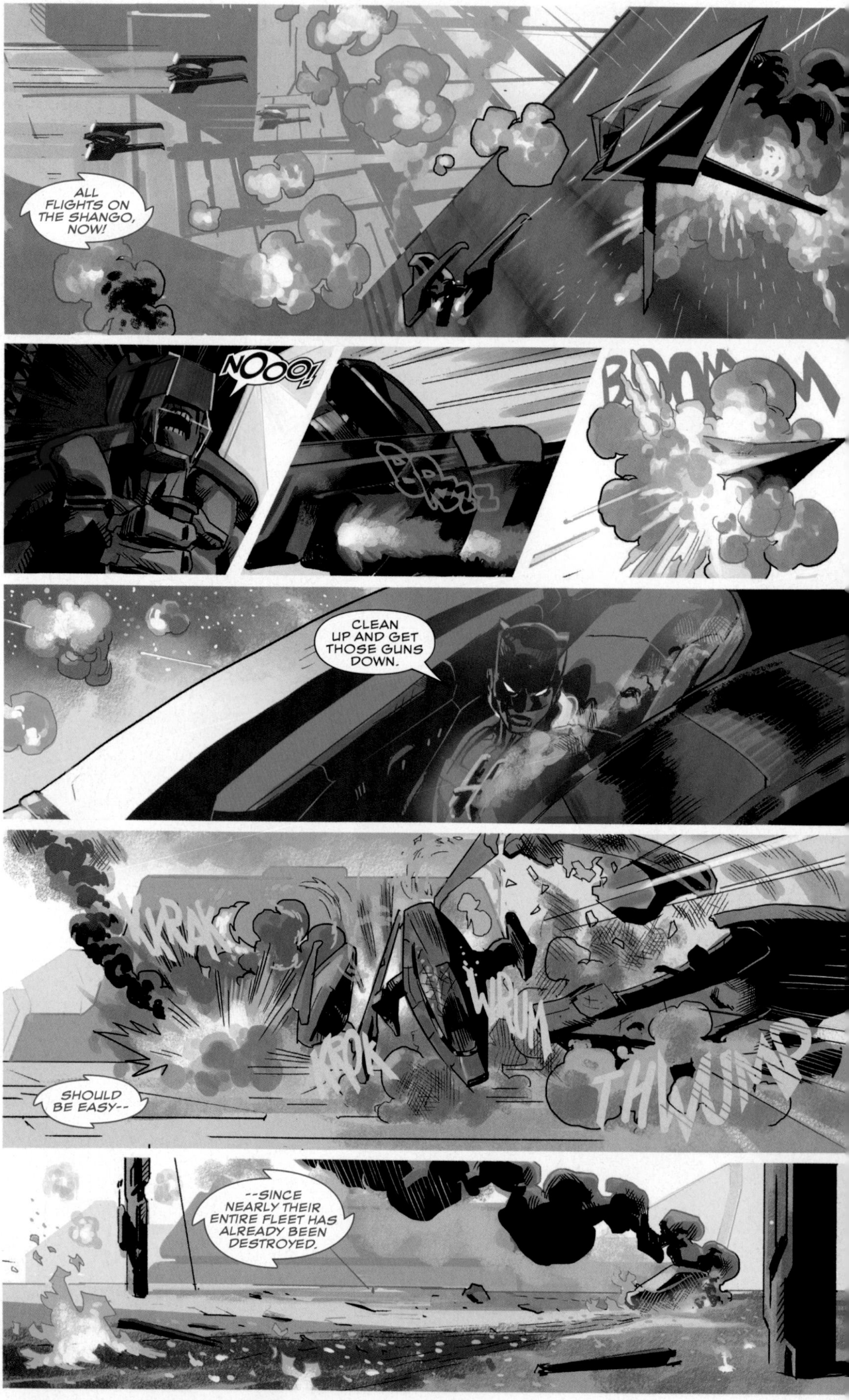
ALL FLIGHTS ON THE SHANGO, NOW!
NOOO!
BOOOM
CLEAN UP AND GET THOSE GUNS DOWN.
KRAK
WRUM
KROK
THWUMP
SHOULD BE EASY--
--SINCE NEARLY THEIR ENTIRE FLEET HAS ALREADY BEEN DESTROYED.

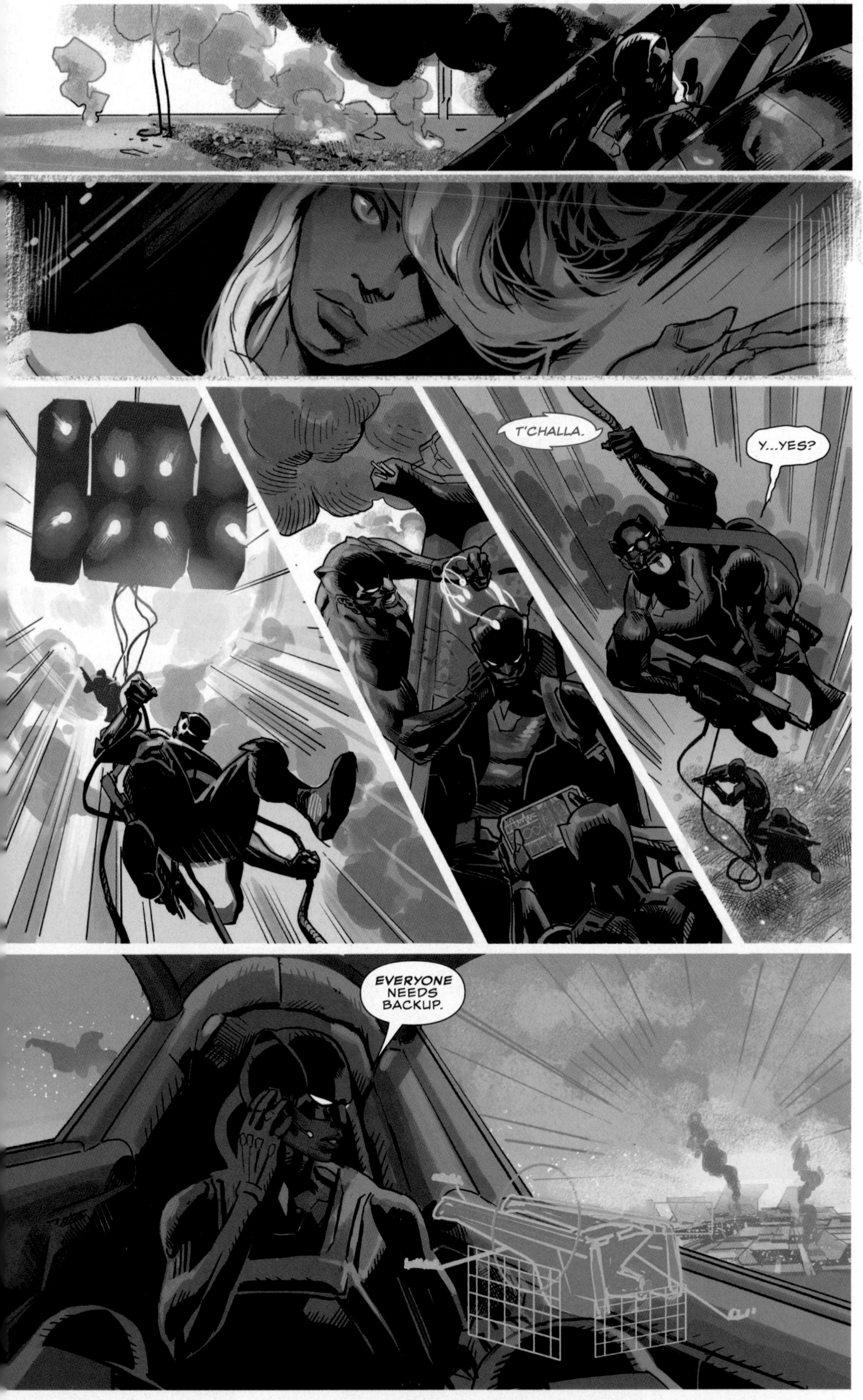
T'CHALLA.
Y...YES?
EVERYONE NEEDS BACKUP.

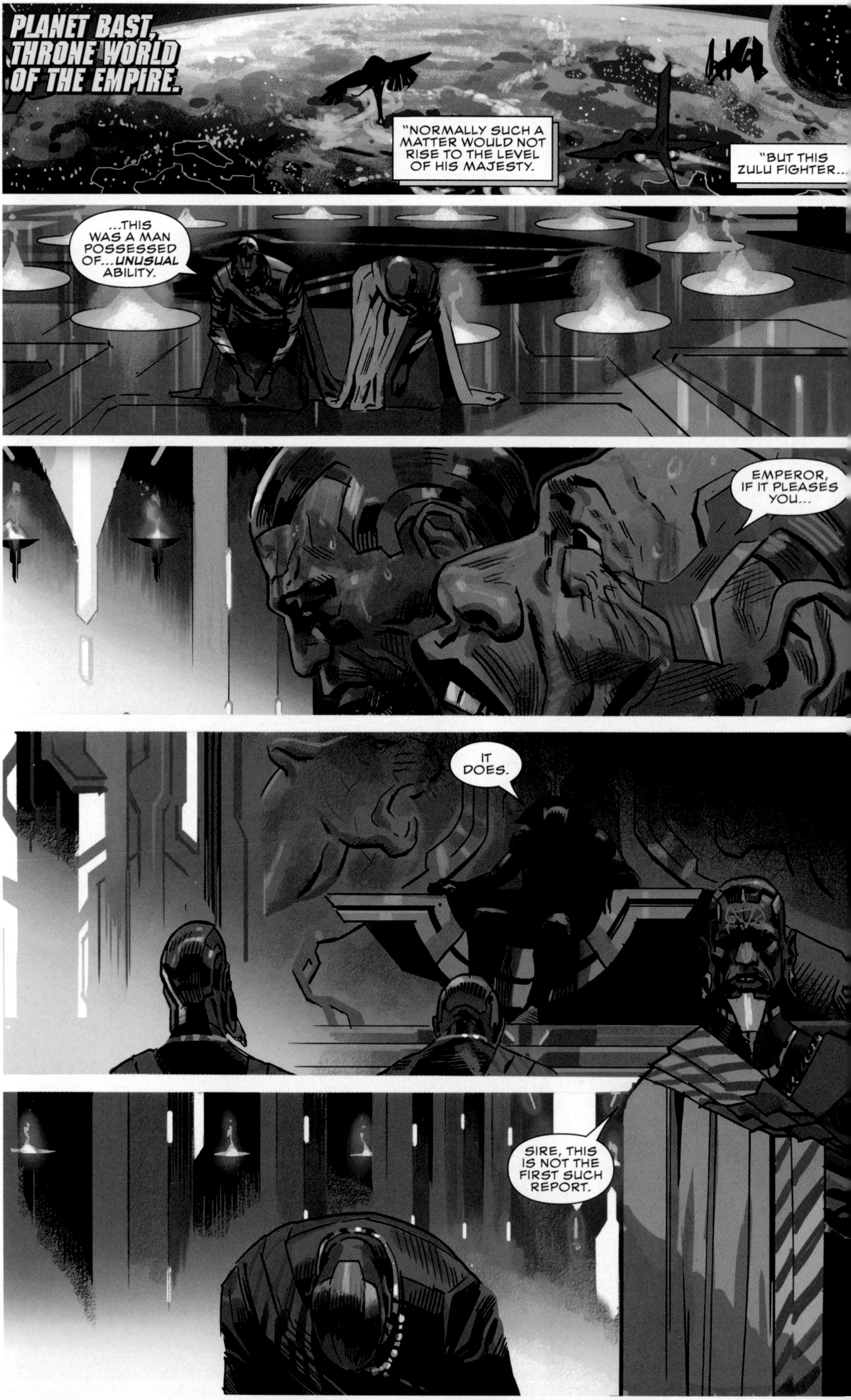
PLANET BAST, THRONE WORLD OF THE EMPIRE.
"NORMALLY SUCH A MATTER WOULD NOT RISE TO THE LEVEL OF HIS MAJESTY.
"BUT THIS ZULU FIGHTER...
...THIS WAS A MAN POSSESSED OF... *UNUSUAL* ABILITY.
EMPEROR, IF IT PLEASES YOU...
IT DOES.
SIRE, THIS IS NOT THE FIRST SUCH REPORT.

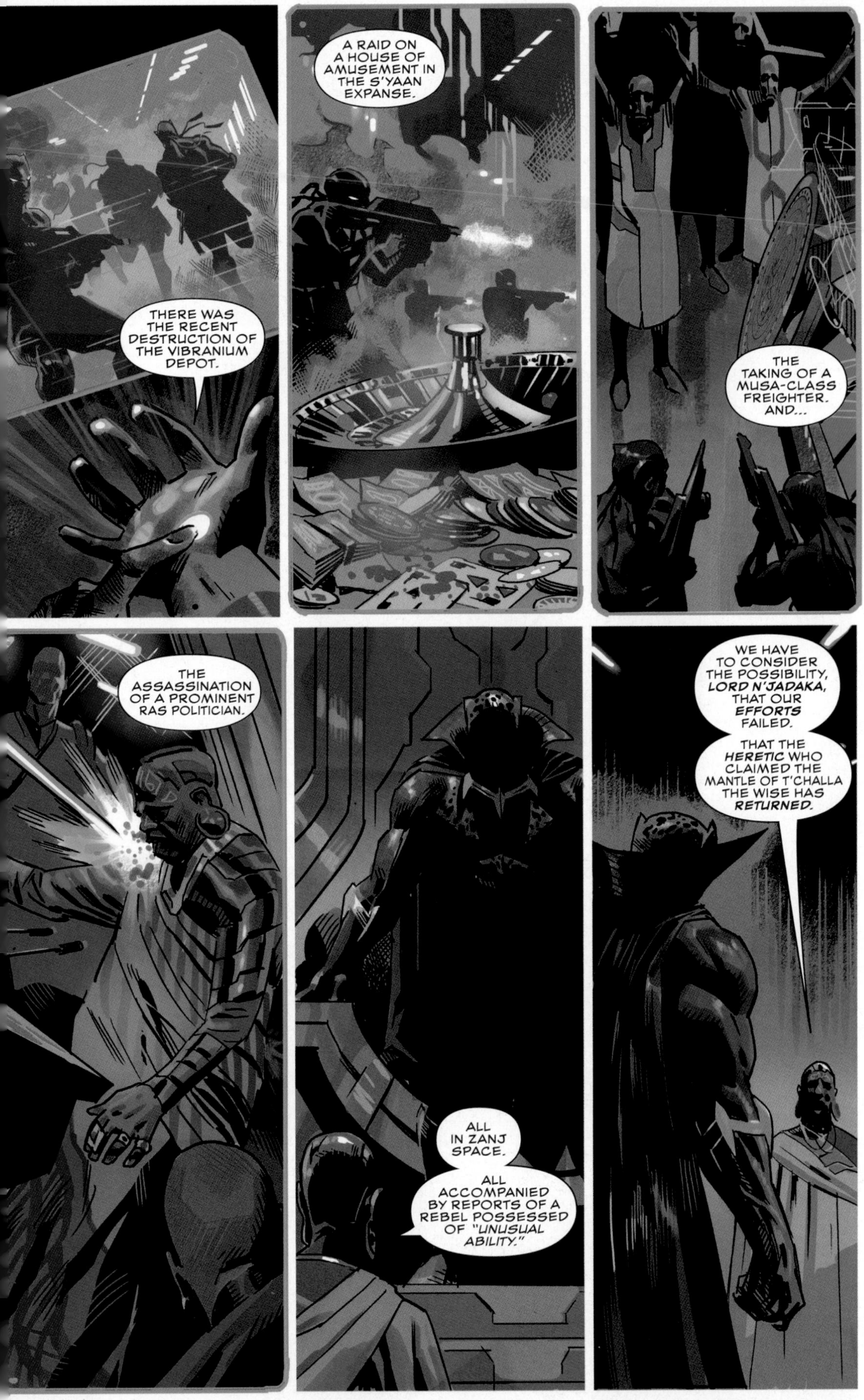
THERE WAS THE RECENT DESTRUCTION OF THE VIBRANIUM DEPOT.
A RAID ON A HOUSE OF AMUSEMENT IN THE S'YAAN EXPANSE.
THE TAKING OF A MUSA-CLASS FREIGHTER. AND...
THE ASSASSINATION OF A PROMINENT RAS POLITICIAN.
ALL IN ZANJ SPACE.
ALL ACCOMPANIED BY REPORTS OF A REBEL POSSESSED OF "UNUSUAL ABILITY."
WE HAVE TO CONSIDER THE POSSIBILITY, LORD N'JADAKA, THAT OUR EFFORTS FAILED.
THAT THE HERETIC WHO CLAIMED THE MANTLE OF T'CHALLA THE WISE HAS RETURNED.

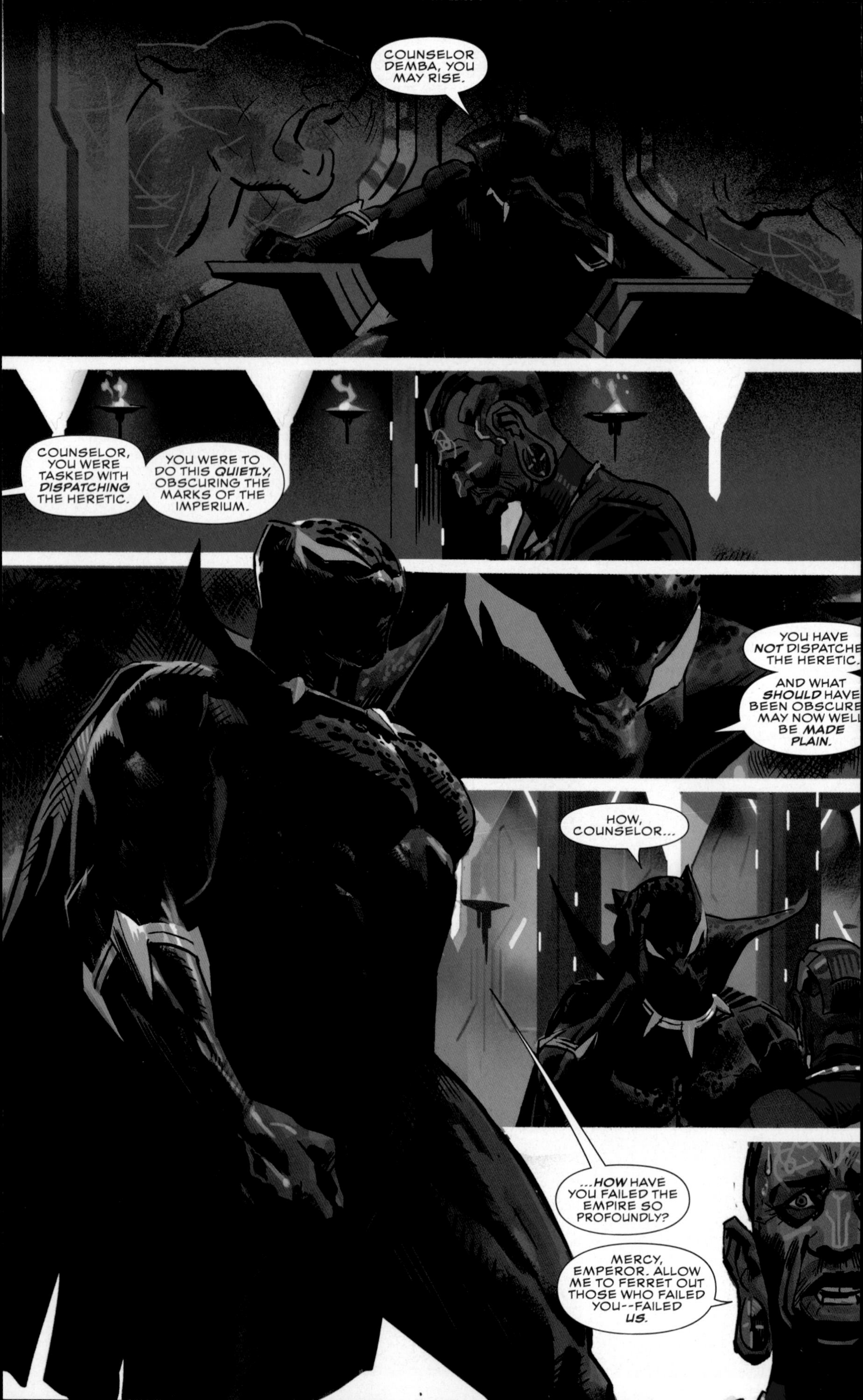
COUNSELOR DEMBA, YOU MAY RISE.
COUNSELOR, YOU WERE TASKED WITH *DISPATCHING* THE HERETIC.
YOU WERE TO DO THIS *QUIETLY,* OBSCURING THE MARKS OF THE IMPERIUM.
YOU HAVE *NOT* DISPATCHE THE HERETIC.
AND WHAT *SHOULD* HAVE BEEN OBSCURE MAY NOW WELL BE *MADE PLAIN.*
HOW, COUNSELOR...
...*HOW* HAVE YOU FAILED THE EMPIRE SO PROFOUNDLY?
MERCY, EMPEROR. ALLOW ME TO FERRET OUT THOSE WHO FAILED YOU--FAILED *US.*

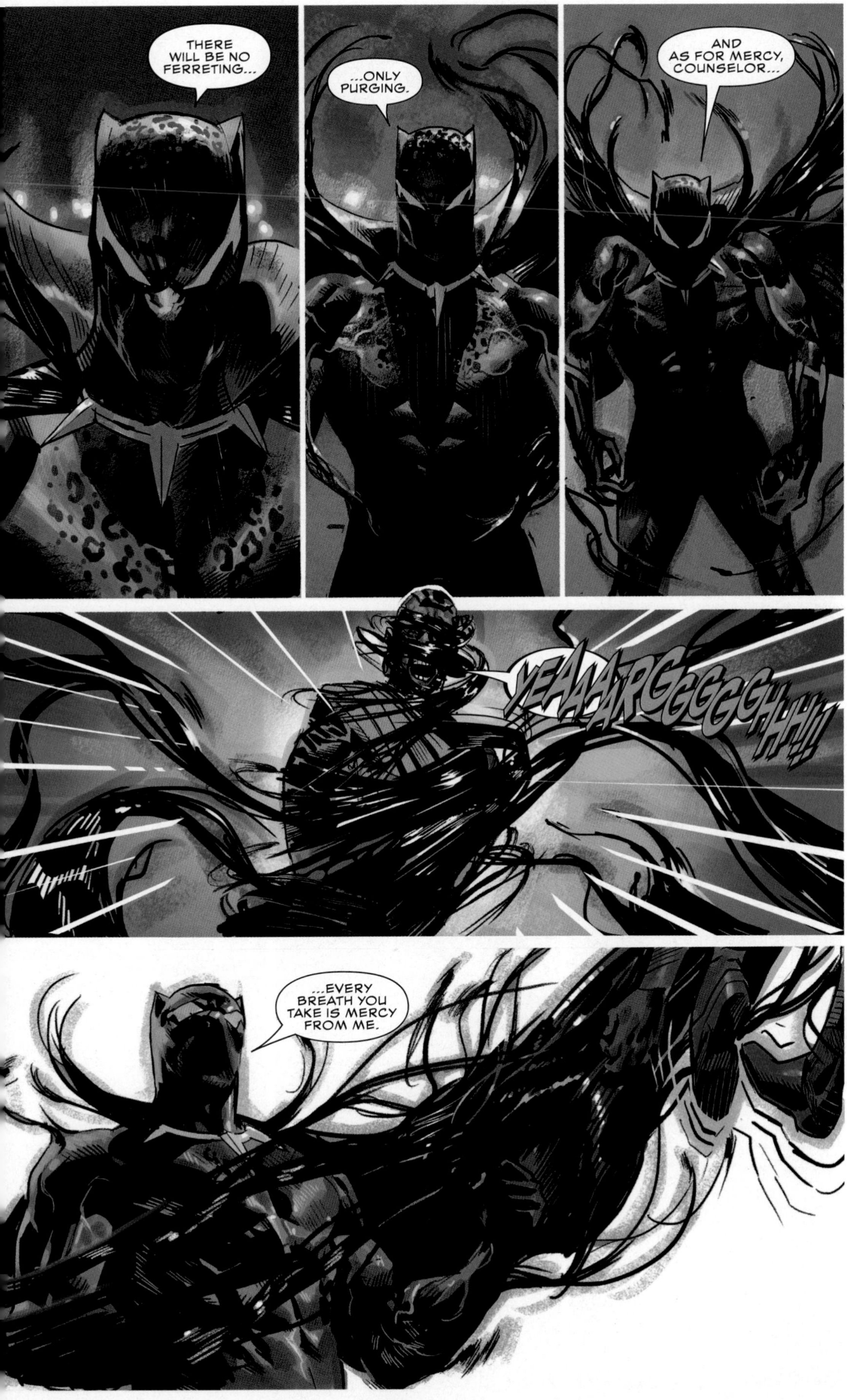
THERE WILL BE NO FERRETING...
...ONLY PURGING.
AND AS FOR MERCY, COUNSELOR...
YEAAAARGGGGGHHH!!
...EVERY BREATH YOU TAKE IS MERCY FROM ME.

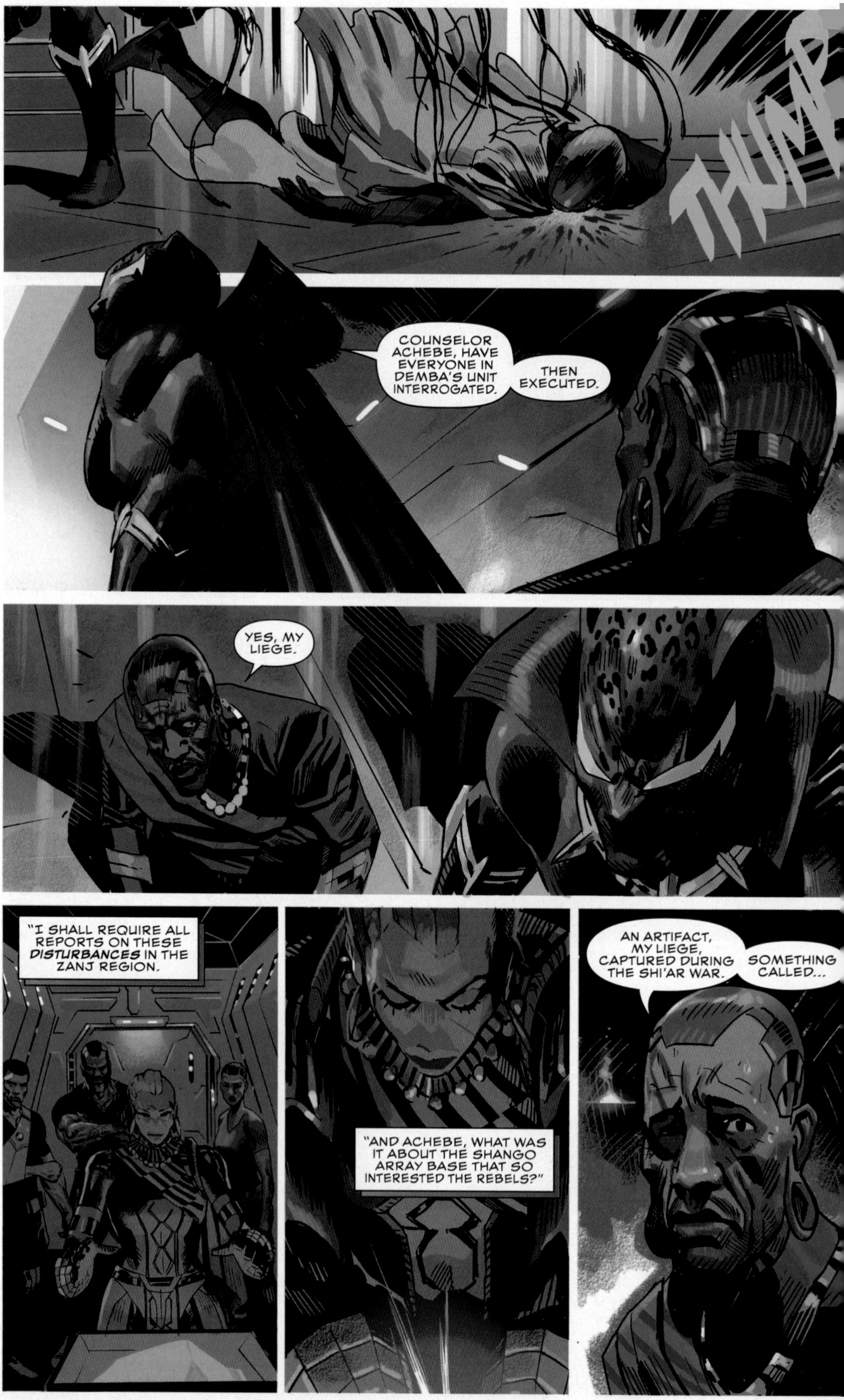
THUMP
COUNSELOR ACHEBE, HAVE EVERYONE IN DEMBA'S UNIT INTERROGATED.
THEN EXECUTED.
YES, MY LIEGE.
"I SHALL REQUIRE ALL REPORTS ON THESE DISTURBANCES IN THE ZANJ REGION.
"AND ACHEBE, WHAT WAS IT ABOUT THE SHANGO ARRAY BASE THAT SO INTERESTED THE REBELS?"
AN ARTIFACT, MY LIEGE, CAPTURED DURING THE SHI'AR WAR.
SOMETHING CALLED...

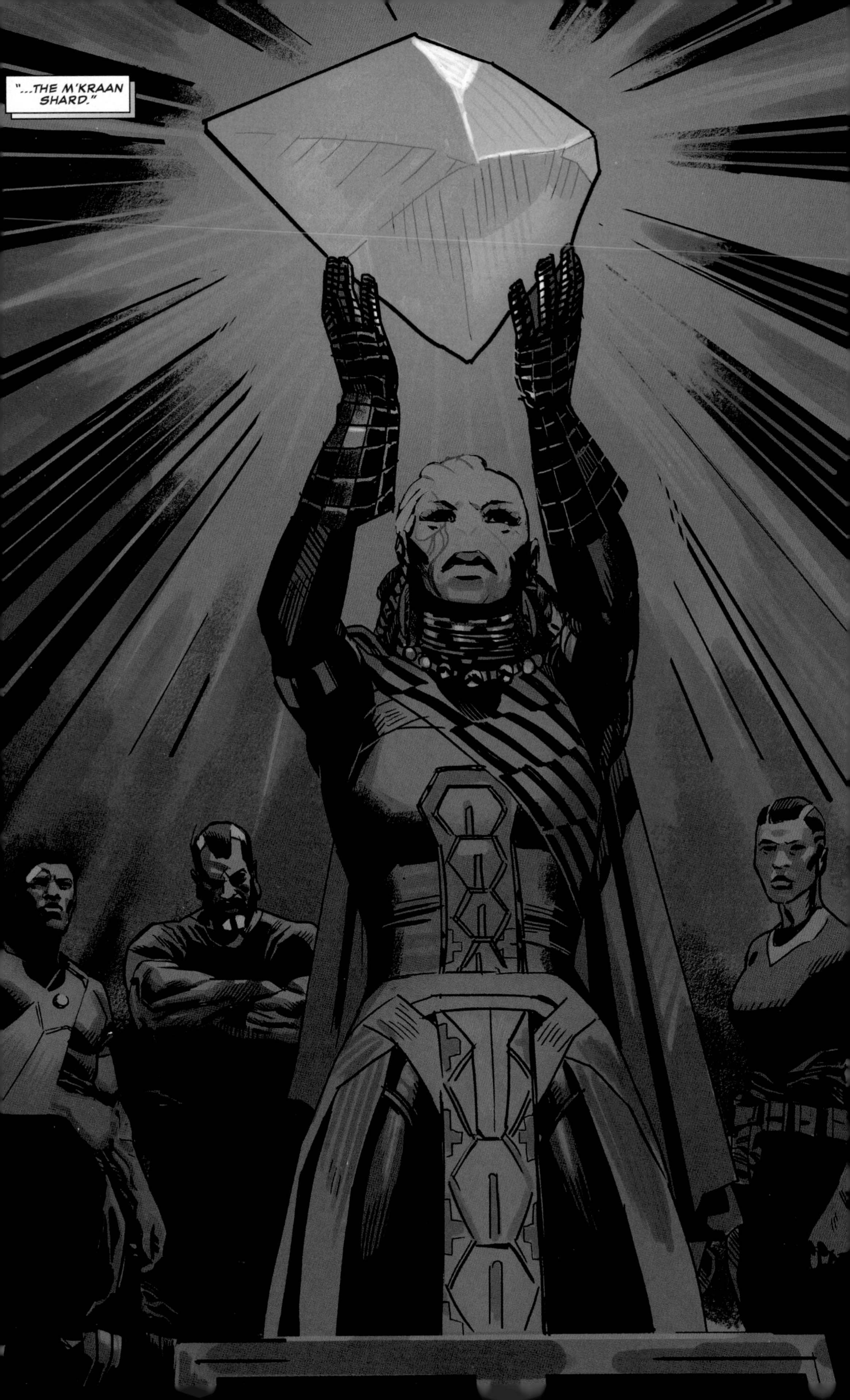
"...THE M'KRAAN SHARD."

WELCOME BACK TO THE EMPIRE! IN THIS ISSUE, YOU FINALLY MEET THE BIG BAD — EMPEROR N'JADAKA HIMSELF! YOU'LL LEARN MORE ABOUT HIM AS WE GO ALONG, BUT IN THE MEANTIME, HERE'S A LITTLE INTRODUCTION BY TA-NEHISI COATES TO THE MAJOR PLAYERS IN THE MAROONS — THE REBEL FACTION FIGHTING FOR THEIR LIVES AND THEIR HISTORIES — ALONG WITH SOME OF DANIEL ACUÑA'S STELLAR DESIGNS!

T'CHALLA:

A WARRIOR IN SEARCH OF HIMSELF, T'CHALLA, LIKE HIS NAMELESS BRETHREN, WAS MIND-WIPED AND ENSLAVED. NO ONE KNOWS HOW LONG THIS MAN WITHOUT A PAST TOILED AWAY IN THE EMPIRE'S VIBRANIUM MINES. WHAT IS KNOWN IS HE LATELY TOOK UP ARMS AGAINST THE EMPIRE AND ALLIED HIMSELF WITH THE REBELLIOUS MAROONS. HAUNTED BY VISIONS OF A VERY DIFFERENT LIFE, T'CHALLA IS DRIVEN TO REGAIN HIS MEMORY AND DESTROY THE EMPIRE THAT STRIPPED HIM OF IT.

NAKIA:

TACTICAL LEADER OF THE MAROONS, IT WAS NAKIA WHO LED THE RAID THAT FREED T'CHALLA. SHE IS AN IMPERIAL — THAT SECT OF WAKANDANS WHO CLAIM TO ORIGINATE SOMEWHERE ACROSS THE STARS ON A MYSTERIOUS WORLD KNOWN ONLY AS WAKANDA PRIME. NAKIA, UNLIKE MOST OF HER FELLOW MAROONS, REMEMBERS HER FORMER LIFE — ONE OF ARISTOCRATIC PRIVILEGE — BUT IS DRIVEN BY HER HATRED OF IT.

N'YAMI:

CHIEF OF THE MAROONS. N'YAMI LABORED FOR MOST OF HER YOUNG LIFE IN THE VIBRANIUM MINES. N'YAMI IS TAKY-MAZA, AN AMPHIBIOUS SPECIES HAILING FROM THE GALAXY OF NEHANDA'S LATTICE. LIKE T'CHALLA, SHE ESCAPED THE MINES. HER FEROCITY IN COMBAT DISTINGUISHED HER AND EVENTUALLY SHE ROSE TO LEAD THE ENTIRE REBELLION. N'YAMI IS CONSIDERABLY OLDER THAN THE SOLDIERS SHE COMMANDS. BUT SHE IS A DEADLY COMBATANT WHO IS UNDERESTIMATED AT HER OPPONENT'S PERIL.

M'BAKU:

ONE OF THE MAROONS' GREATEST WARRIORS. M'BAKU IS A LARGE MAN, FEARLESS IN BATTLE, WHO WOULD GLADLY SACRIFICE HIS LIFE IN SERVICE OF THE ZANJ REBELLION. UNLIKE HIS FELLOW MAROONS, M'BAKU IS IN NO GREAT HURRY TO RECOVER HIS MEMORY. HE DIMLY PERCEIVES SOME DARKNESS IN HIS PAST, AND PREFERS HIS LIFE AMONG THE MAROONS.

TAKU:

N'YAMI'S CHIEF INTELLIGENCE OFFICER. TAKU IS A RIGELLIAN WHOSE PEOPLE WERE LARGELY NOT ENSLAVED, BUT DRIVEN TO NEAR EXTINCTION BY THE EMPIRE. TAKU LIVED FOR YEARS AMONG A BAND OF RIGELLIAN TRADERS WHO ROAMED THE FIVE GALAXIES HAWKING THEIR WARES. HER KNOWLEDGE, GAINED THROUGH DECADES OF VOYAGING ACROSS THE EMPIRE, HAS PROVEN INDISPENSABLE TO THE MAROONS.

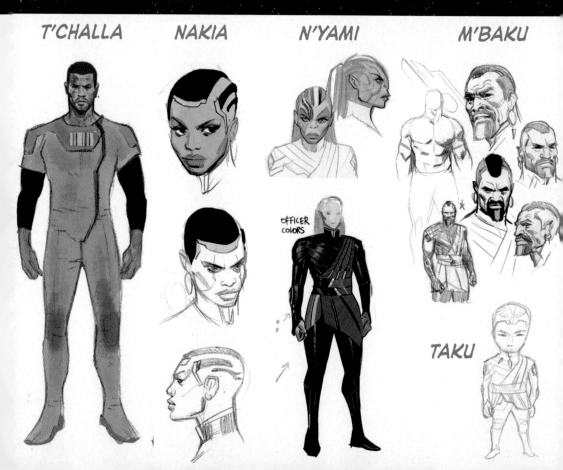

T'CHALLA   NAKIA   N'YAMI   M'BAKU

OFFICER COLORS

TAKU

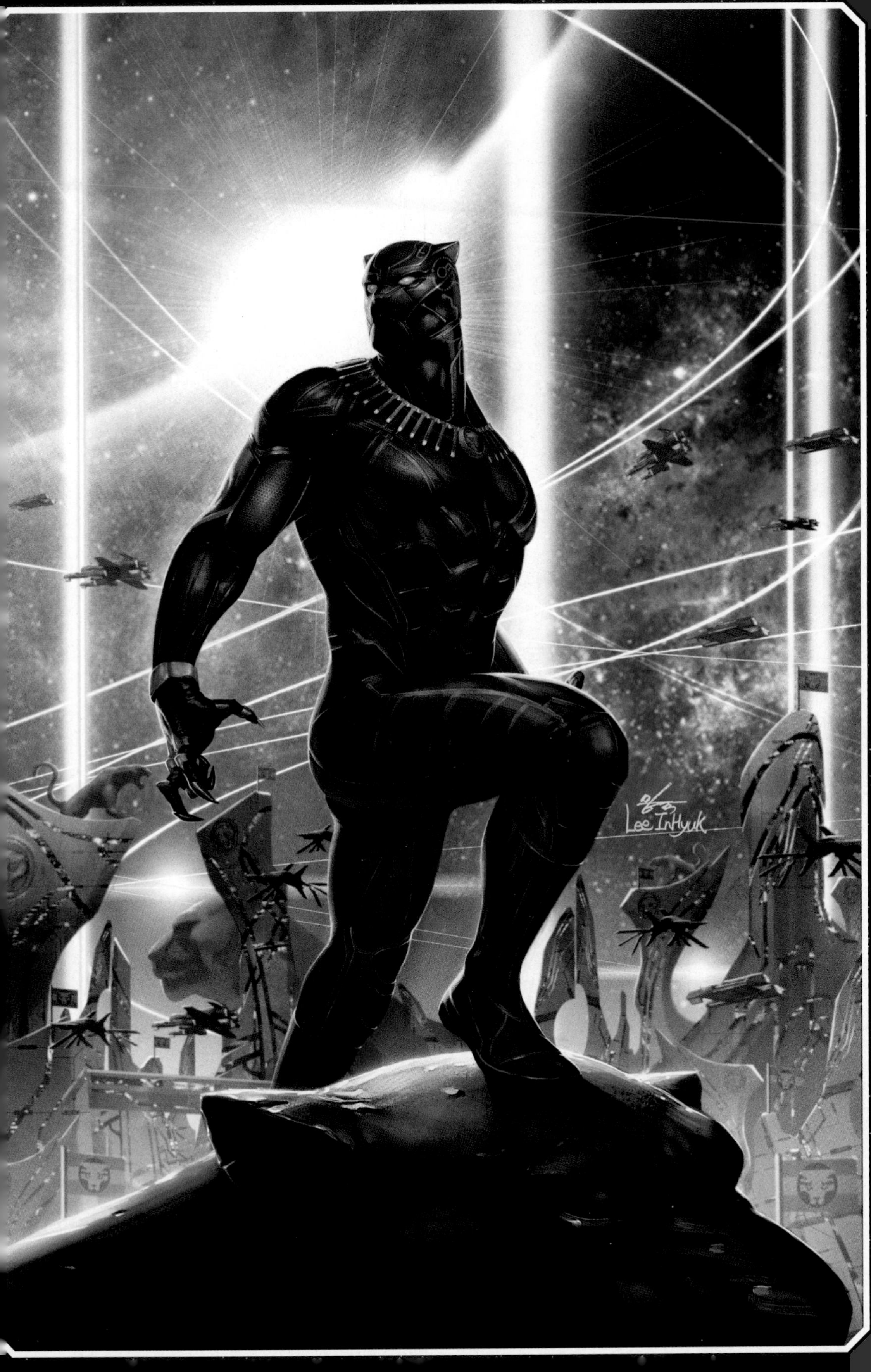
Lee InHyuk

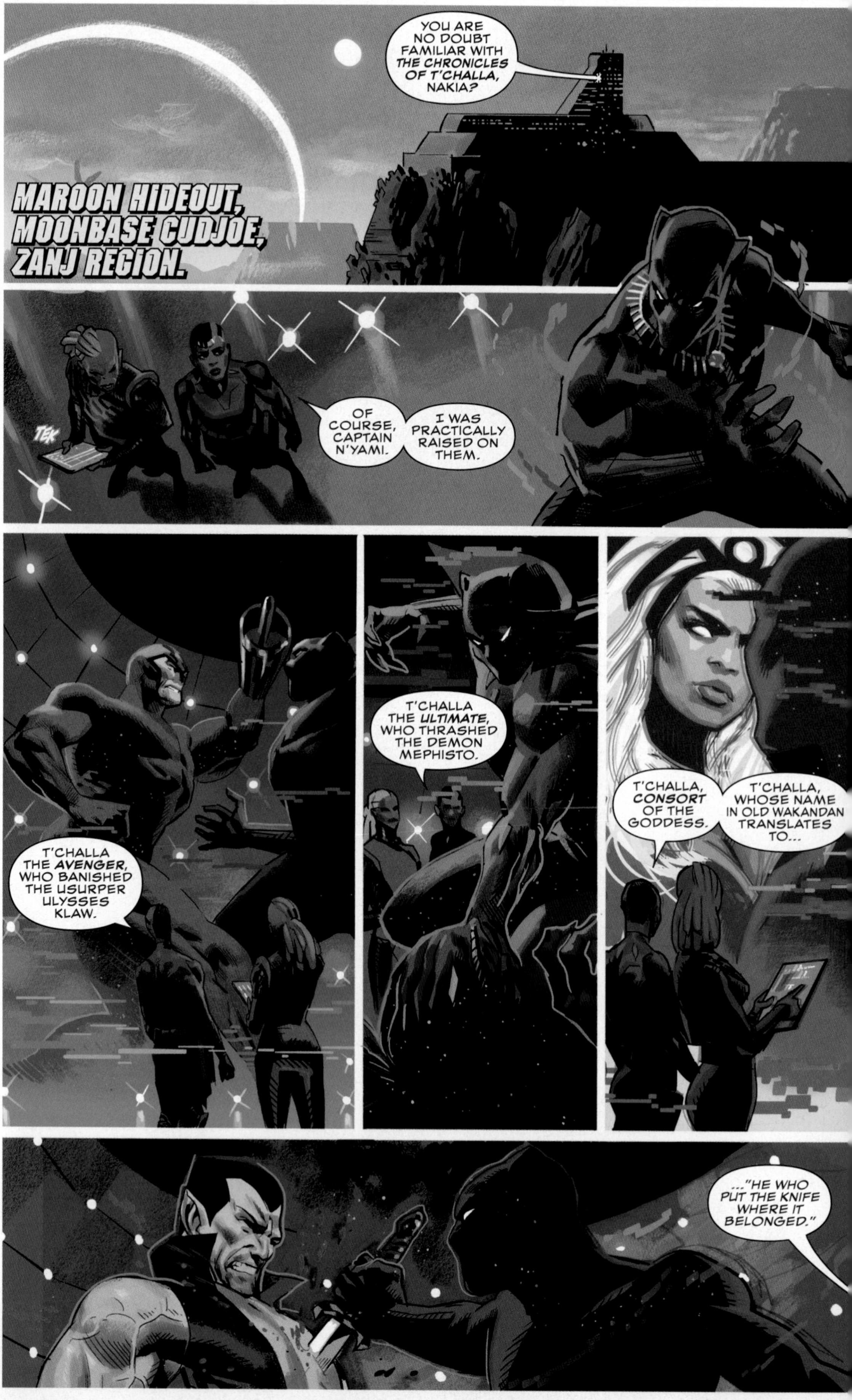
YOU ARE NO DOUBT FAMILIAR WITH *THE CHRONICLES OF T'CHALLA*, NAKIA?
MAROON HIDEOUT, MOONBASE CUDJOE, ZANJ REGION.
TEK
OF COURSE, CAPTAIN N'YAMI.
I WAS PRACTICALLY RAISED ON THEM.
T'CHALLA THE *AVENGER*, WHO BANISHED THE USURPER ULYSSES KLAW.
T'CHALLA THE *ULTIMATE*, WHO THRASHED THE DEMON MEPHISTO.
T'CHALLA, *CONSORT* OF THE GODDESS.
T'CHALLA, WHOSE NAME IN OLD WAKANDAN TRANSLATES TO...
..."HE WHO PUT THE KNIFE WHERE IT BELONGED."

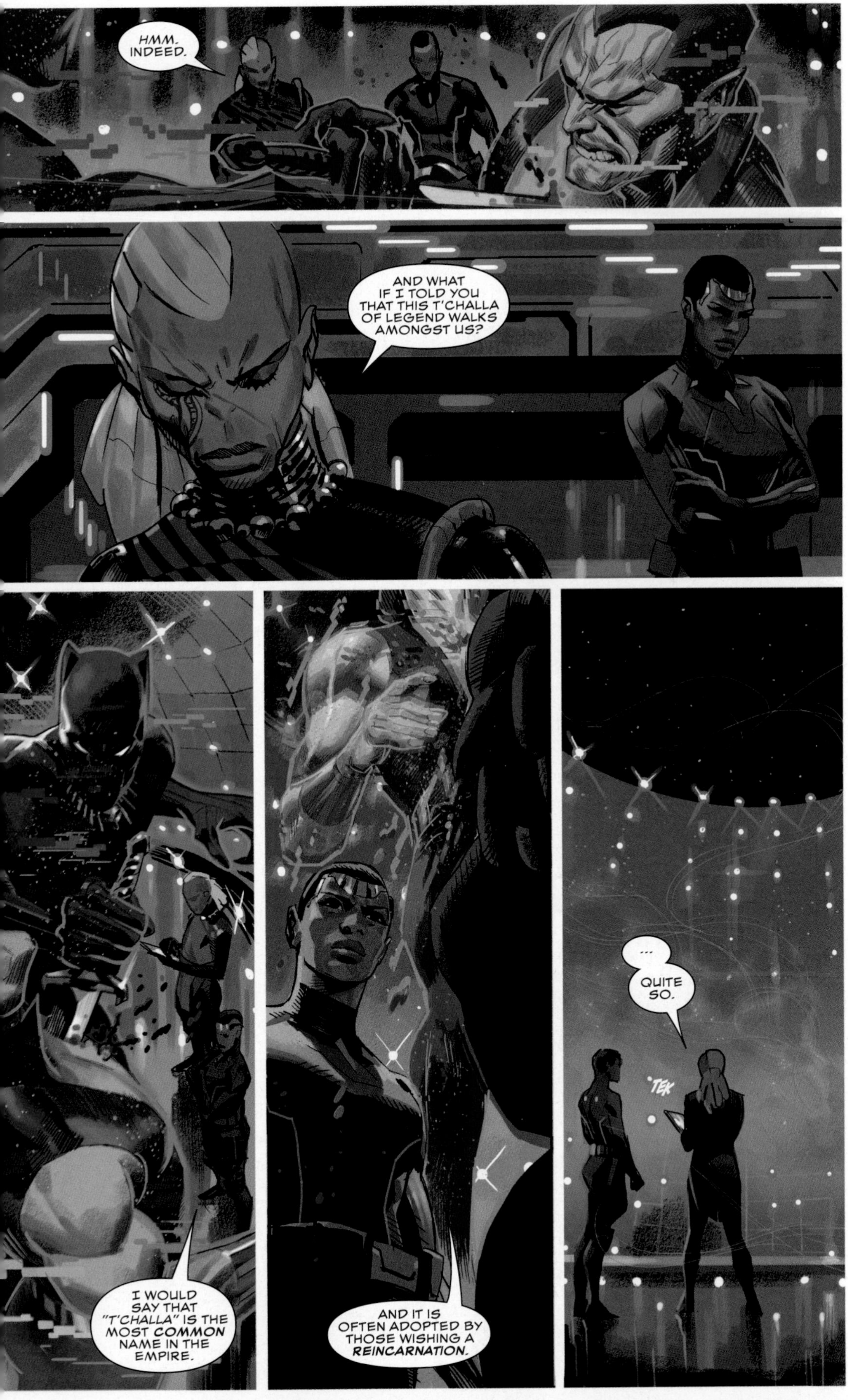
HMM. INDEED.
AND WHAT IF I TOLD YOU THAT THIS T'CHALLA OF LEGEND WALKS AMONGST US?
I WOULD SAY THAT "T'CHALLA" IS THE MOST COMMON NAME IN THE EMPIRE.
AND IT IS OFTEN ADOPTED BY THOSE WISHING A REINCARNATION.
...
QUITE SO.
TEK

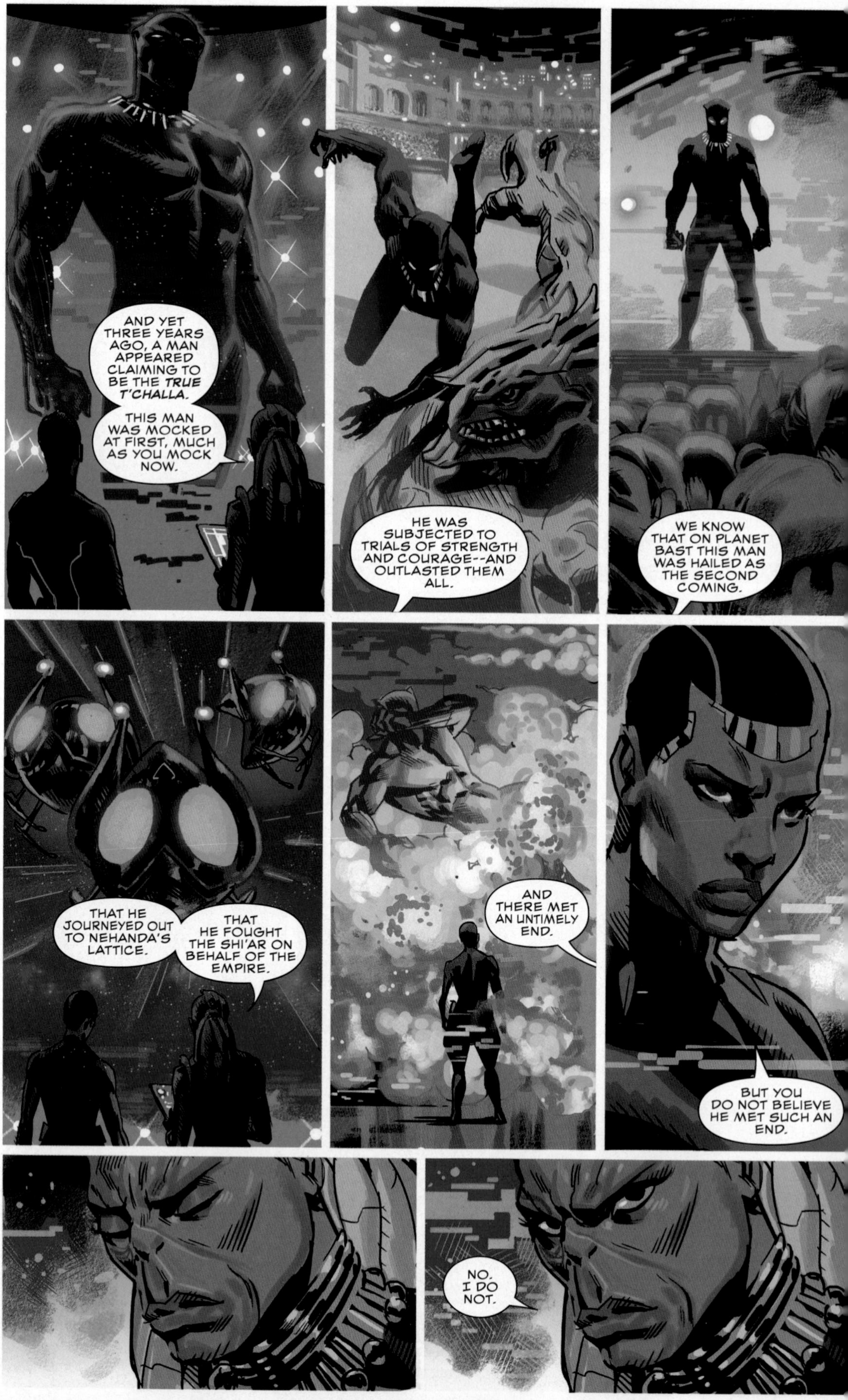
AND YET THREE YEARS AGO, A MAN APPEARED CLAIMING TO BE THE *TRUE T'CHALLA.*
THIS MAN WAS MOCKED AT FIRST, MUCH AS YOU MOCK NOW.
HE WAS SUBJECTED TO TRIALS OF STRENGTH AND COURAGE--AND OUTLASTED THEM ALL.
WE KNOW THAT ON PLANET BAST THIS MAN WAS HAILED AS THE SECOND COMING.
THAT HE JOURNEYED OUT TO NEHANDA'S LATTICE.
THAT HE FOUGHT THE SHI'AR ON BEHALF OF THE EMPIRE.
AND THERE MET AN UNTIMELY END.
BUT YOU DO NOT BELIEVE HE MET SUCH AN END.
NO. I DO NOT.

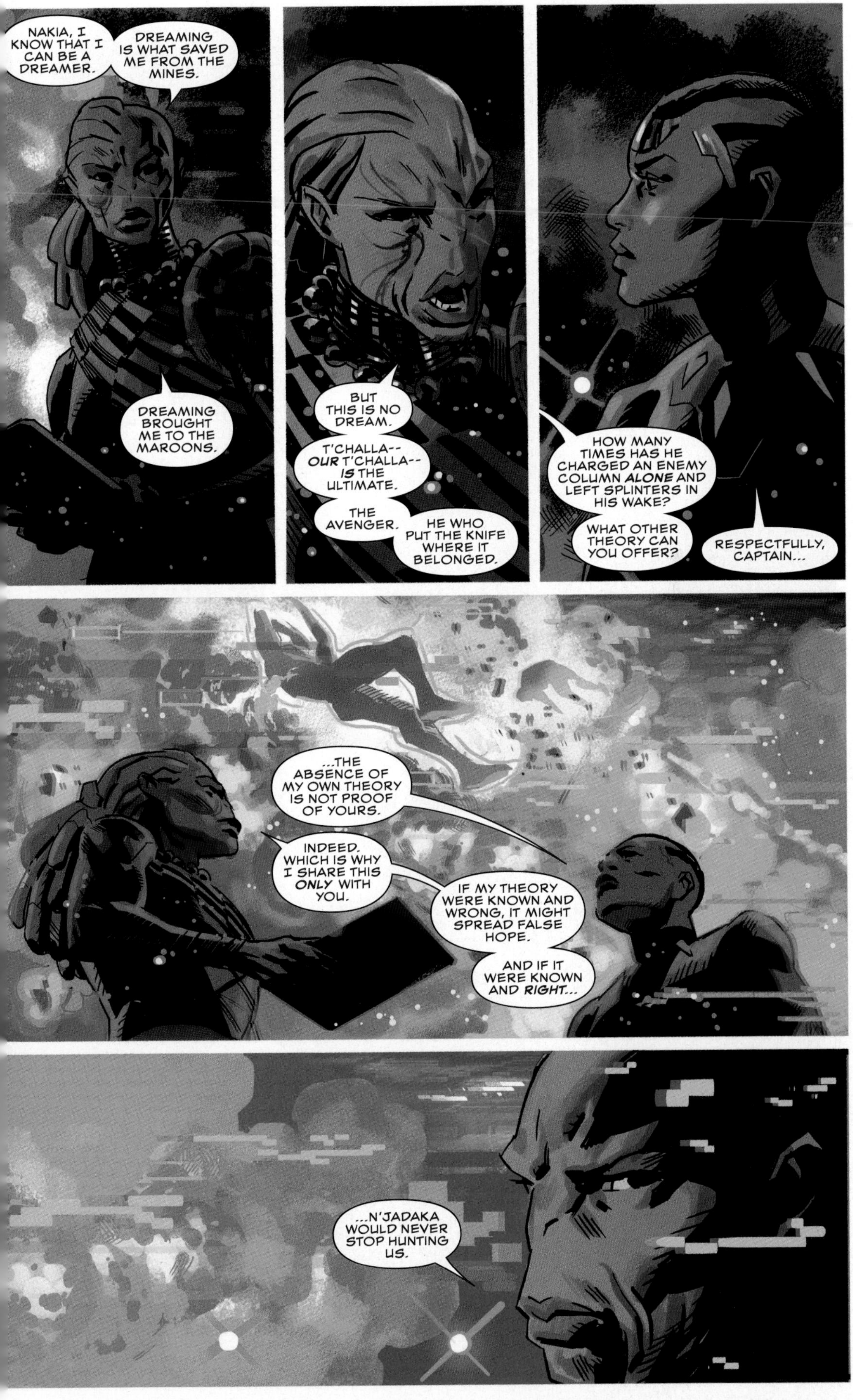
NAKIA, I KNOW THAT I CAN BE A DREAMER.
DREAMING IS WHAT SAVED ME FROM THE MINES.
DREAMING BROUGHT ME TO THE MAROONS.
BUT THIS IS NO DREAM.
T'CHALLA-- *OUR* T'CHALLA-- *IS* THE ULTIMATE.
THE AVENGER.
HE WHO PUT THE KNIFE WHERE IT BELONGED.
HOW MANY TIMES HAS HE CHARGED AN ENEMY COLUMN *ALONE* AND LEFT SPLINTERS IN HIS WAKE?
WHAT OTHER THEORY CAN YOU OFFER?
RESPECTFULLY, CAPTAIN...
...THE ABSENCE OF MY OWN THEORY IS NOT PROOF OF YOURS.
INDEED. WHICH IS WHY I SHARE THIS *ONLY* WITH YOU.
IF MY THEORY WERE KNOWN AND WRONG, IT MIGHT SPREAD FALSE HOPE.
AND IF IT WERE KNOWN AND *RIGHT*...
...N'JADAKA WOULD NEVER STOP HUNTING US.

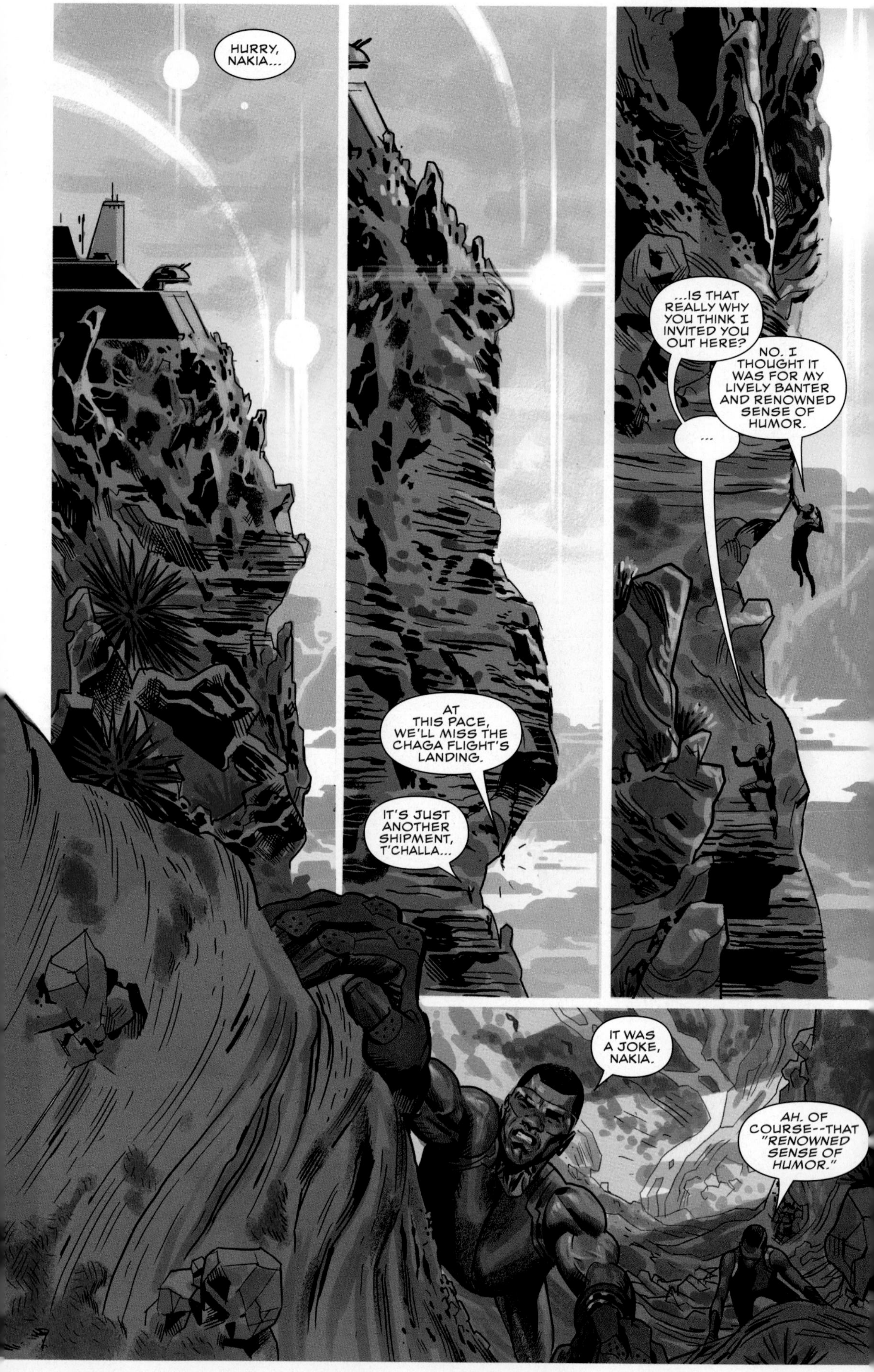
HURRY, NAKIA...
AT THIS PACE, WE'LL MISS THE CHAGA FLIGHT'S LANDING.
IT'S JUST ANOTHER SHIPMENT, T'CHALLA...
...IS THAT REALLY WHY YOU THINK I INVITED YOU OUT HERE?
NO. I THOUGHT IT WAS FOR MY LIVELY BANTER AND RENOWNED SENSE OF HUMOR.
...
IT WAS A JOKE, NAKIA.
AH. OF COURSE--THAT "RENOWNED SENSE OF HUMOR."

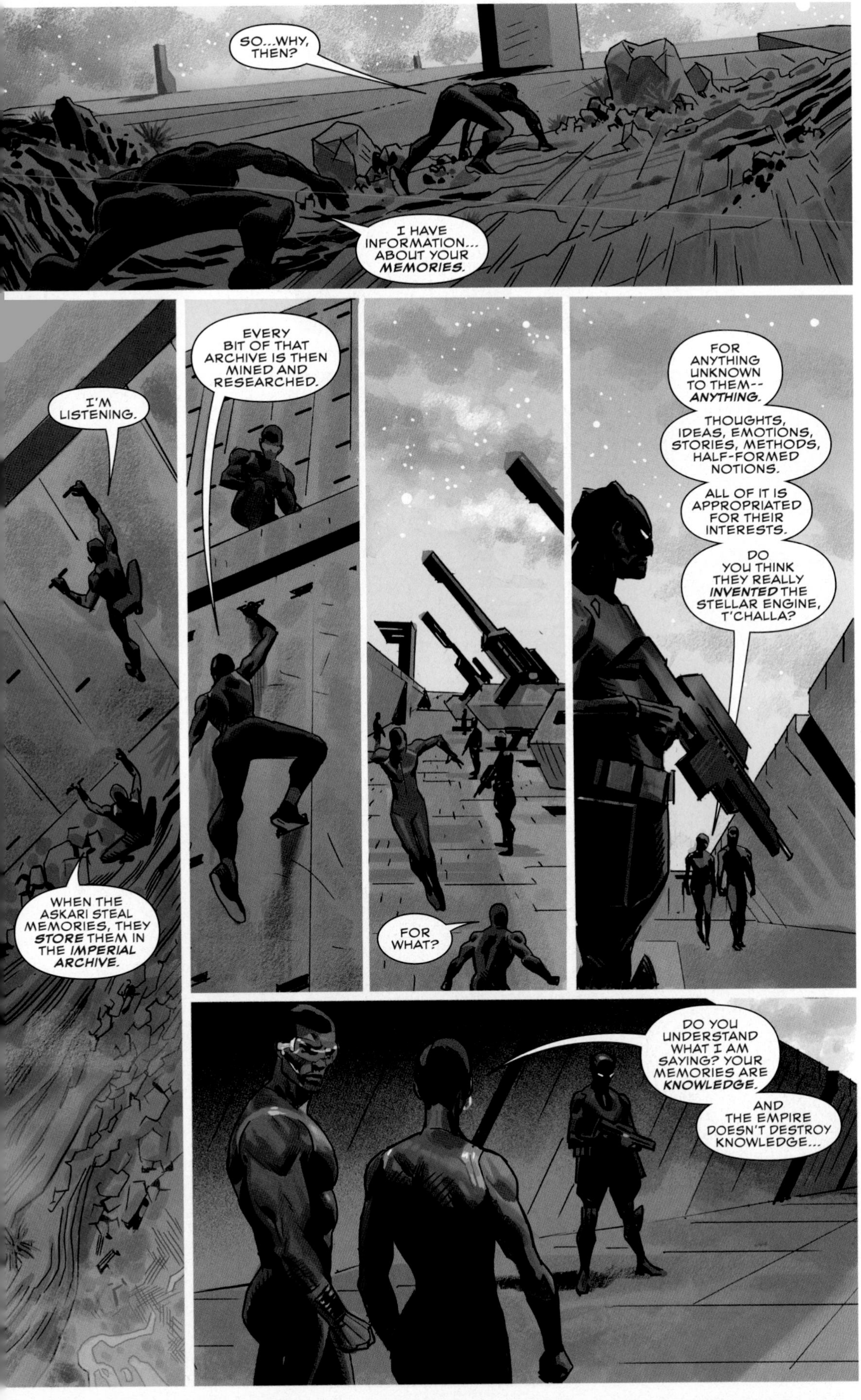

SO...WHY, THEN?
I HAVE INFORMATION... ABOUT YOUR MEMORIES.
I'M LISTENING.
WHEN THE ASKARI STEAL MEMORIES, THEY STORE THEM IN THE IMPERIAL ARCHIVE.
EVERY BIT OF THAT ARCHIVE IS THEN MINED AND RESEARCHED.
FOR WHAT?
FOR ANYTHING UNKNOWN TO THEM-- ANYTHING.
THOUGHTS, IDEAS, EMOTIONS, STORIES, METHODS, HALF-FORMED NOTIONS.
ALL OF IT IS APPROPRIATED FOR THEIR INTERESTS.
DO YOU THINK THEY REALLY INVENTED THE STELLAR ENGINE, T'CHALLA?
DO YOU UNDERSTAND WHAT I AM SAYING? YOUR MEMORIES ARE KNOWLEDGE.
AND THE EMPIRE DOESN'T DESTROY KNOWLEDGE...

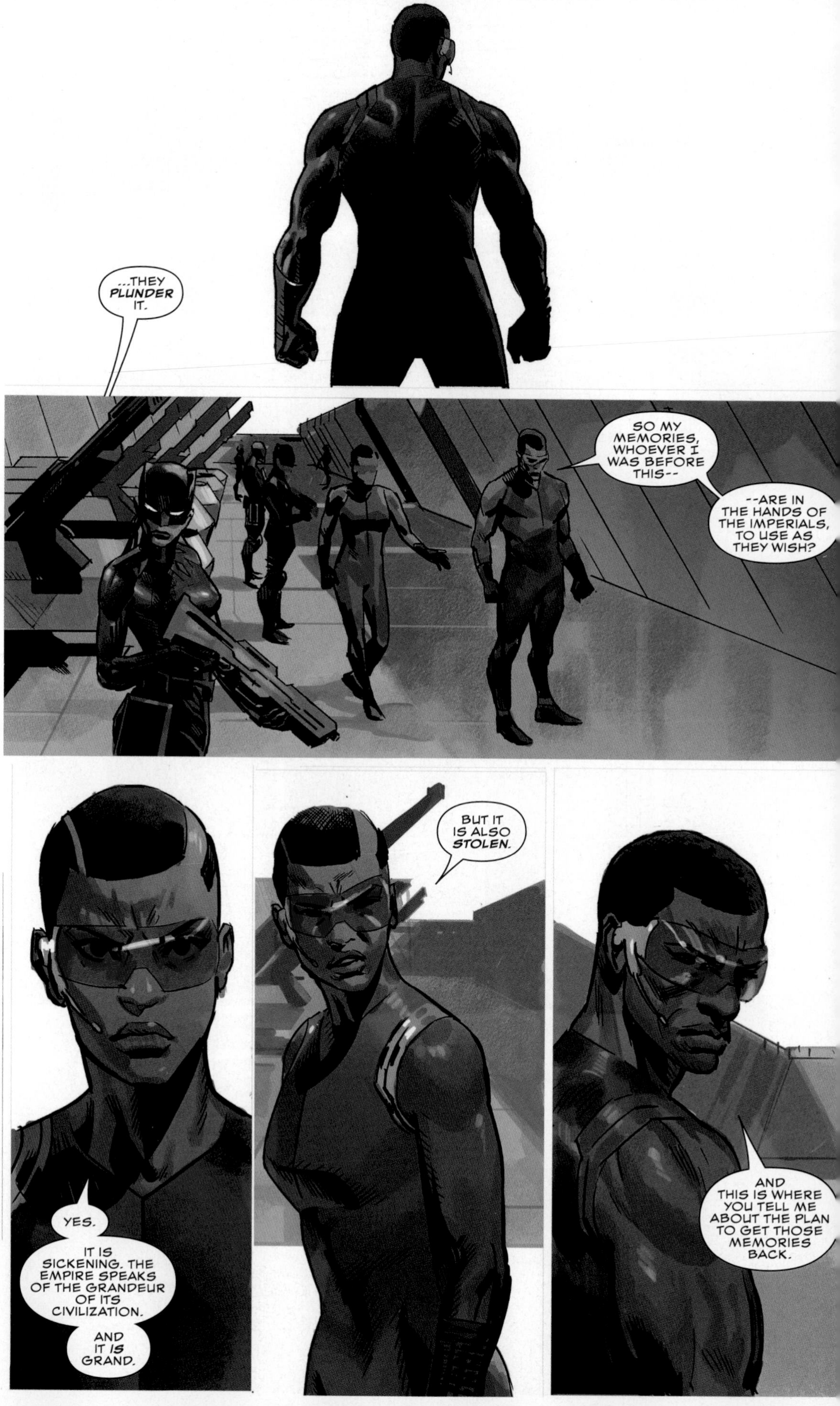
...THEY PLUNDER IT.
SO MY MEMORIES, WHOEVER I WAS BEFORE THIS--
--ARE IN THE HANDS OF THE IMPERIALS, TO USE AS THEY WISH?
YES.
IT IS SICKENING. THE EMPIRE SPEAKS OF THE GRANDEUR OF ITS CIVILIZATION.
AND IT IS GRAND.
BUT IT IS ALSO STOLEN.
AND THIS IS WHERE YOU TELL ME ABOUT THE PLAN TO GET THOSE MEMORIES BACK.

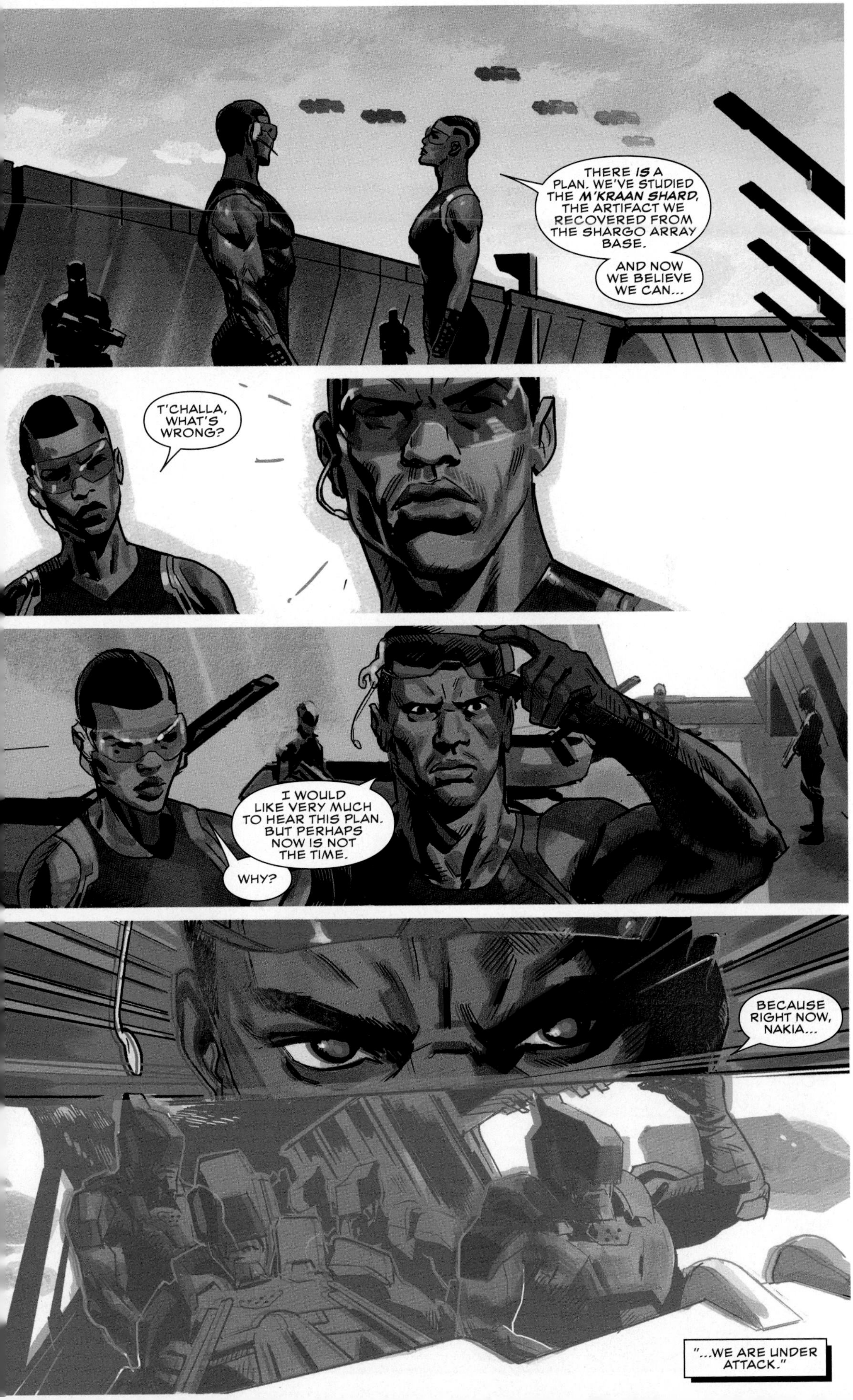

THERE IS A PLAN. WE'VE STUDIED THE M'KRAAN SHARD, THE ARTIFACT WE RECOVERED FROM THE SHARGO ARRAY BASE.
AND NOW WE BELIEVE WE CAN...
T'CHALLA, WHAT'S WRONG?
I WOULD LIKE VERY MUCH TO HEAR THIS PLAN. BUT PERHAPS NOW IS NOT THE TIME.
WHY?
BECAUSE RIGHT NOW, NAKIA...
"...WE ARE UNDER ATTACK."

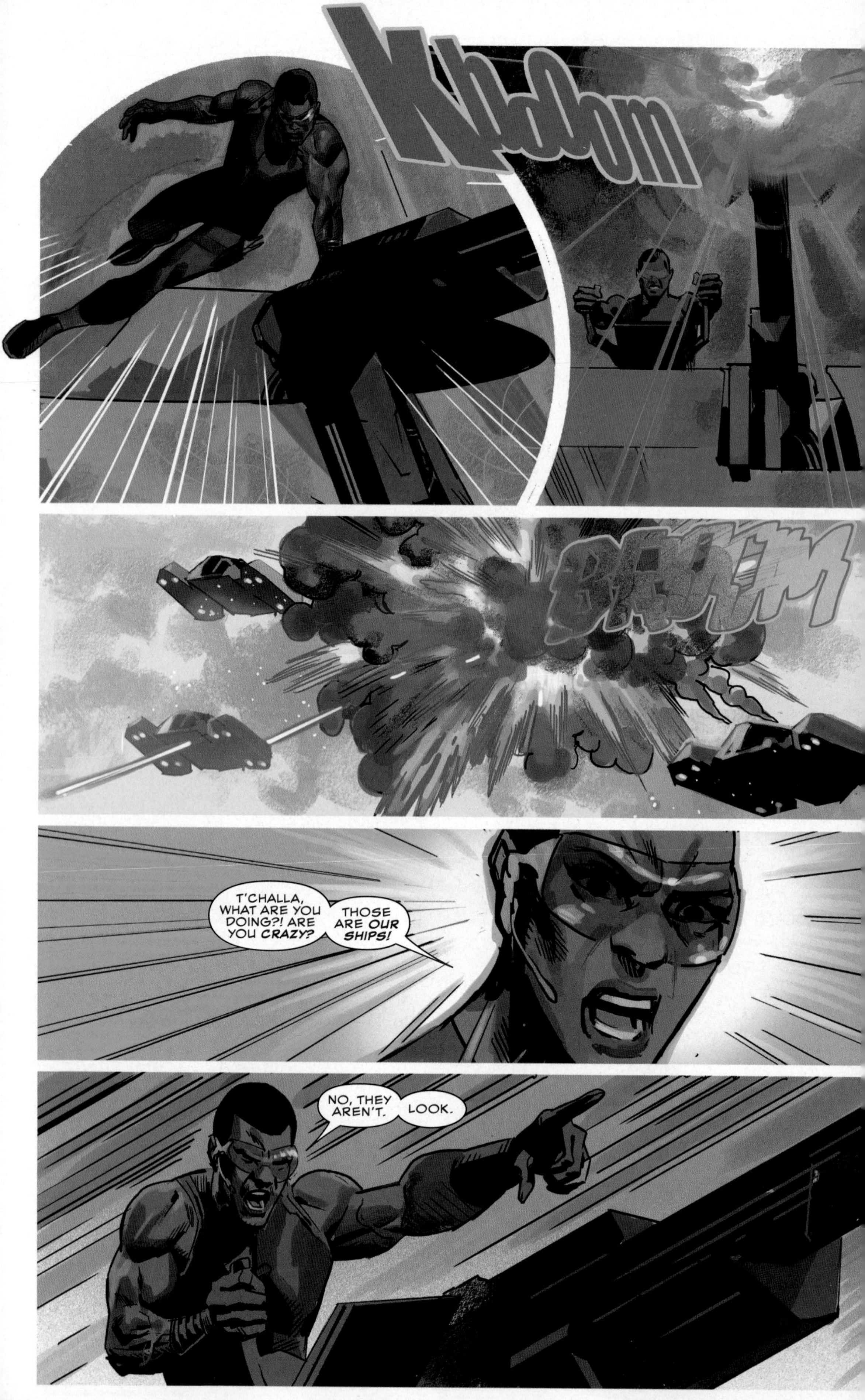
KHOOOM
T'CHALLA, WHAT ARE YOU DOING?! ARE YOU CRAZY?
THOSE ARE OUR SHIPS!
NO, THEY AREN'T.
LOOK.

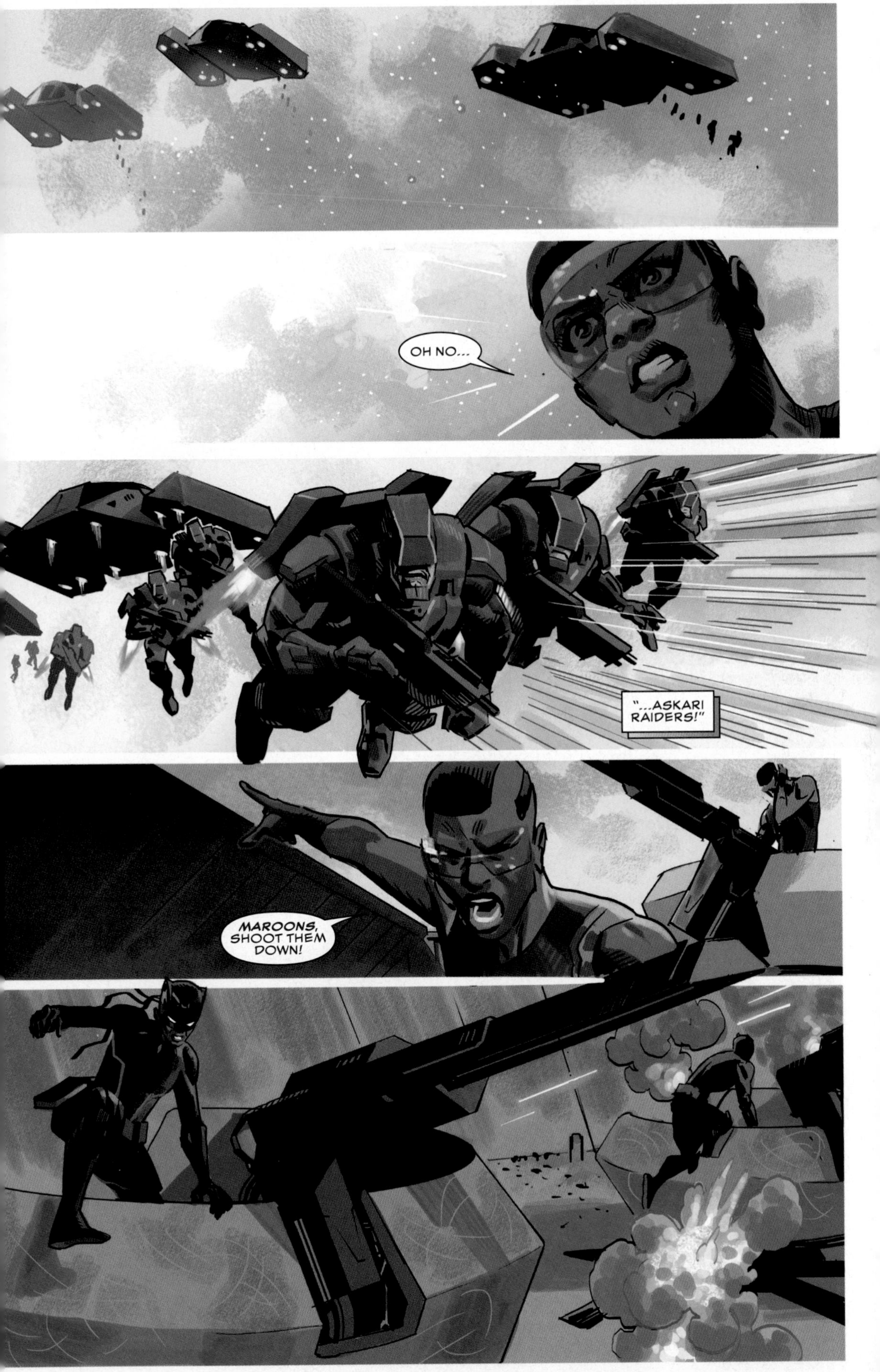
OH NO...
"...ASKARI RAIDERS!"
MAROONS, SHOOT THEM DOWN!

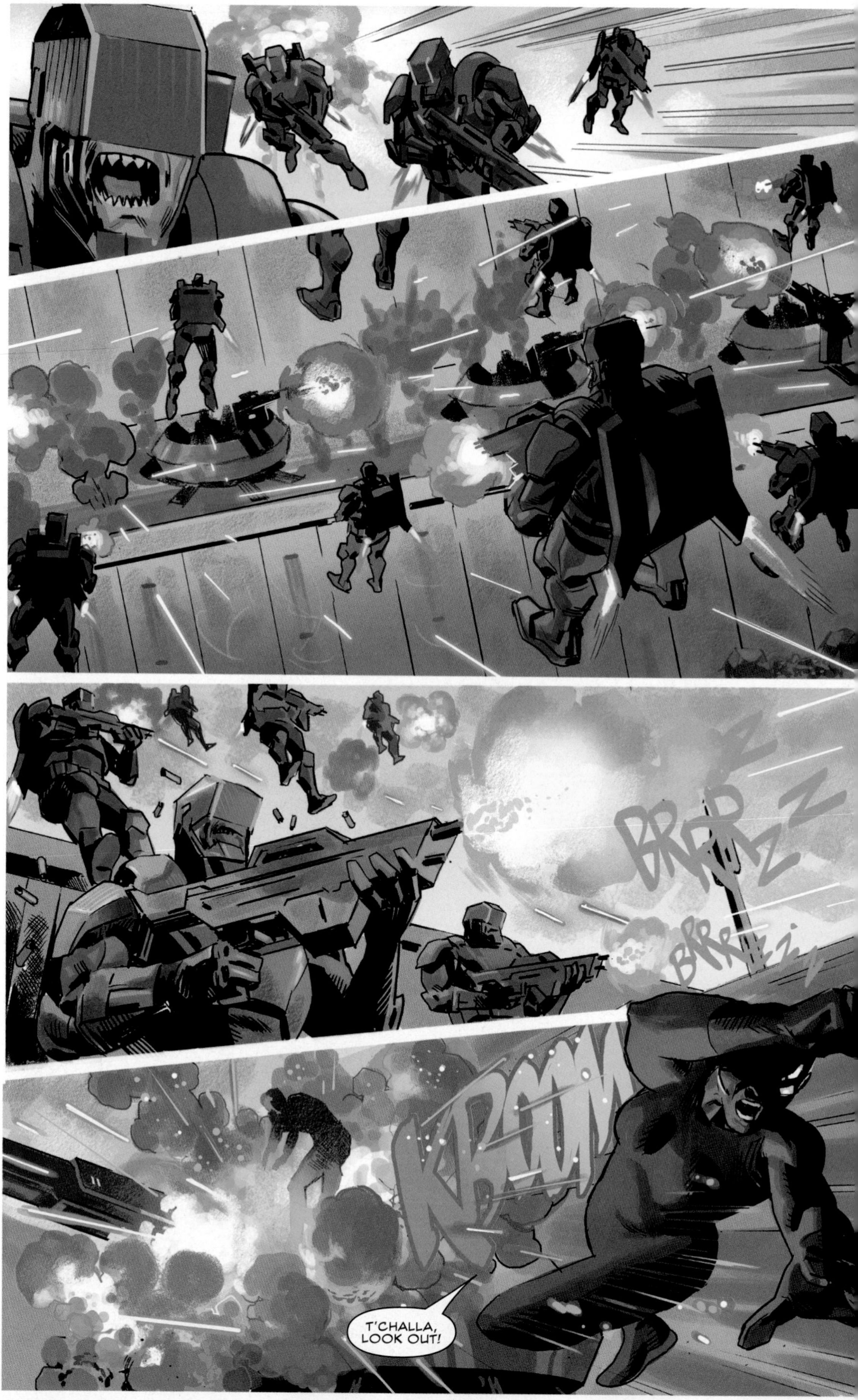
BRRRZZZ
BRRRZZ
KRAOOM
T'CHALLA, LOOK OUT!

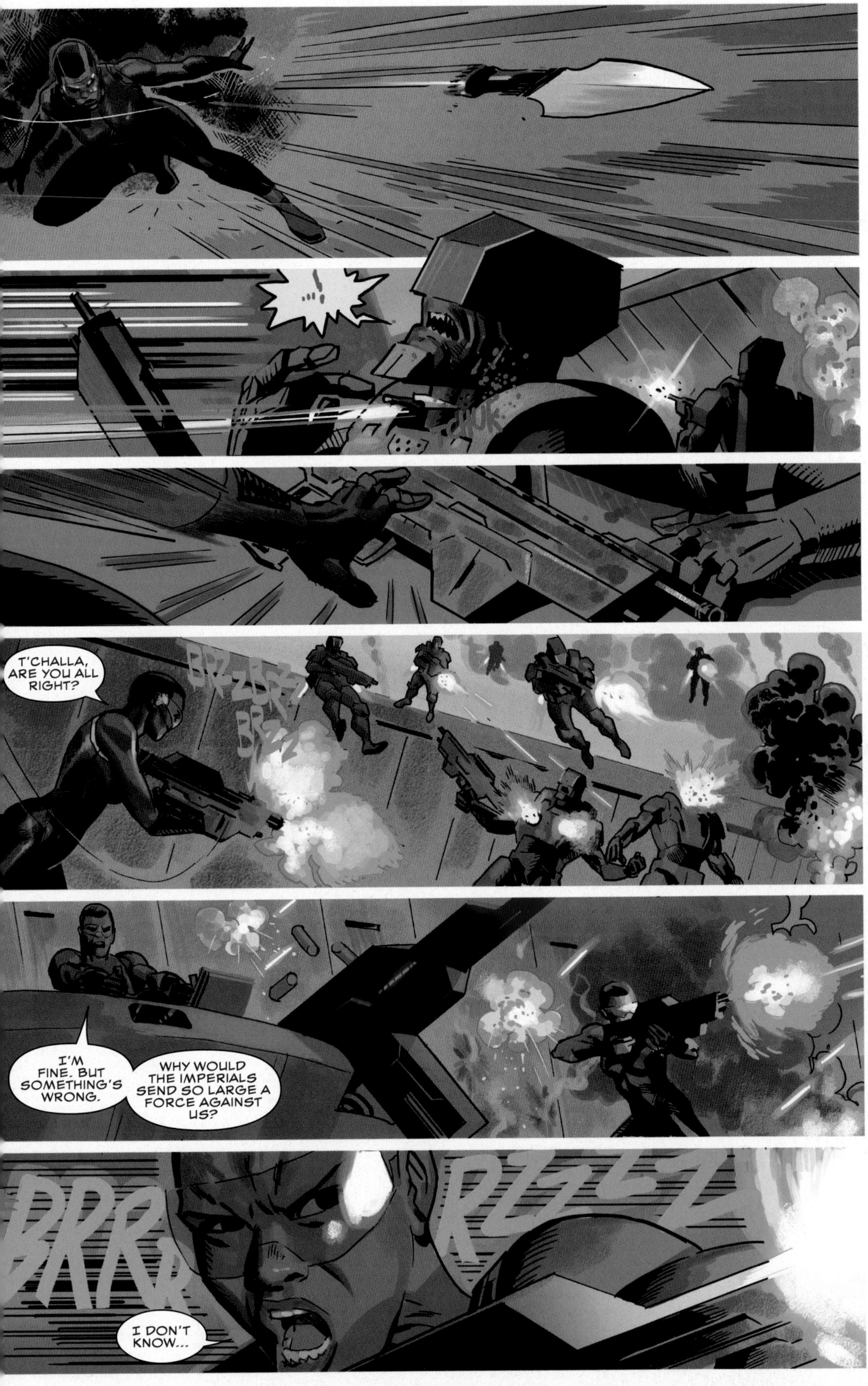
!
T'CHALLA, ARE YOU ALL RIGHT?
I'M FINE. BUT SOMETHING'S WRONG.
WHY WOULD THE IMPERIALS SEND SO LARGE A FORCE AGAINST US?
I DON'T KNOW...

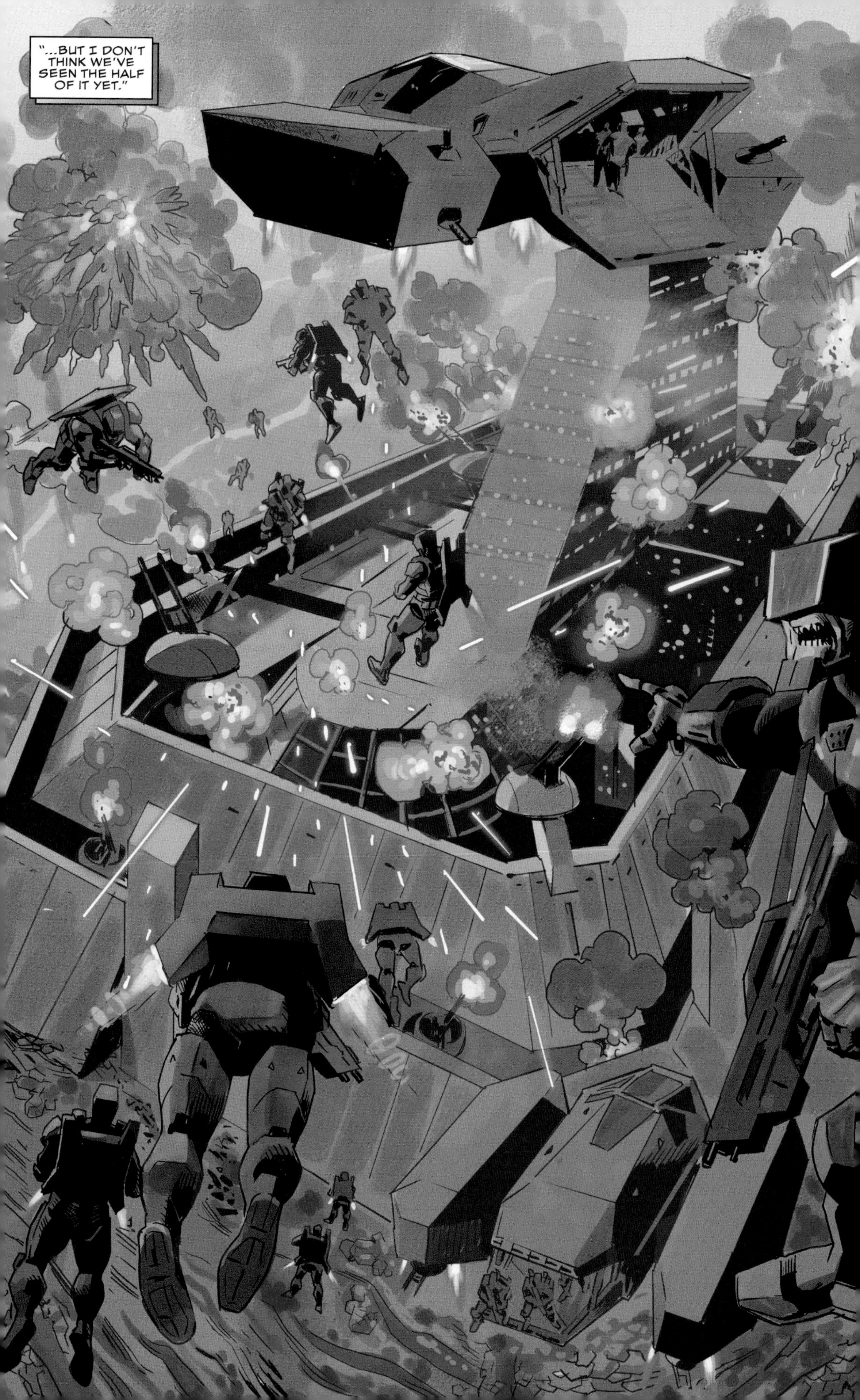
"...BUT I DON'T THINK WE'VE SEEN THE HALF OF IT YET."

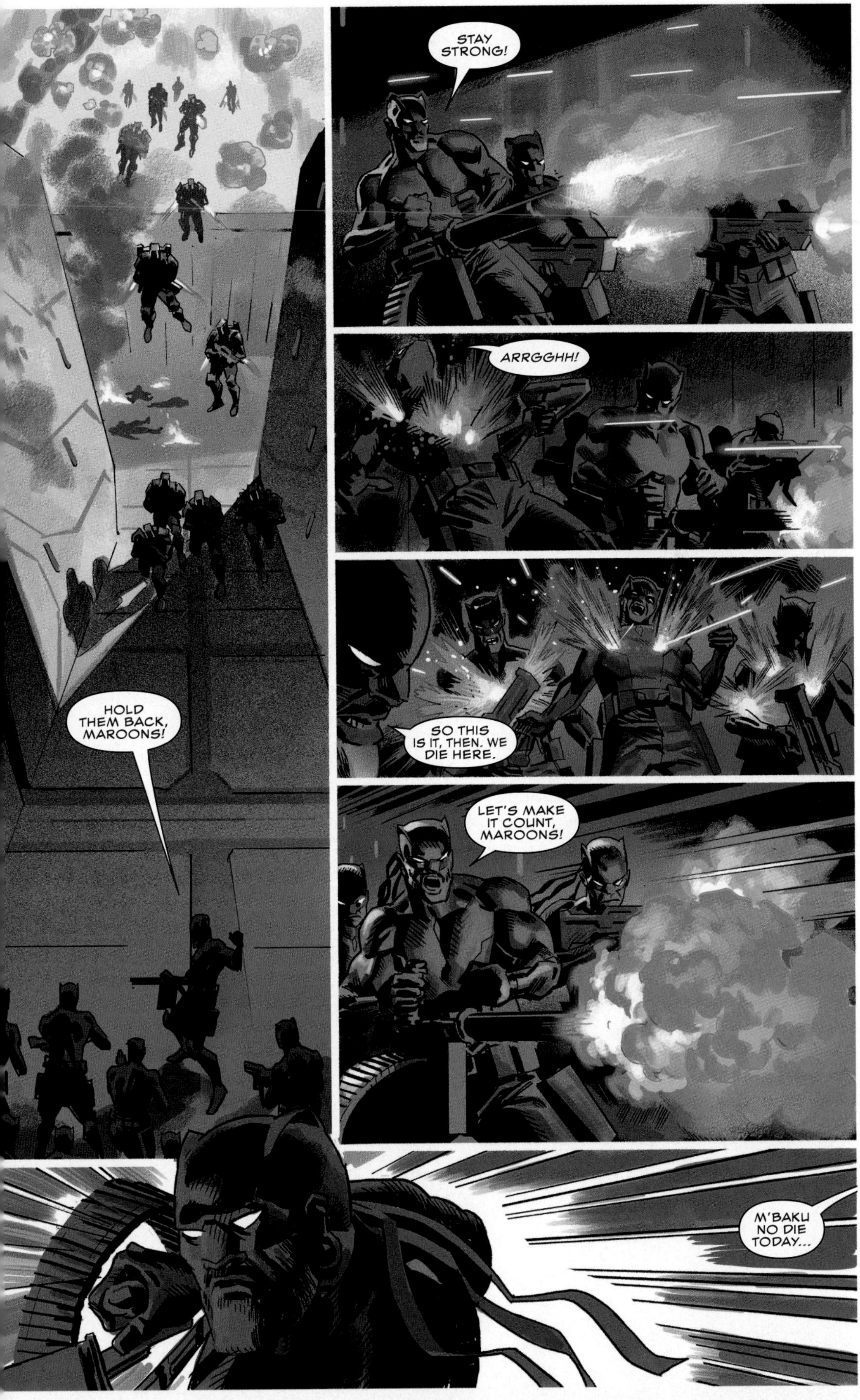
HOLD THEM BACK, MAROONS!
STAY STRONG!
ARRGGHH!
SO THIS IS IT, THEN. WE DIE HERE.
LET'S MAKE IT COUNT, MAROONS!
M'BAKU NO DIE TODAY...

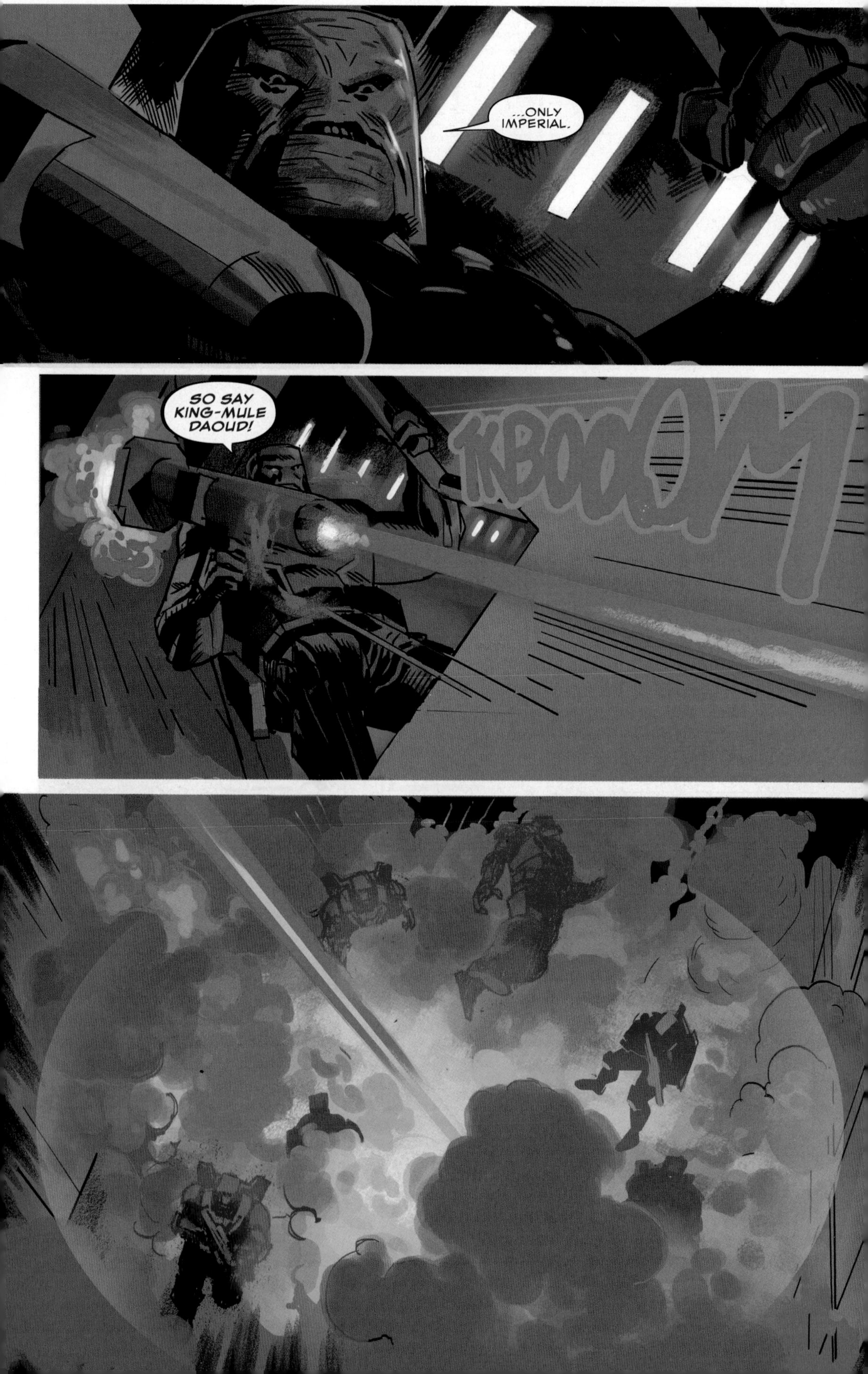
...ONLY IMPERIAL.
SO SAY KING-MULE DAOUD!
KBOOOM

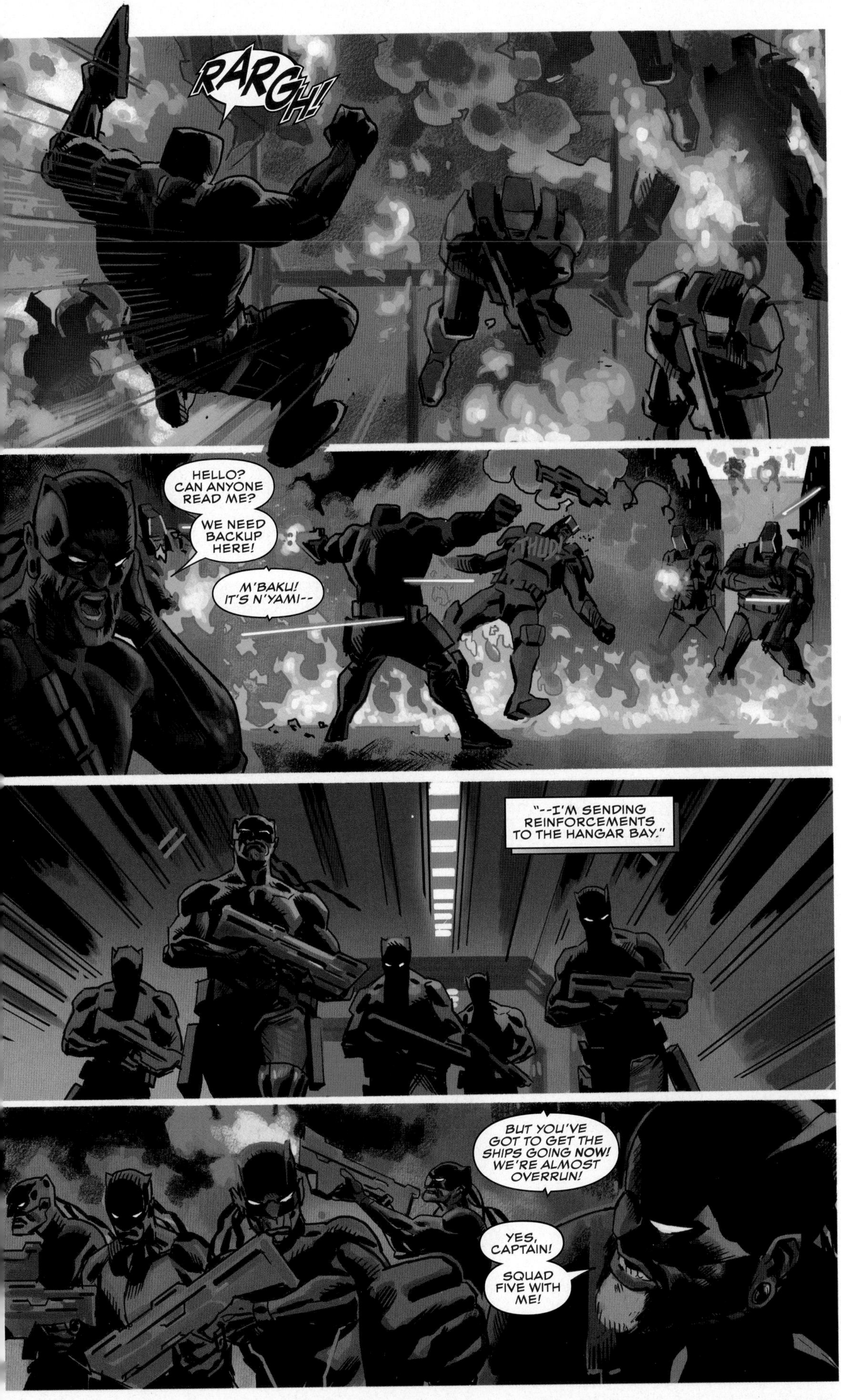
RARGH!
HELLO? CAN ANYONE READ ME?
WE NEED BACKUP HERE!
M'BAKU! IT'S N'YAMI--
THUD!
"--I'M SENDING REINFORCEMENTS TO THE HANGAR BAY."
BUT YOU'VE GOT TO GET THE SHIPS GOING NOW! WE'RE ALMOST OVERRUN!
YES, CAPTAIN!
SQUAD FIVE WITH ME!

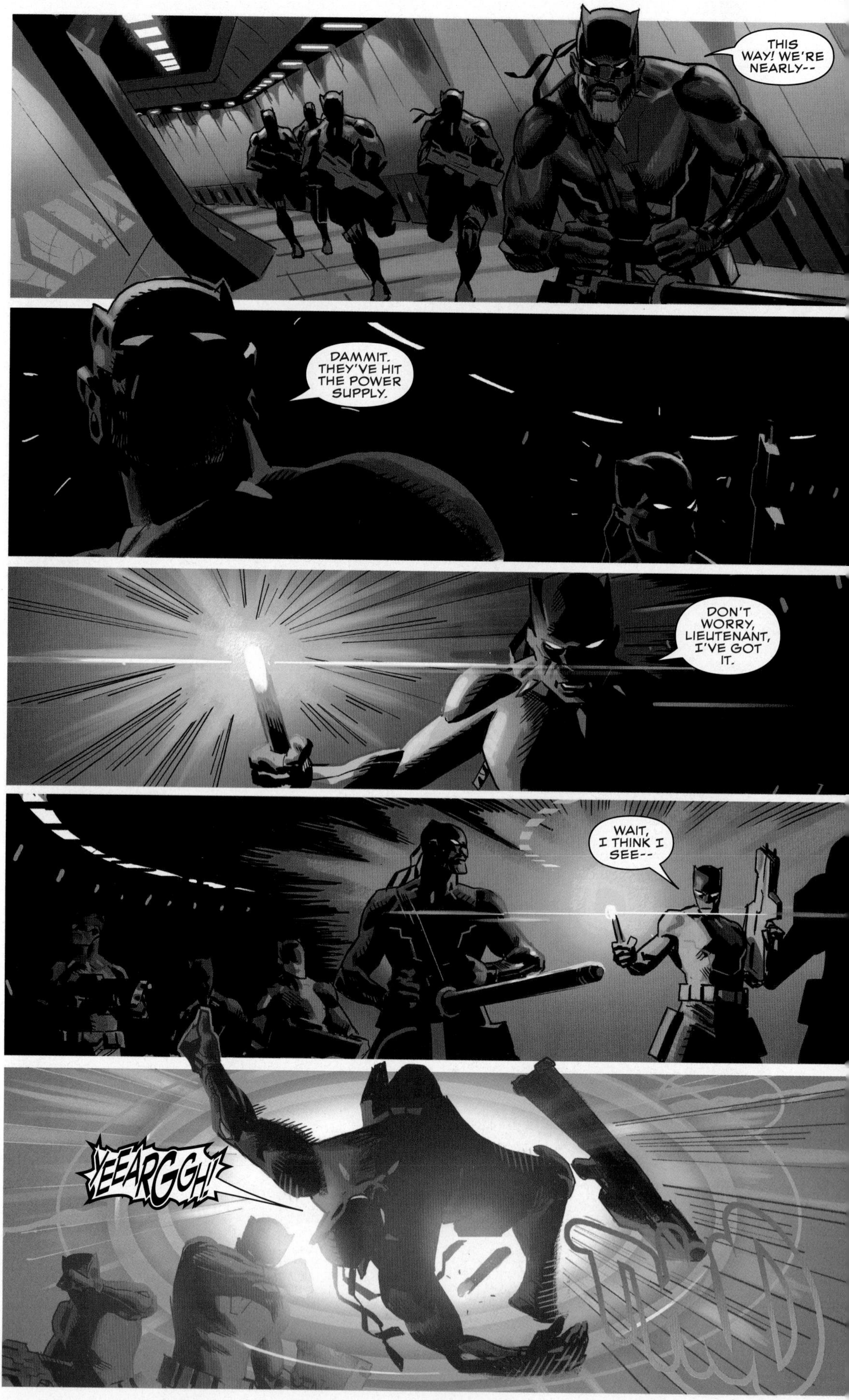
THIS WAY! WE'RE NEARLY--
DAMMIT. THEY'VE HIT THE POWER SUPPLY.
DON'T WORRY, LIEUTENANT, I'VE GOT IT.
WAIT, I THINK I SEE--
YEEARGGH!

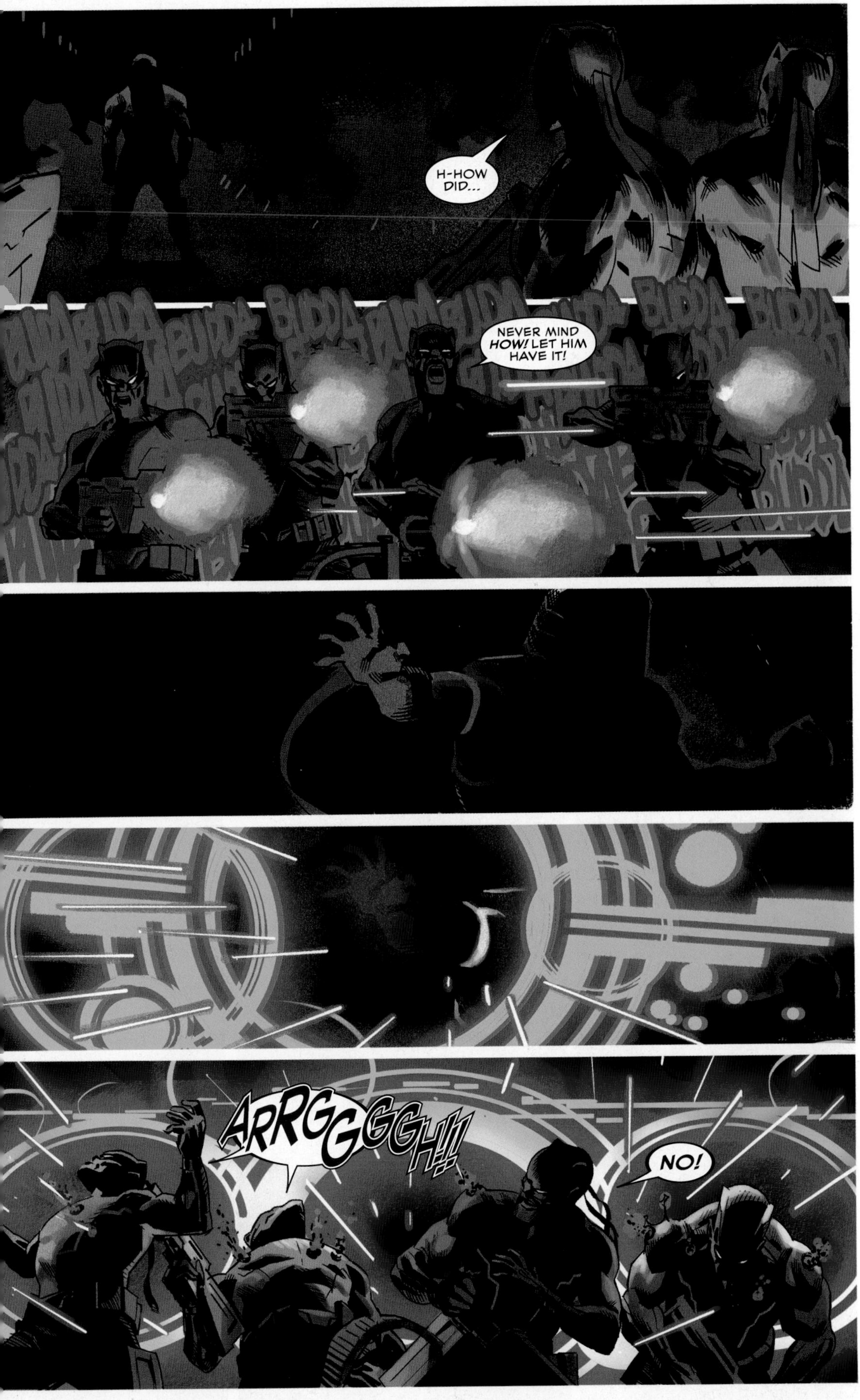
H-HOW DID...
BUDDA BUDDA BUDDA BUDDA
NEVER MIND HOW! LET HIM HAVE IT!
ARRGGGGH!!!
NO!

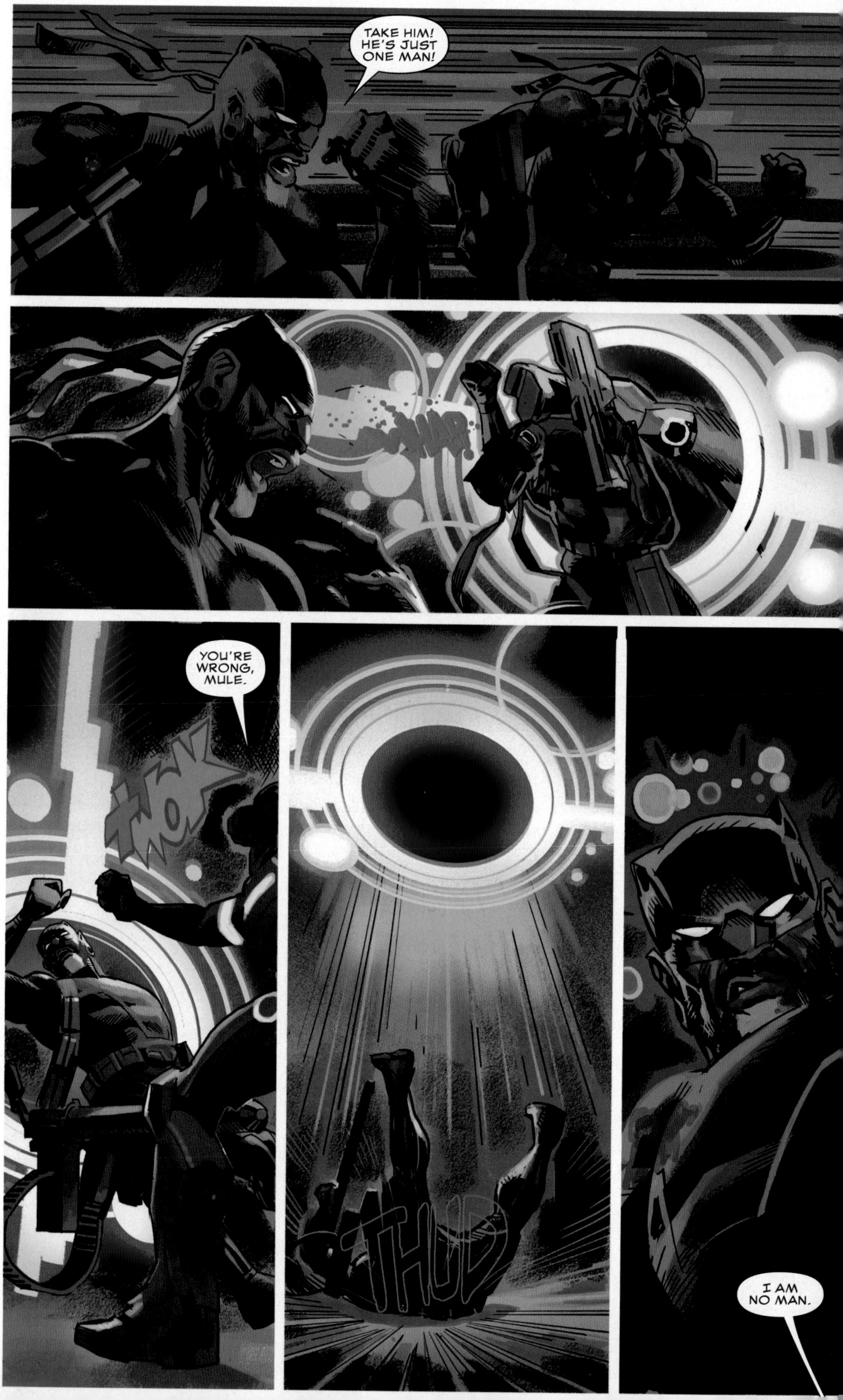
TAKE HIM! HE'S JUST ONE MAN!
YOU'RE WRONG, MULE.
THOK
THUD
I AM NO MAN.

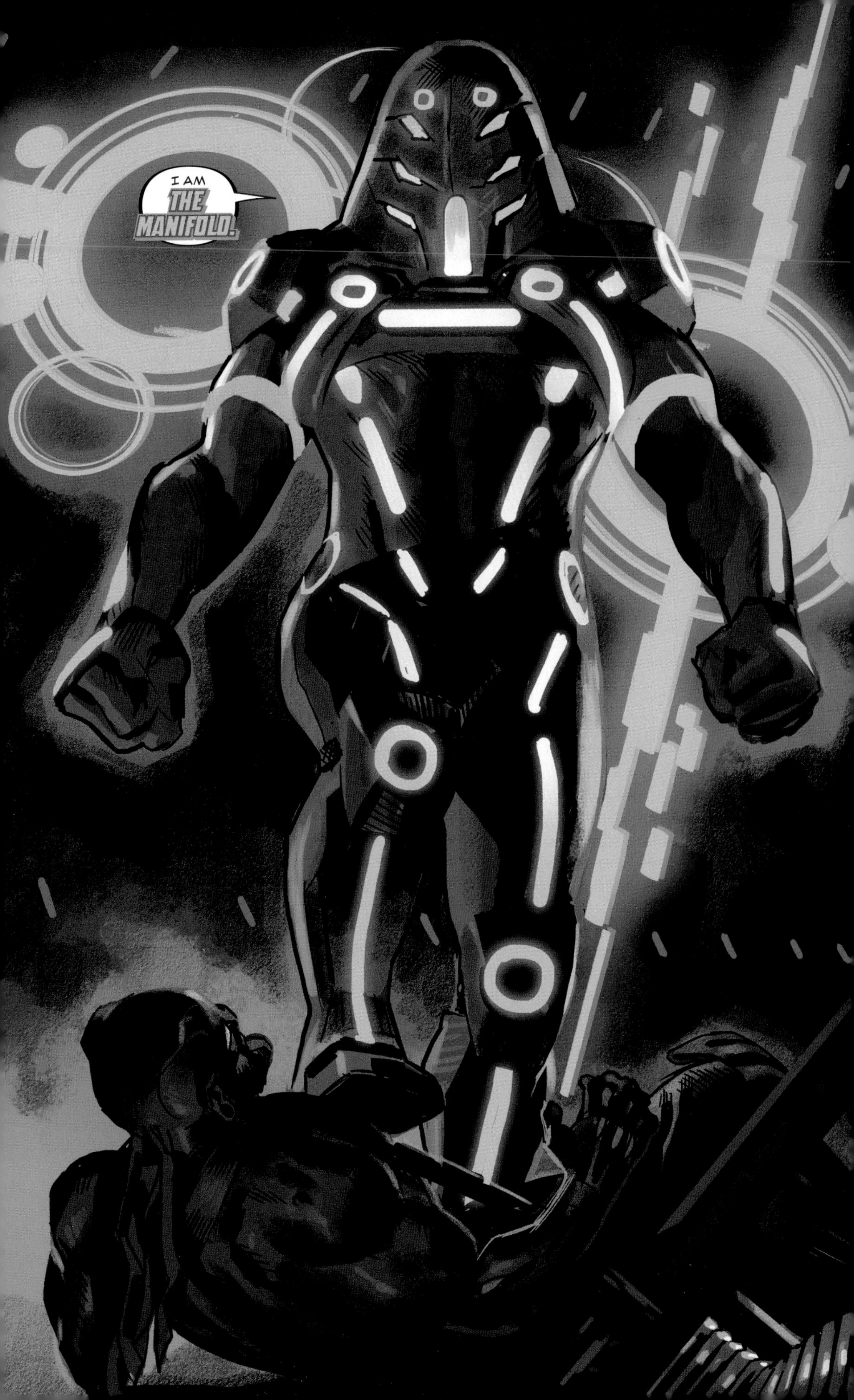
I AM THE MANIFOLD.

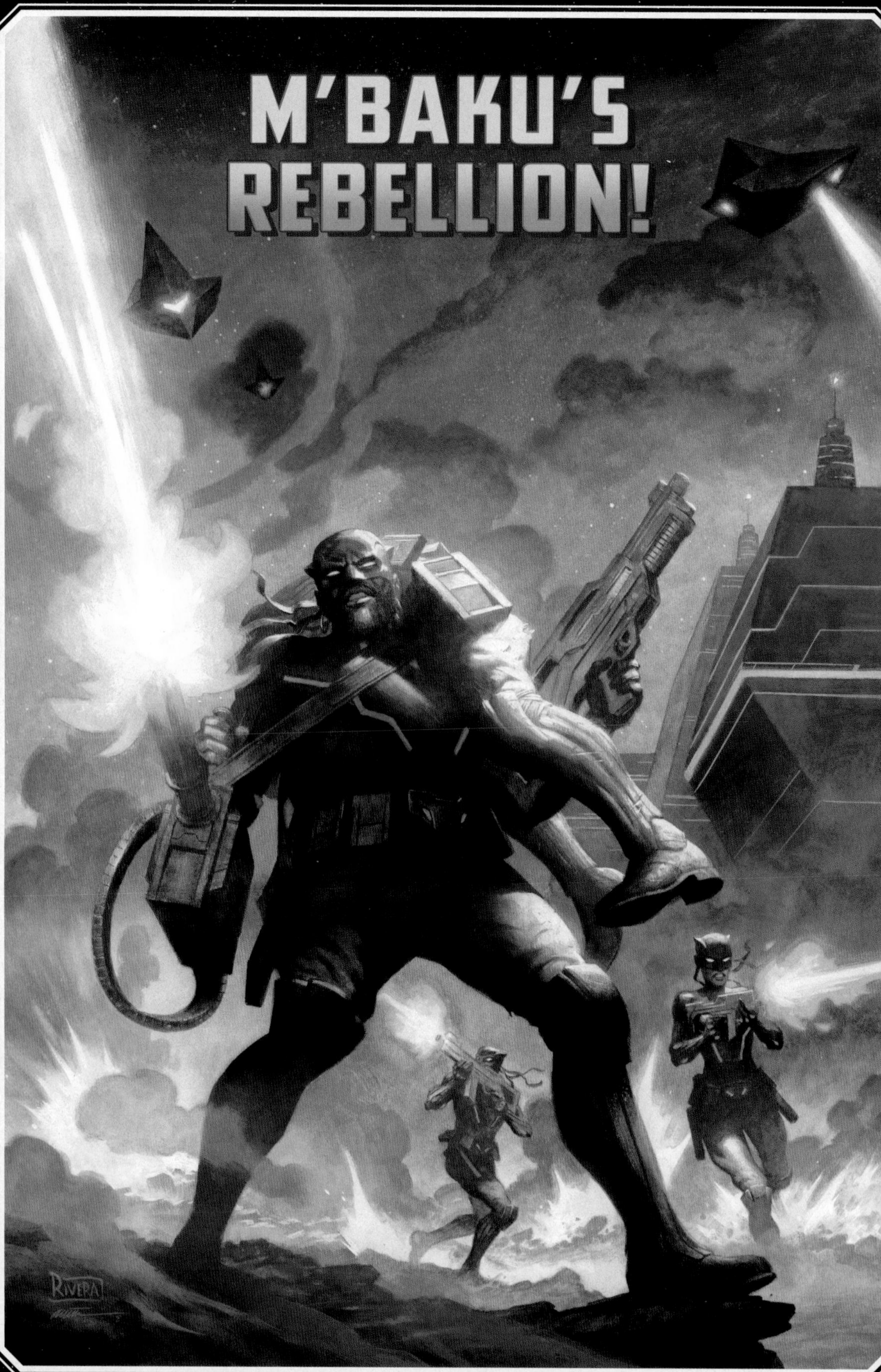
M'BAKU'S
REBELLION!
RIVERA

4

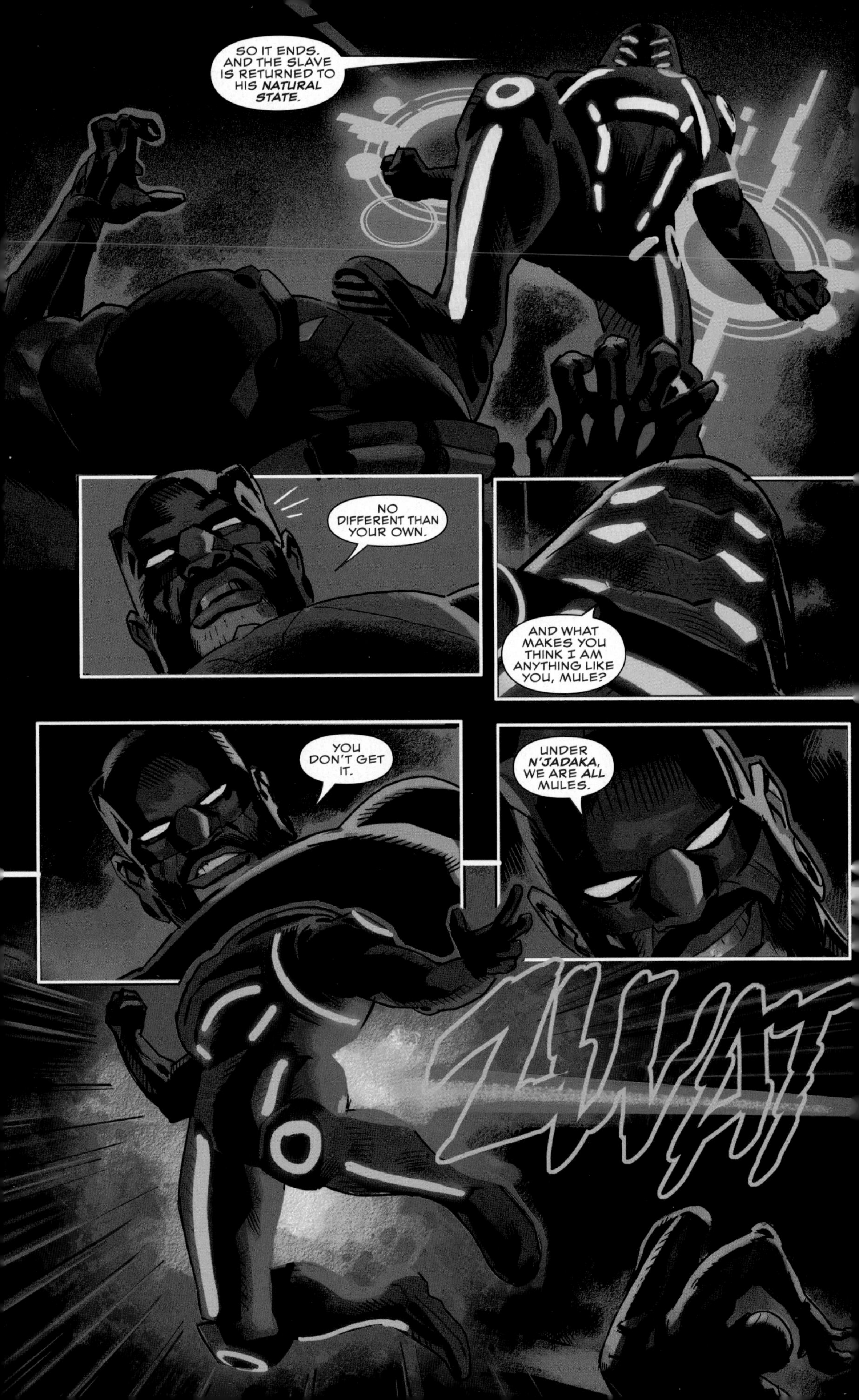
SO IT ENDS. AND THE SLAVE IS RETURNED TO HIS NATURAL STATE.
NO DIFFERENT THAN YOUR OWN.
AND WHAT MAKES YOU THINK I AM ANYTHING LIKE YOU, MULE?
YOU DON'T GET IT.
UNDER N'JADAKA, WE ARE ALL MULES.
ZWAT

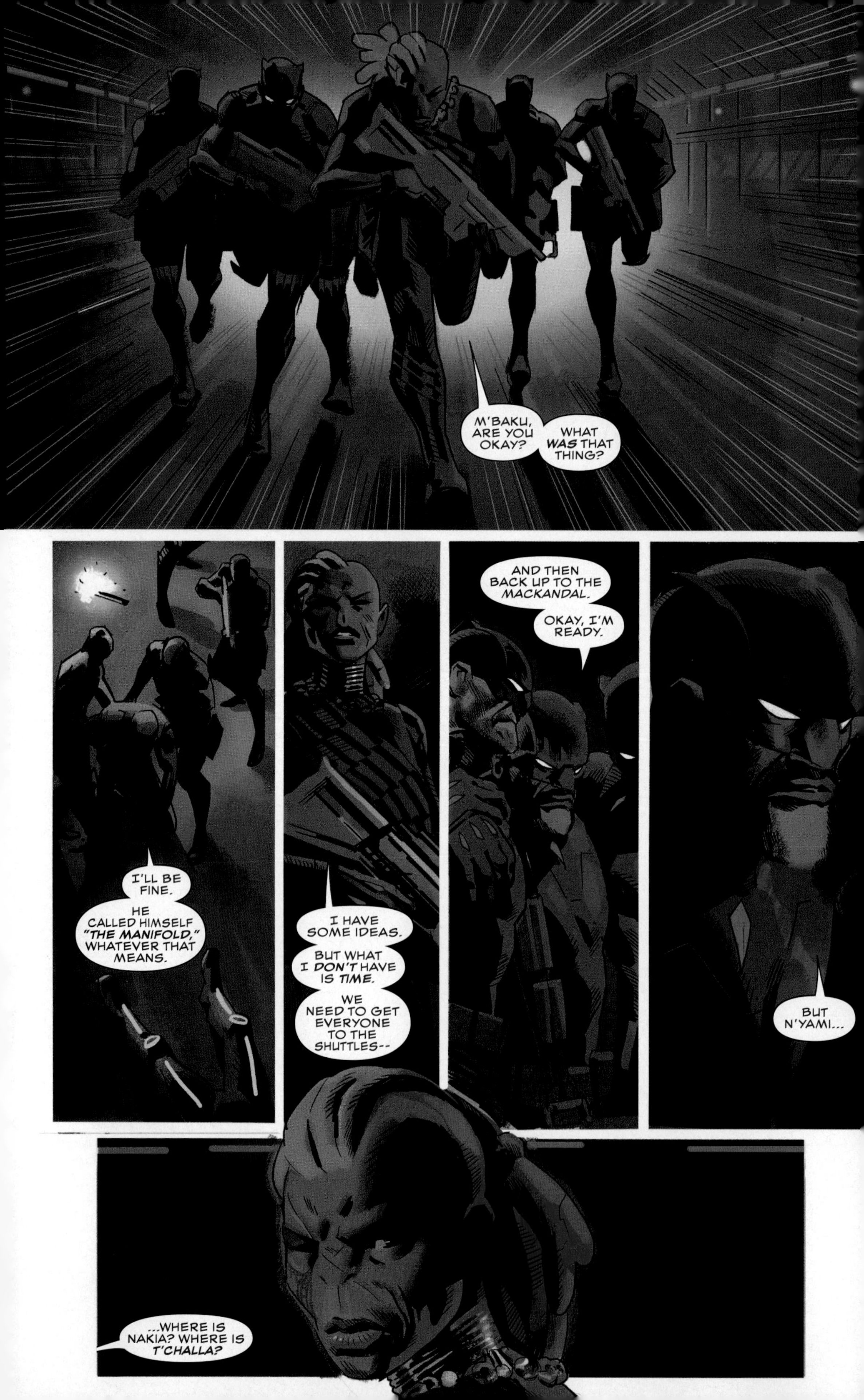
M'BAKU, ARE YOU OKAY?
WHAT *WAS* THAT THING?
I'LL BE FINE.
HE CALLED HIMSELF *"THE MANIFOLD,"* WHATEVER THAT MEANS.
I HAVE SOME IDEAS.
BUT WHAT I *DON'T* HAVE IS *TIME.*
WE NEED TO GET EVERYONE TO THE SHUTTLES--
AND THEN BACK UP TO THE *MACKANDAL.*
OKAY, I'M READY.
BUT N'YAMI...
...WHERE IS NAKIA? WHERE IS *T'CHALLA?*

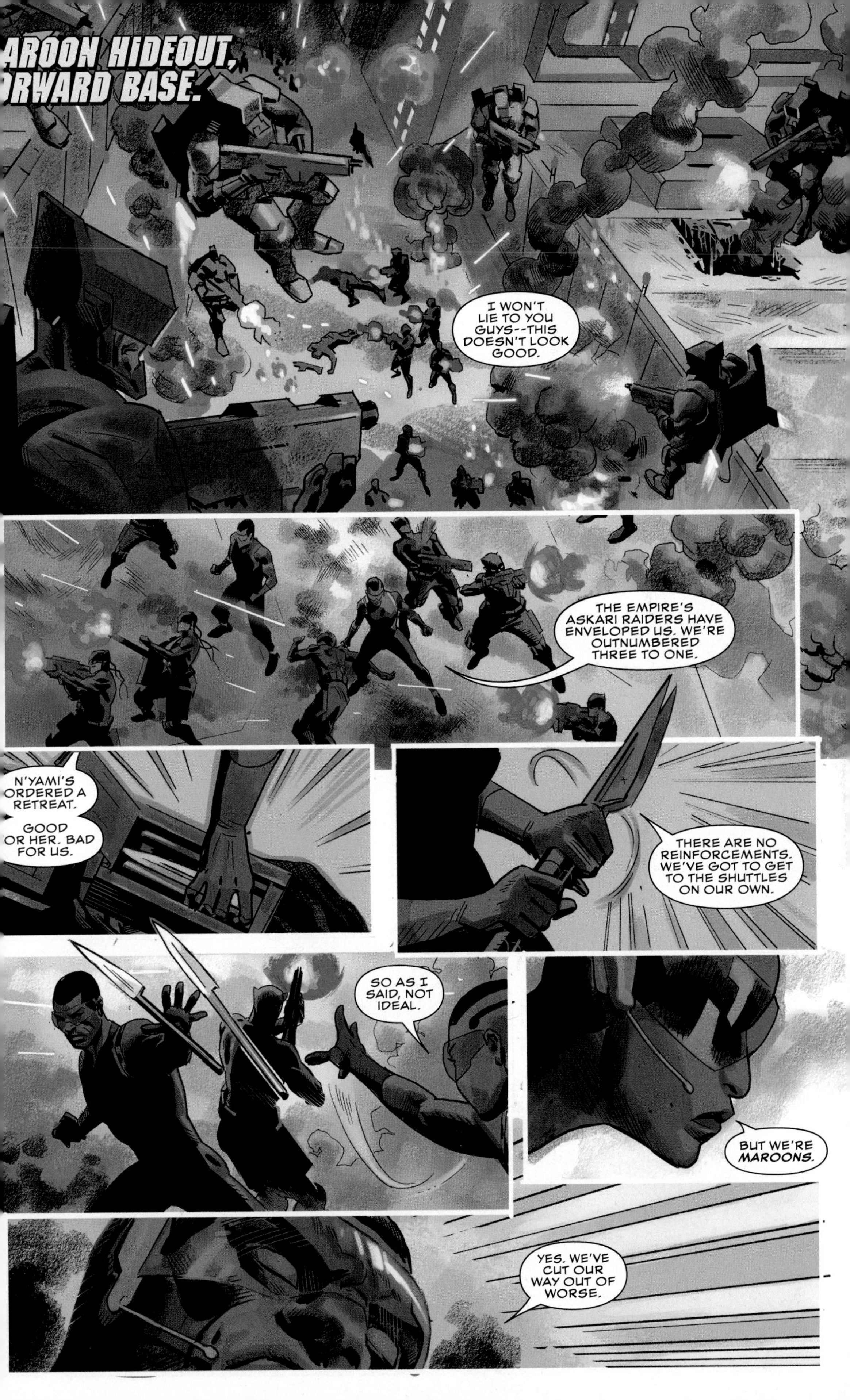

AROON HIDEOUT,
ORWARD BASE.
I WON'T LIE TO YOU GUYS--THIS DOESN'T LOOK GOOD.
THE EMPIRE'S ASKARI RAIDERS HAVE ENVELOPED US. WE'RE OUTNUMBERED THREE TO ONE.
N'YAMI'S ORDERED A RETREAT.
GOOD OR HER. BAD FOR US.
THERE ARE NO REINFORCEMENTS. WE'VE GOT TO GET TO THE SHUTTLES ON OUR OWN.
SO AS I SAID, NOT IDEAL.
BUT WE'RE MAROONS.
YES. WE'VE CUT OUR WAY OUT OF WORSE.

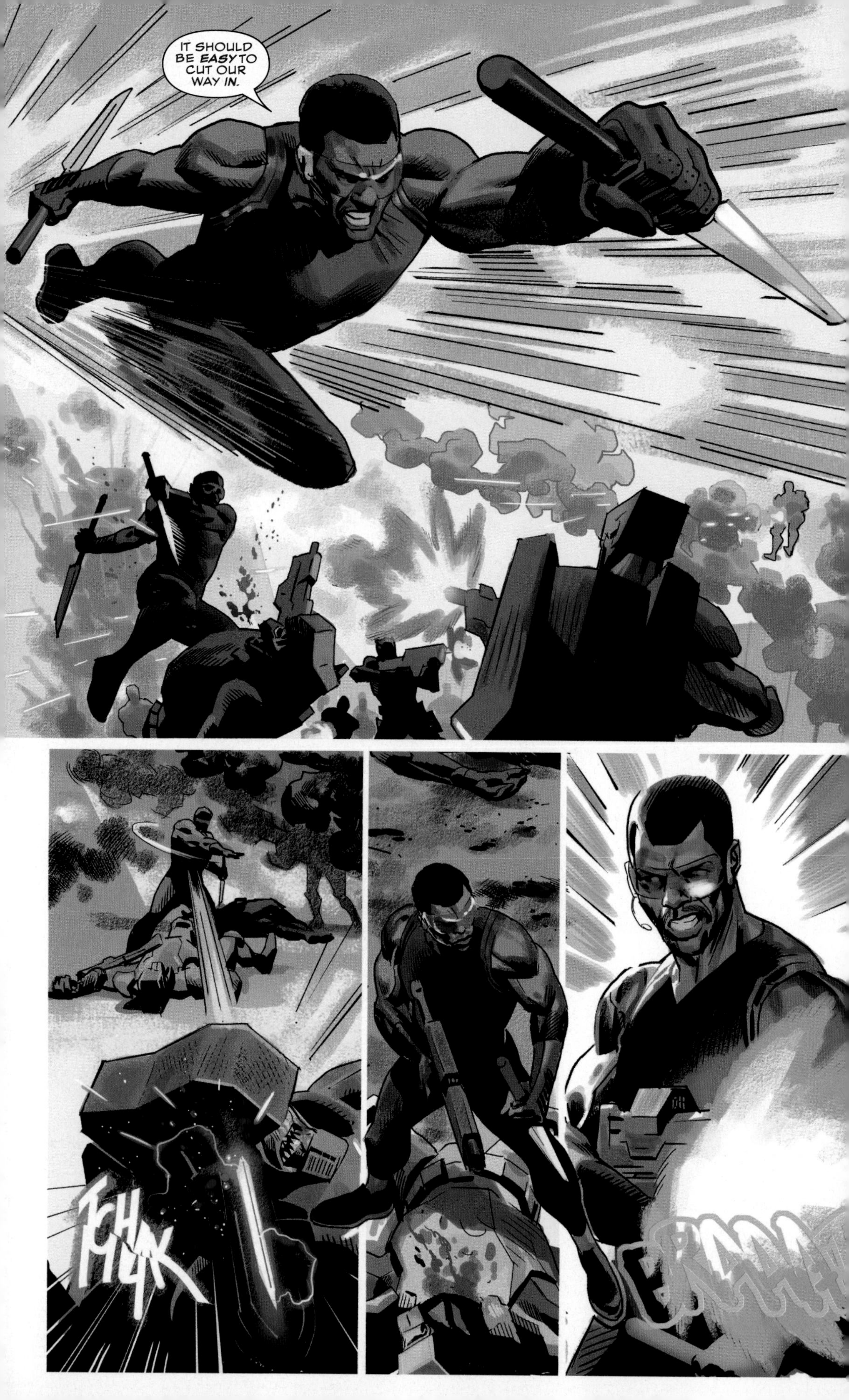
IT SHOULD BE EASY TO CUT OUR WAY IN.
TCHUK

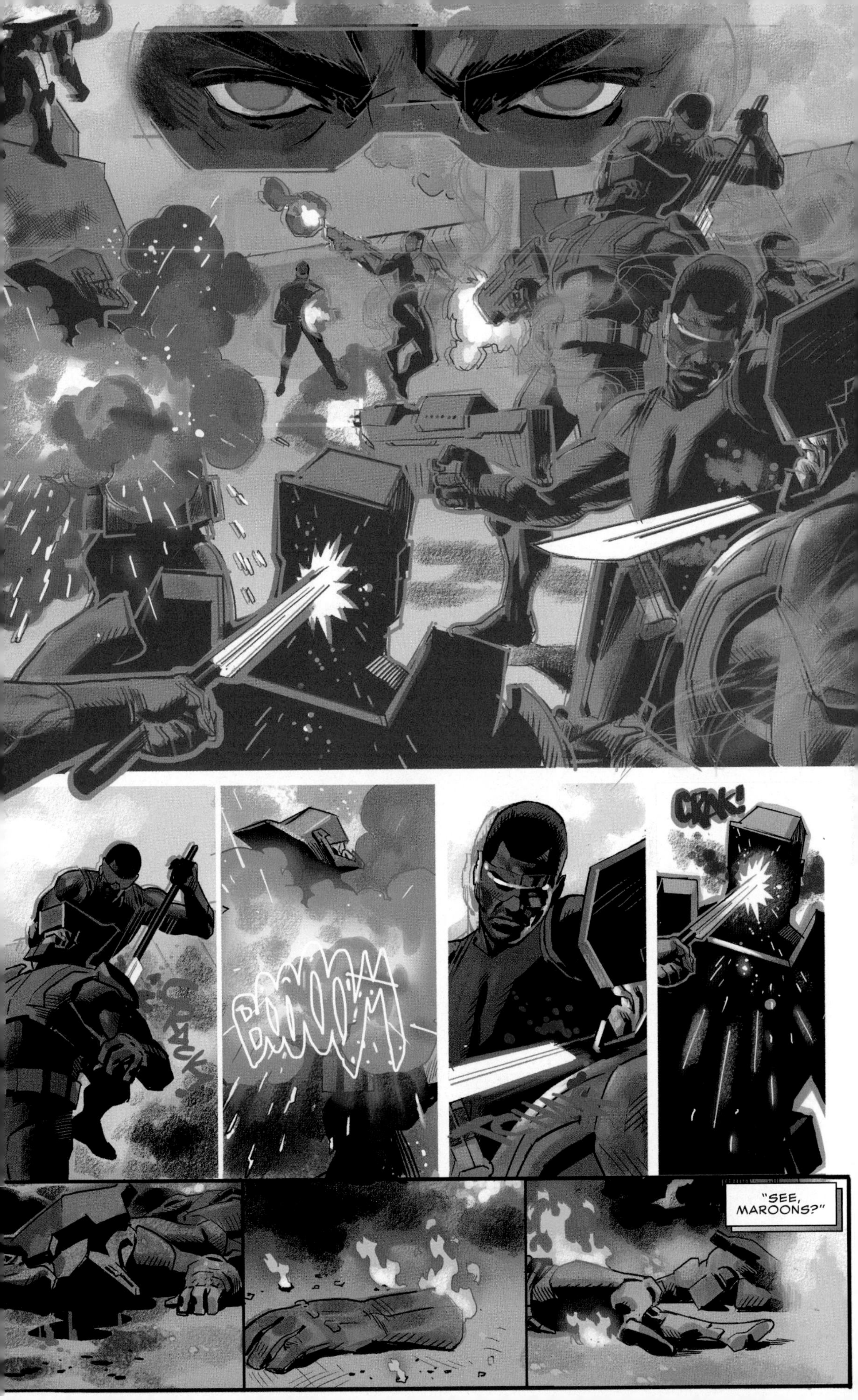
CRACK
BOOOM
CRAK!
"SEE, MAROONS?"

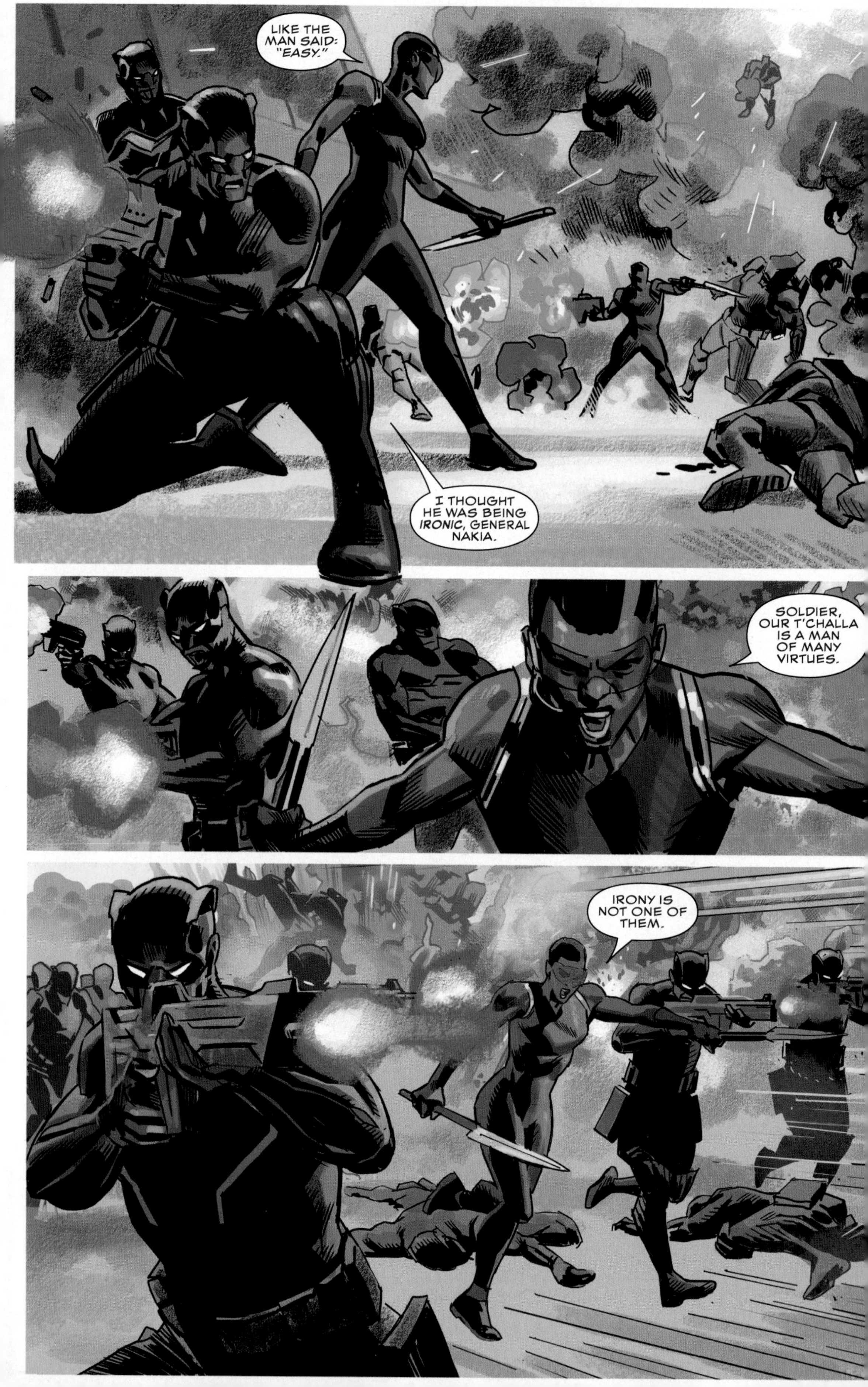
LIKE THE MAN SAID: "EASY."
I THOUGHT HE WAS BEING IRONIC, GENERAL NAKIA.
SOLDIER, OUR T'CHALLA IS A MAN OF MANY VIRTUES.
IRONY IS NOT ONE OF THEM.

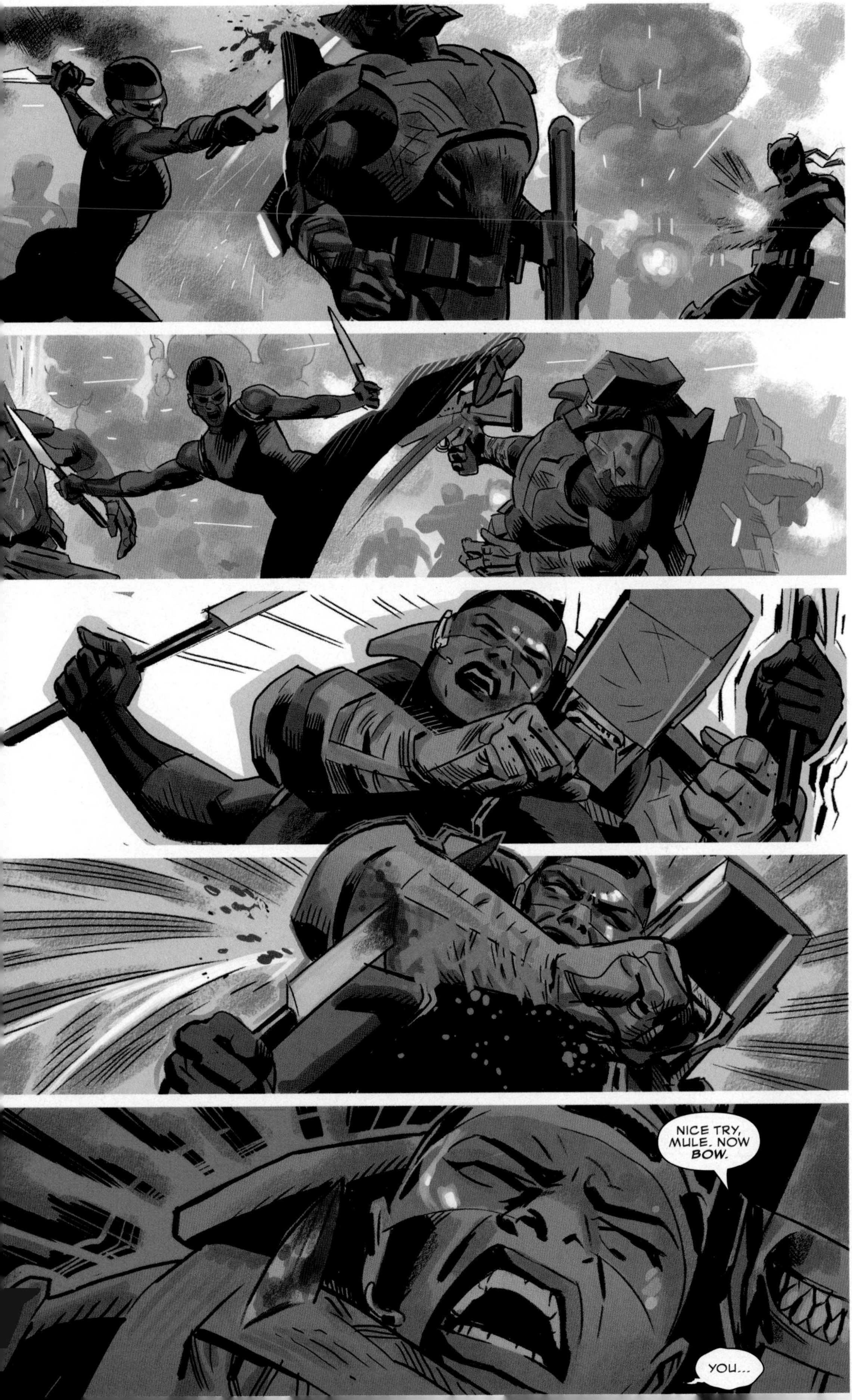
NICE TRY, MULE. NOW BOW.
YOU...

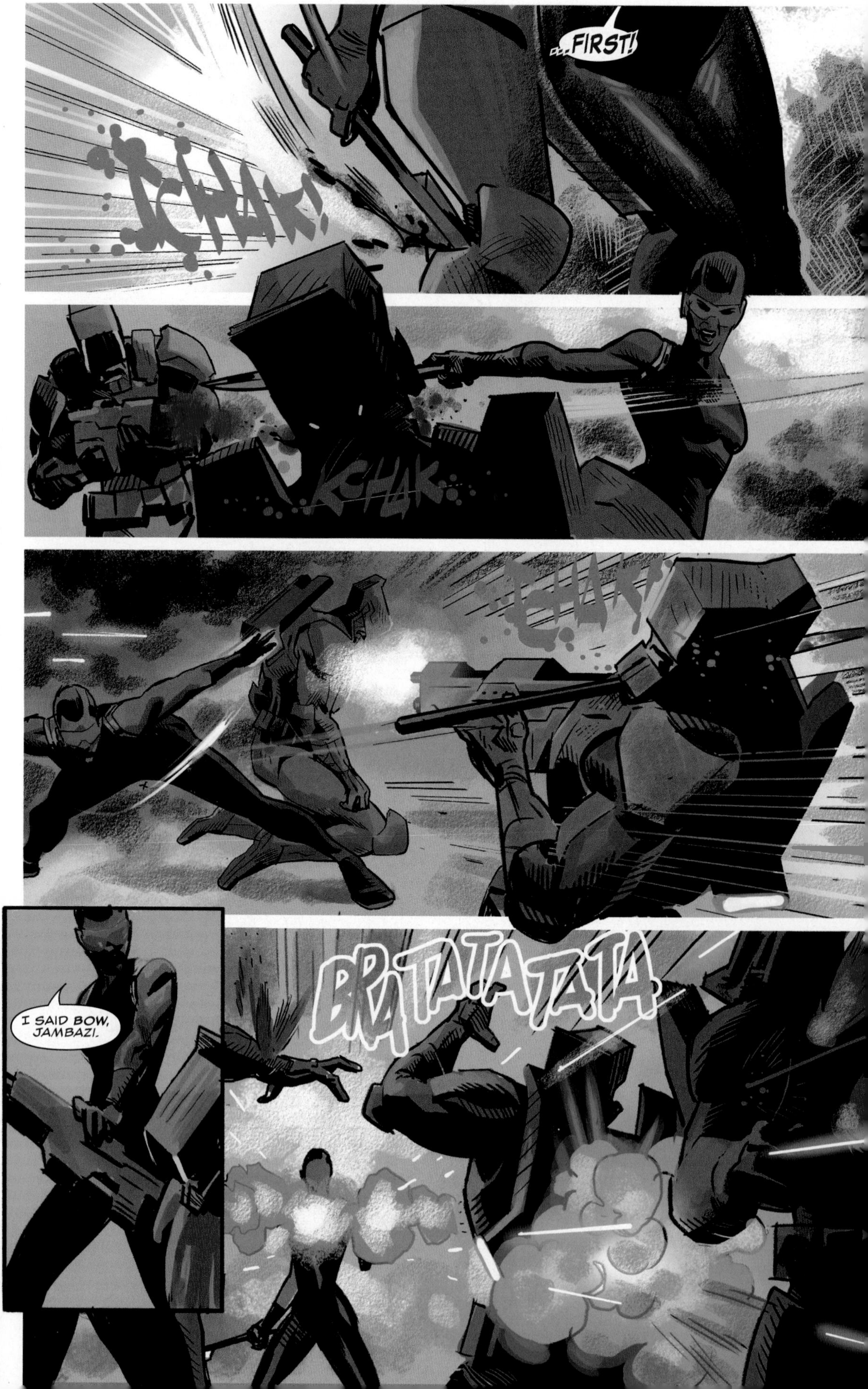
...FIRST!
TCHAK!
KCHAK
TCHAK!
I SAID BOW, JAMBAZI.
BRATATATATA

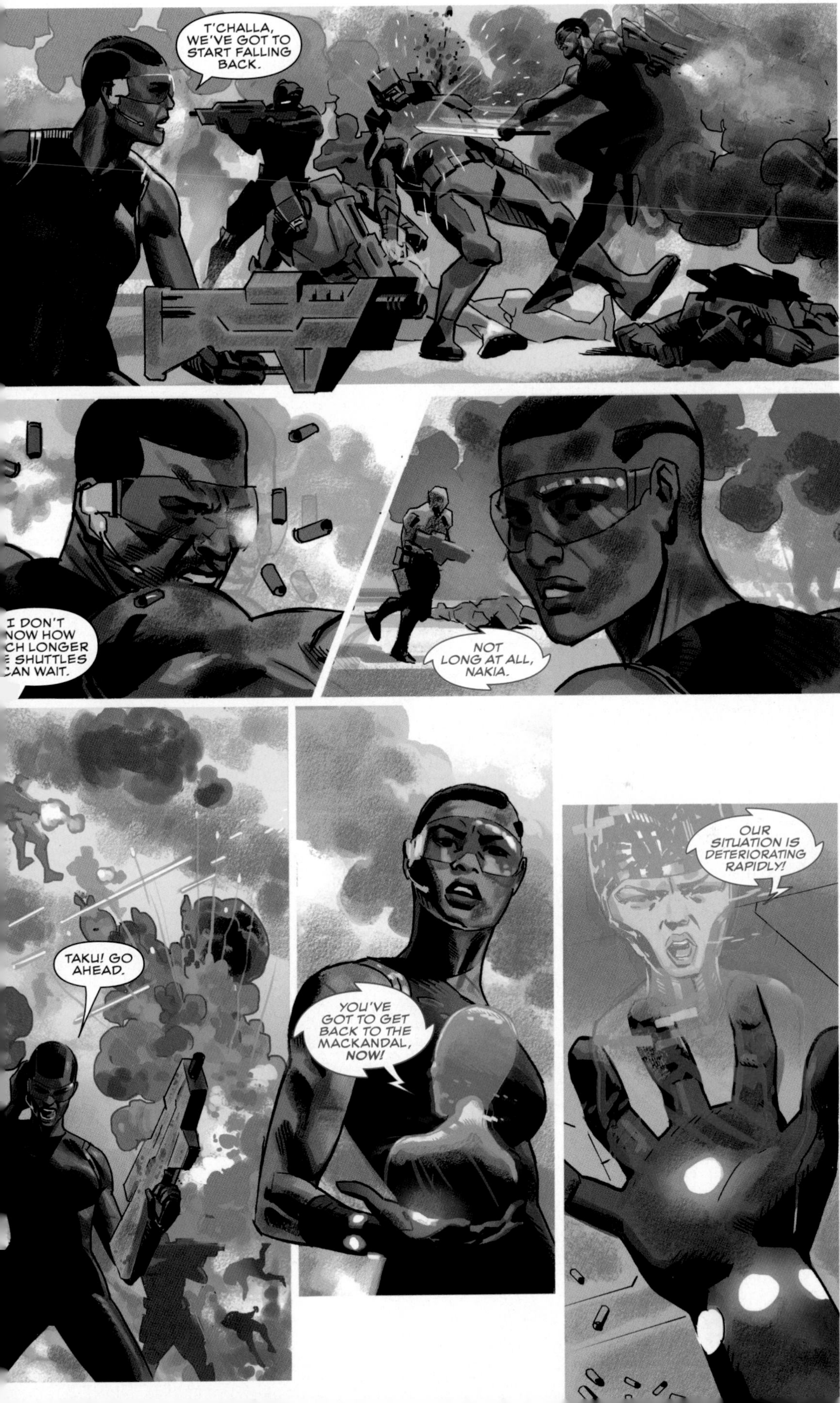
T'CHALLA, WE'VE GOT TO START FALLING BACK.
I DON'T NOW HOW CH LONGER E SHUTTLES CAN WAIT.
NOT LONG AT ALL, NAKIA.
TAKU! GO AHEAD.
YOU'VE GOT TO GET BACK TO THE MACKANDAL, NOW!
OUR SITUATION IS DETERIORATING RAPIDLY!

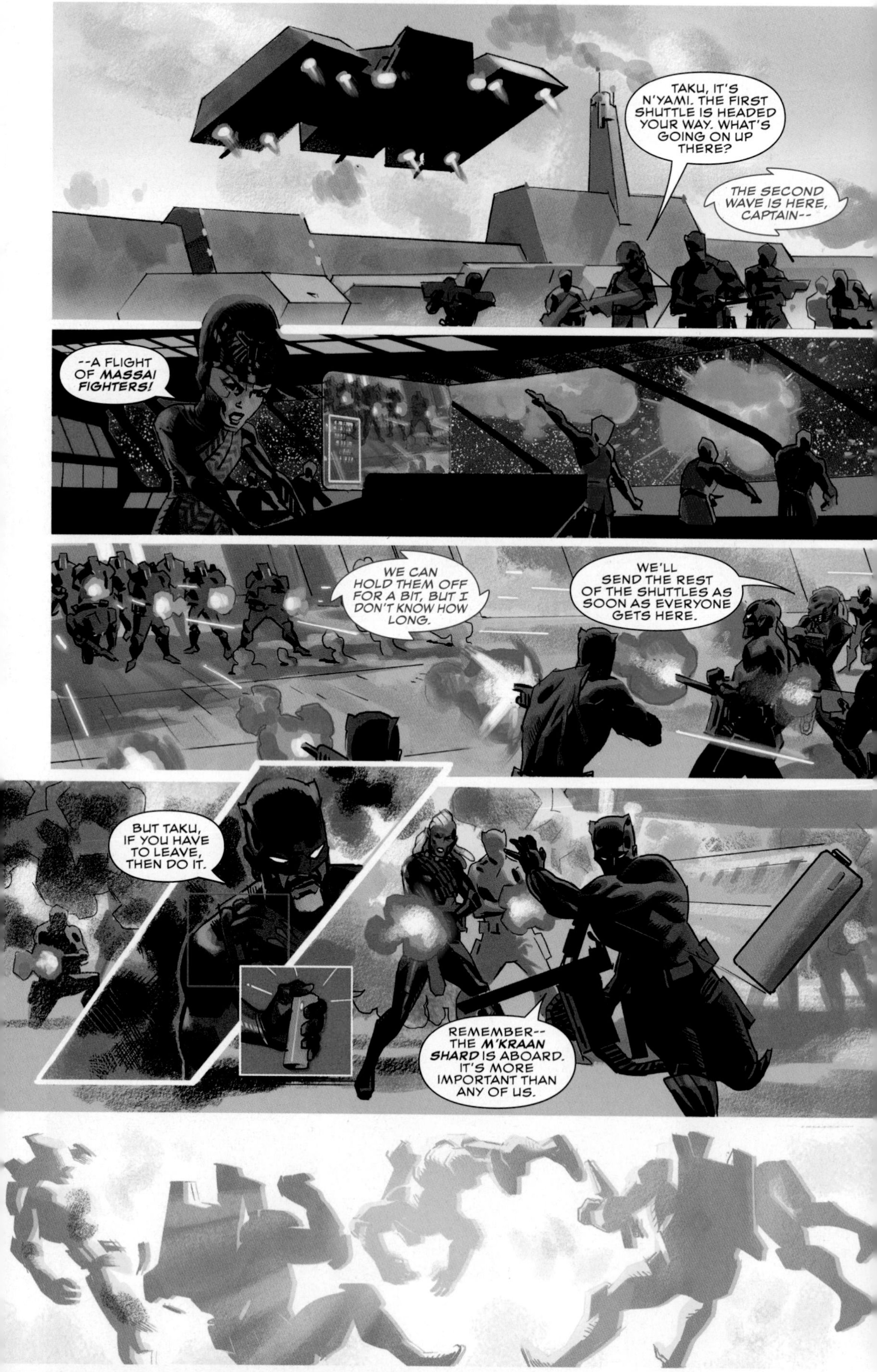
TAKU, IT'S N'YAMI. THE FIRST SHUTTLE IS HEADED YOUR WAY. WHAT'S GOING ON UP THERE?
THE SECOND WAVE IS HERE, CAPTAIN--
--A FLIGHT OF MASSAI FIGHTERS!
WE CAN HOLD THEM OFF FOR A BIT, BUT I DON'T KNOW HOW LONG.
WE'LL SEND THE REST OF THE SHUTTLES AS SOON AS EVERYONE GETS HERE.
BUT TAKU, IF YOU HAVE TO LEAVE, THEN DO IT.
REMEMBER-- THE M'KRAAN SHARD IS ABOARD. IT'S MORE IMPORTANT THAN ANY OF US.

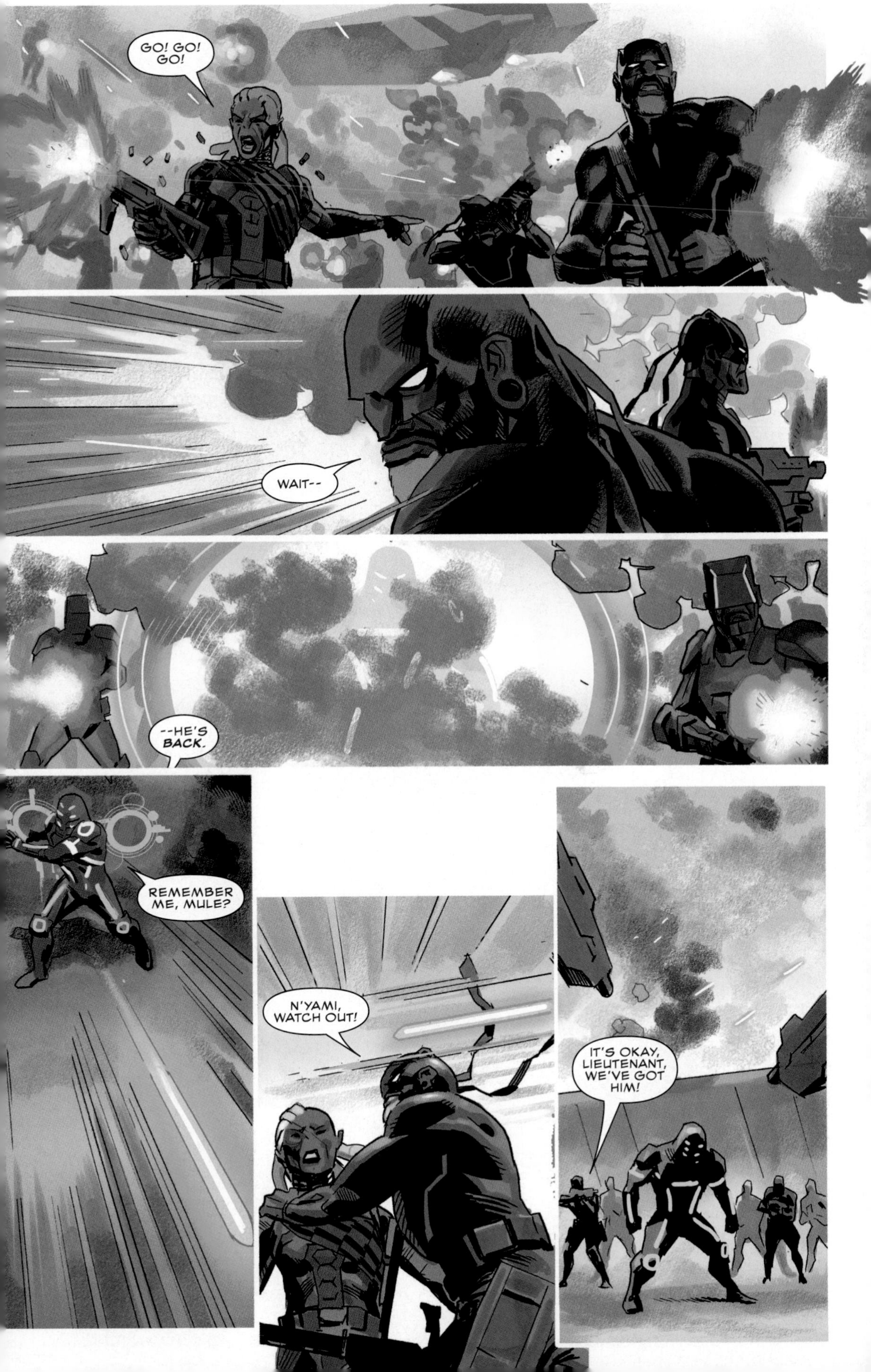
GO! GO! GO!
WAIT--
--HE'S BACK.
REMEMBER ME, MULE?
N'YAMI, WATCH OUT!
IT'S OKAY, LIEUTENANT, WE'VE GOT HIM!

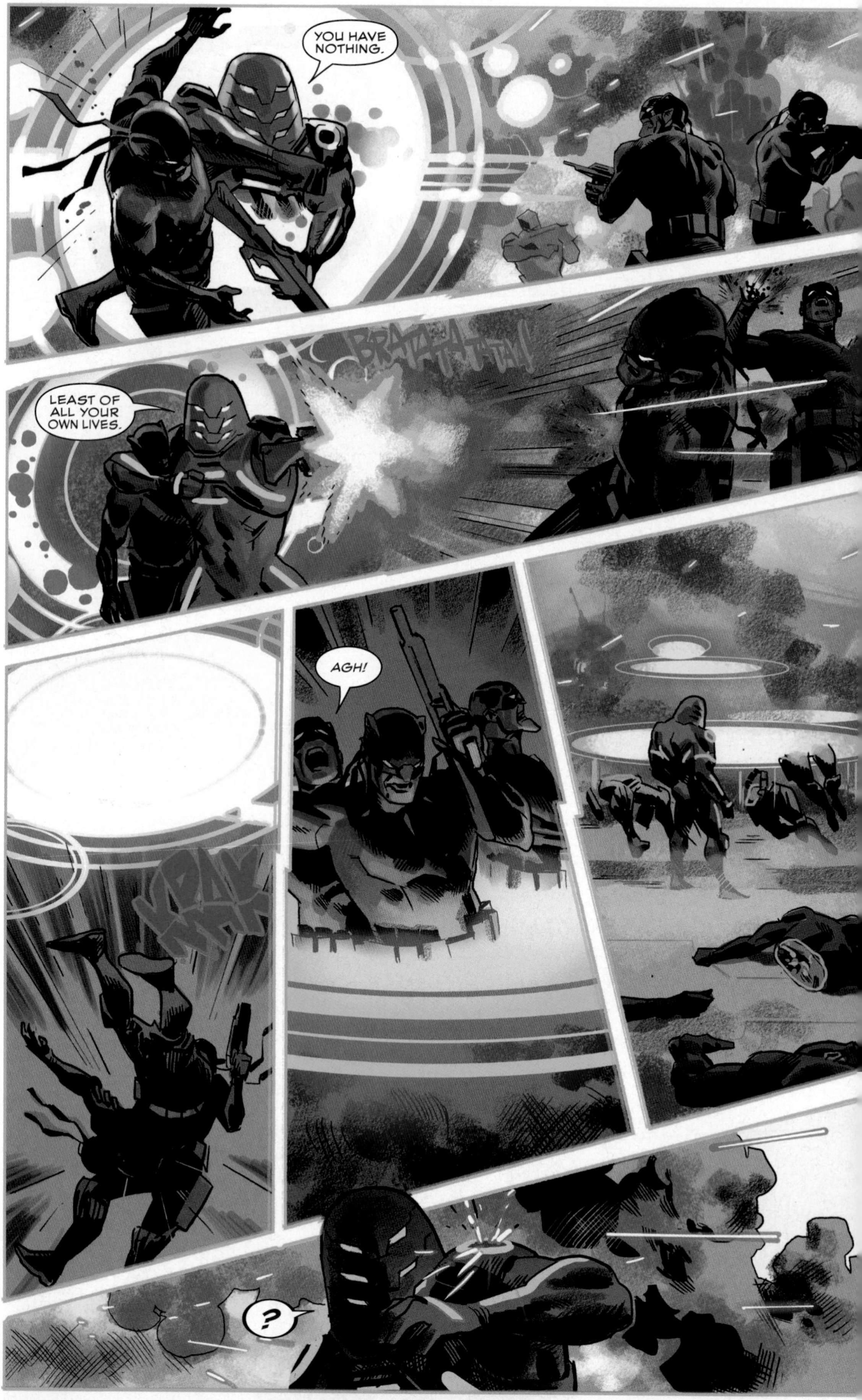
YOU HAVE NOTHING.
BRATATATATATAT!
LEAST OF ALL YOUR OWN LIVES.
AGH!
?

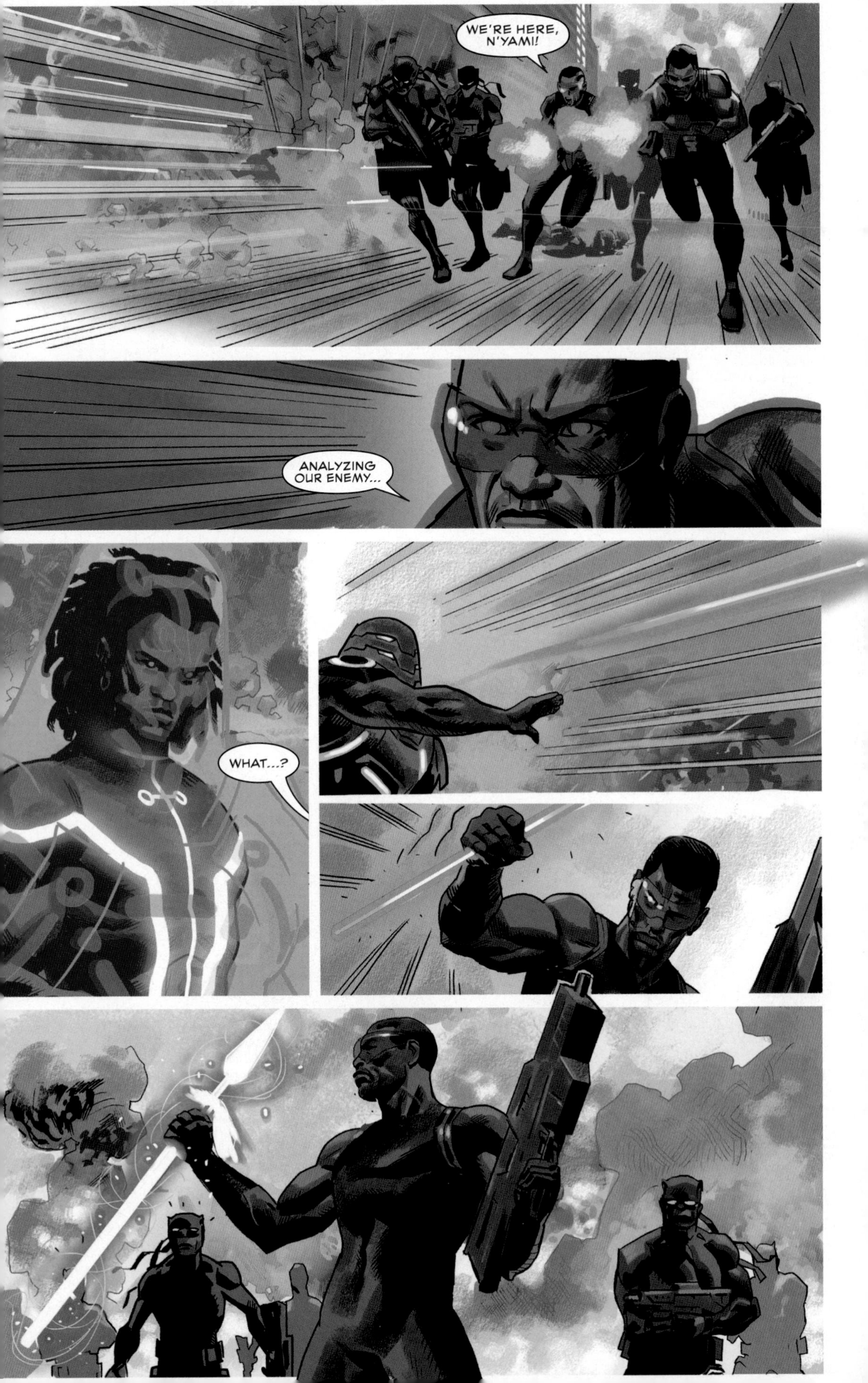
WE'RE HERE, N'YAMI!
ANALYZING OUR ENEMY...
WHAT...?

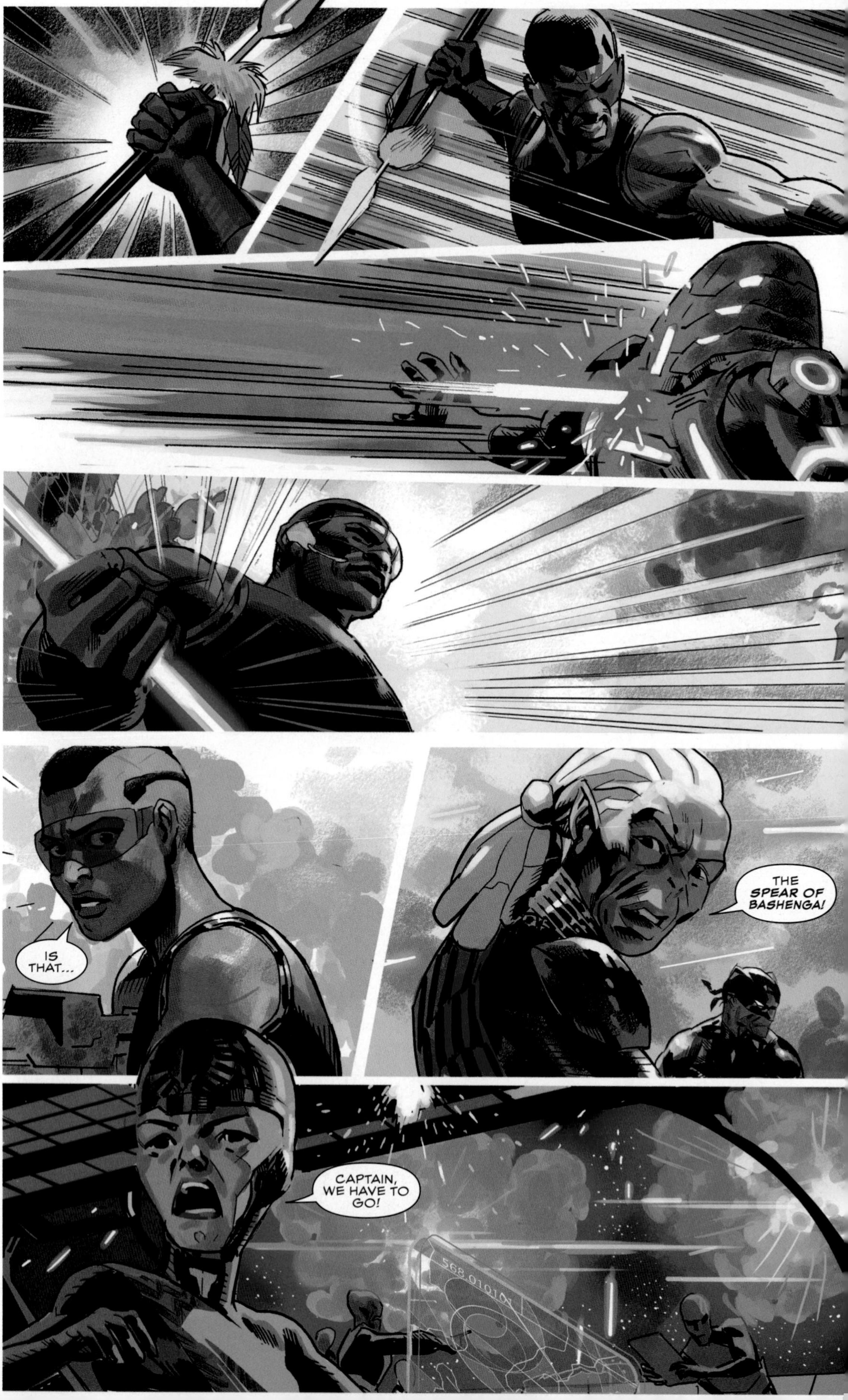
IS THAT...
THE SPEAR OF BASHENGA!
CAPTAIN, WE HAVE TO GO!
568 010101

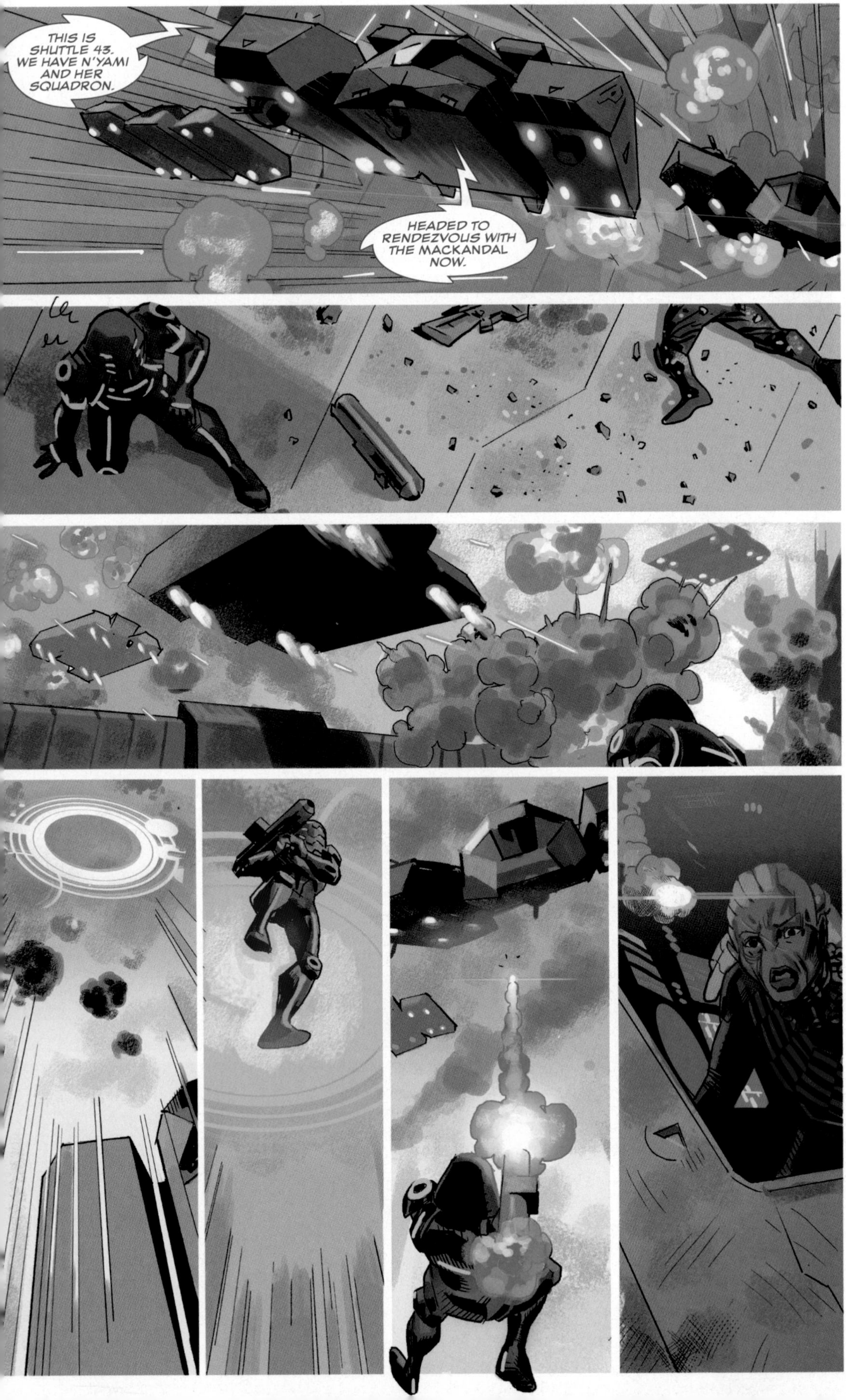
THIS IS SHUTTLE 43. WE HAVE N'YAMI AND HER SQUADRON.
HEADED TO RENDEZVOUS WITH THE MACKANDAL NOW.

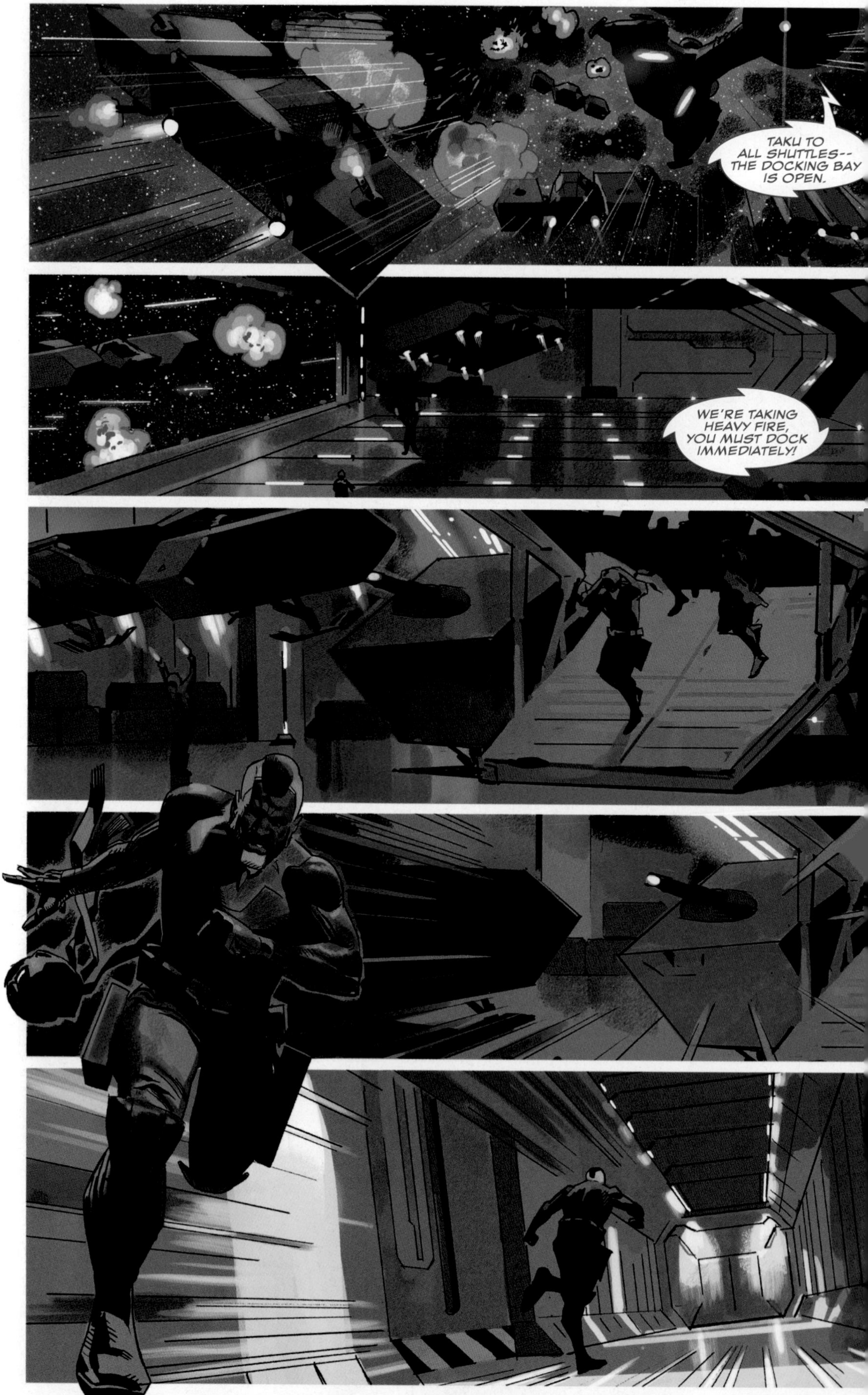
TAKU TO ALL SHUTTLES-- THE DOCKING BAY IS OPEN.
WE'RE TAKING HEAVY FIRE, YOU MUST DOCK IMMEDIATELY!

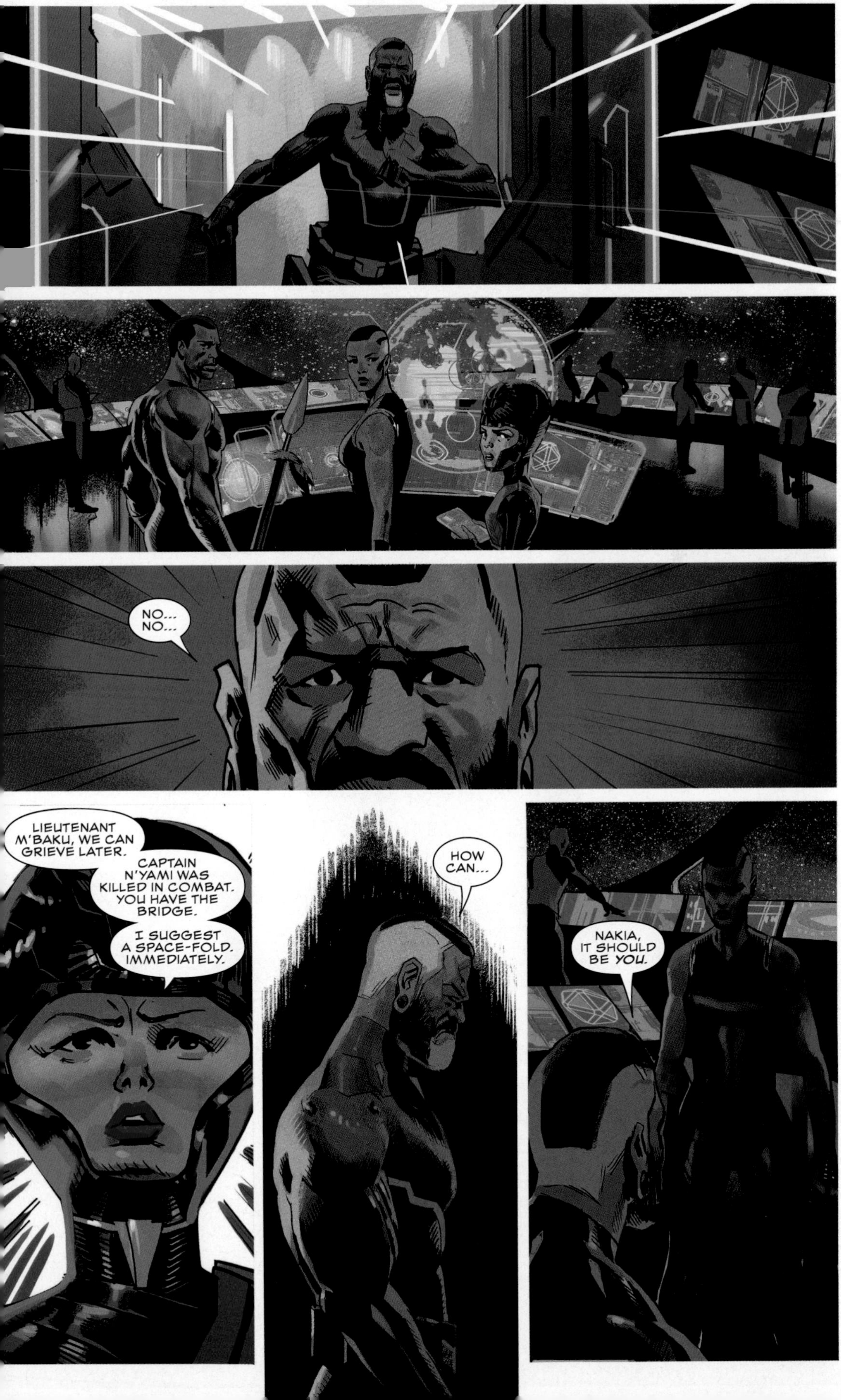
NO...
NO...
LIEUTENANT M'BAKU, WE CAN GRIEVE LATER.
CAPTAIN N'YAMI WAS KILLED IN COMBAT. YOU HAVE THE BRIDGE.
I SUGGEST A SPACE-FOLD. IMMEDIATELY.
HOW CAN...
NAKIA, IT SHOULD BE YOU.

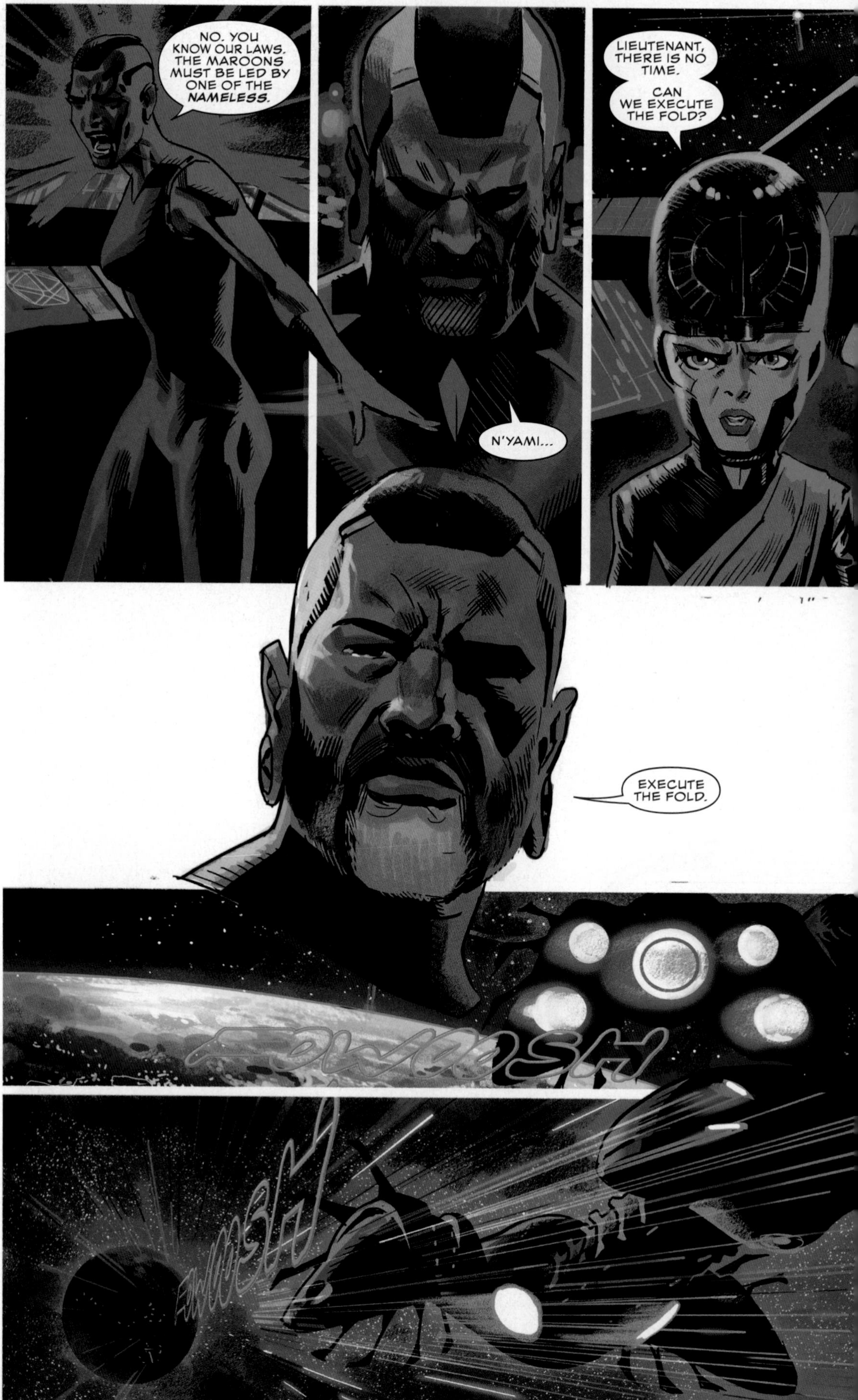
NO. YOU KNOW OUR LAWS. THE MAROONS MUST BE LED BY ONE OF THE *NAMELESS*.
LIEUTENANT, THERE IS NO TIME.
CAN WE EXECUTE THE FOLD?
N'YAMI...
EXECUTE THE FOLD.

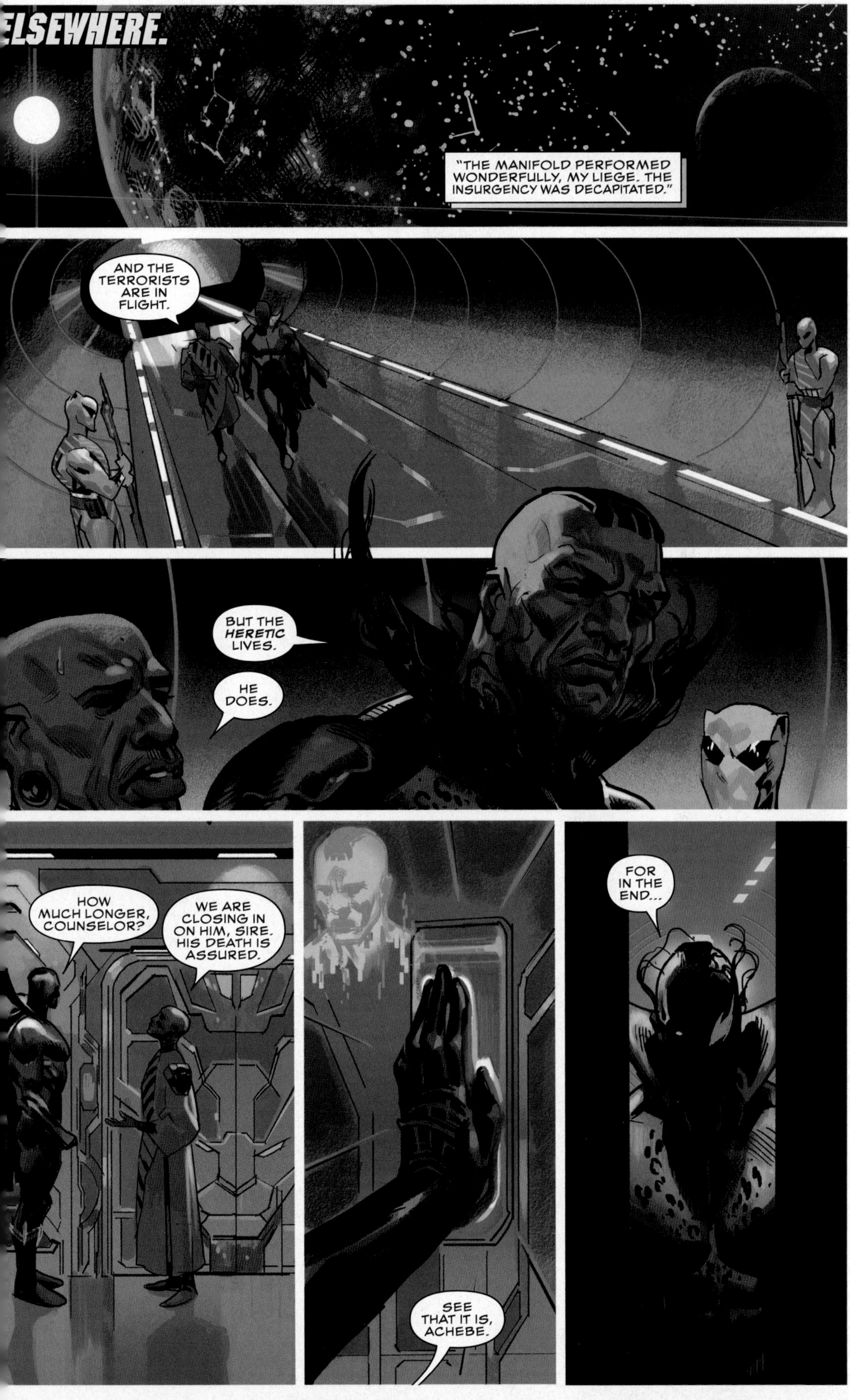
ELSEWHERE.
"THE MANIFOLD PERFORMED WONDERFULLY, MY LIEGE. THE INSURGENCY WAS DECAPITATED."
AND THE TERRORISTS ARE IN FLIGHT.
BUT THE *HERETIC* LIVES.
HE DOES.
HOW MUCH LONGER, COUNSELOR?
WE ARE CLOSING IN ON HIM, SIRE. HIS DEATH IS ASSURED.
SEE THAT IT IS, ACHEBE.
FOR IN THE END...

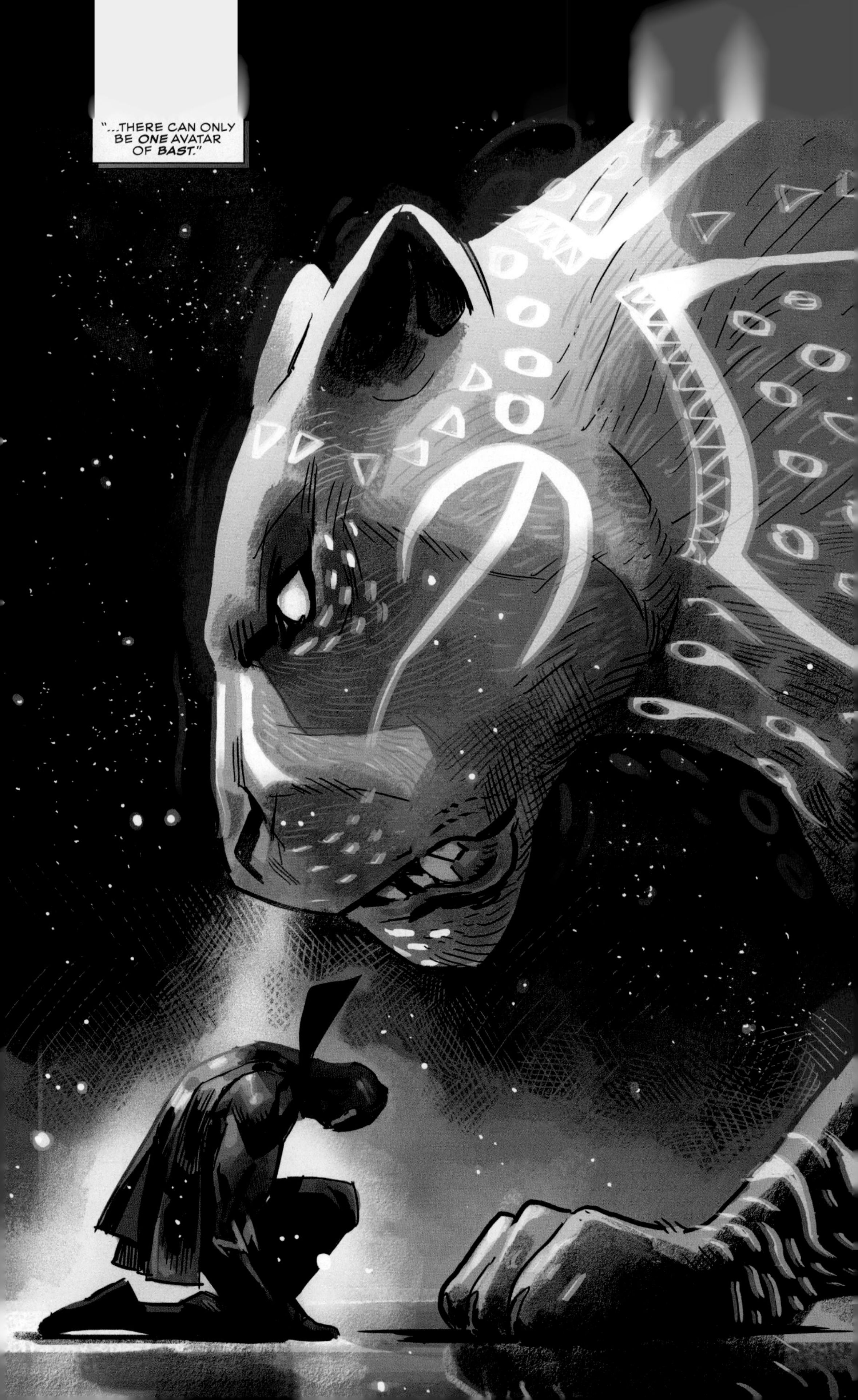
"...THERE CAN ONLY BE *ONE* AVATAR OF *BAST*."

OCCUPYING THE FAR REACHES OF THE UNIVERSE, THE INTERGALACTIC EMPIRE OF WAKANDA
IS A SPRAWLING IMPERIUM MADE UP OF FIVE STAR CLUSTERS.

HE EARLY WAKANDAN SETTLERS OF THE BENHAZIN SYSTEM WERE INITIALLY PEACEFUL, PREFERRING TO REMAIN AMONG
EIR OWN, AS WAS THE WAY OF THEIR FOREFATHERS. BUT A SERIES OF ATTEMPTED INVASIONS CONVINCED THE SETTLERS
HAT SELF-DEFENSE WOULD NOT BE ENOUGH FOR THIS BARBARIC PORTION OF SPACE — PREVENTIVE STRIKES MUST BE
DE. THEN, AFTER THE WAKANDANS MASTERED THE TECHNOLOGY OF DEEP-SPACE PASSAGE, THOSE PREVENTIVE STRIKES
BECAME PREVENTIVE OCCUPATION AND FINALLY PREVENTIVE CONQUEST.

ARMED WITH SUPERIOR TECHNOLOGY AND A TYPICAL WAKANDAN FEROCITY IN BATTLE, THE CONQUERORS
QUICKLY BECAME MASTERS OF THEIR CORNER OF THE UNIVERSE — AND THERE IS NO REASON TO BELIEVE THEY WILL
SIMPLY SETTLE FOR THAT CORNER.

THE FIVE GALAXIES OF THE EMPIRE:

THE BENHAZIN SYSTEM:

OME GALAXY OF PLANET BAST, THE BENHAZIN SYSTEM IS THE ORIGINATING GALAXY FOR THE INTERGALACTIC EMPIRE OF WAKANDA. THE
TEM WAS ONCE RICH IN VIBRANIUM — INDEED, JUST OUTSIDE THE SOLAR SYSTEM OF PLANET BAST THERE ONCE WAS A RING OF ASTEROIDS
ADE OF NEARLY PURE VIBRANIUM. THE ASTEROID BELT IS LONG GONE, HAVING BEEN STRIP-MINED BY THE WAKANDANS A MILLENNIA AGO.

T'CHAKA'S REACH:

CLOSEST GALAXY TO THE BENHAZIN SYSTEM, AND THE FIRST TO FALL UNDER THE SWAY OF THE EMPIRE, T'CHAKA'S REACH WAS ONCE HOME
) A GREAT INTERPLANETARY EMPIRE RULED BY THE RIGELLIANS. THE WAKANDANS MADE SHORT WORK OF THEM; HOWEVER, AND THE STAR
STEM IS NOW DOTTED WITH PLANETARY RUINS. THE RIGELLIANS ARE NOW NOMADS OF THEIR HOME GALAXY, THOROUGHLY DISPLACED BY
THE CONQUERING WAKANDANS.

THE S'YAAN EXPANSE:

A RICH NETWORK OF STAR SYSTEMS SUPPORTING PLANETS IN THE "GOLDILOCKS ZONE," OR PLANETS CAPABLE OF SUPPORTING CARBON-
SED LIFEFORMS. THE WAKANDANS SEIZED UPON THE S'YAAN EXPANSE NOT FOR ITS VIBRANIUM BUT FOR ITS LUSH AND BEAUTIFUL PLANETS,
W OF WHICH REQUIRED TERRAFORMING. THE S'YAAN EXPANSE IS THOUGHT TO BE THE MOST BEAUTIFUL GALAXY IN THE EMPIRE, HOME TO
AGNIFICENT STELLAR PHENOMENON. THE S'YAAN EXPANSE WAS THE SECOND GALAXY TO FALL TO THE WAKANDANS AND PROVED CRUCIAL
THE MASSIVE POPULATION BOOM THAT ALLOWED THEIR CONQUESTS TO CONTINUE. NOTHING IS RECORDED OF THE EXPANSE'S ORIGINAL
INHABITANTS. WHOEVER THEY WERE, IT APPEARS THE WAKANDANS DEALT WITH THEM MERCILESSLY.

THE MATRIX OF MAMADOU:

NCE HOME TO A WARRING SET OF POWERS, THE MATRIX OF MAMADOU WAS CONQUERED BY THE WAKANDANS AT CONSIDERABLE COSTS.
HE FEROCIOUS KRONAN WERE ONCE BASED HERE, AS WELL AS A COLONY OF KLYNTAR AND ANOTHER OF MYSTERIOUS SHADOW-PEOPLE.
E KRONAN HAVE SINCE BEEN ENSLAVED, WHILE THE SHADOW-PEOPLE HAVE ACCEPTED WAKANDAN RULE AND INTEGRATED THEMSELVES IN
VIRTUALLY ALL LEVELS OF WAKANDAN SOCIETY. THE FATE OF THE KLYNTAR COLONY REMAINS A MYSTERY TO THIS DAY.

NEHANDA'S LATTICE:

EOGRAPHICALLY IT IS THE GALAXY MOST DISTANT FROM THE BENHAZIN SYSTEM. IT CONTAINS WITHIN IT THE ZANJ REGION, HOME TO THE
ADQUARTERS OF THE MAROONS, THE MOST SUSTAINED AND THREATENING REBELLION EVER LAUNCHED AGAINST THE EMPIRE. NEHANDA'S
ICE WAS ORIGINALLY DOMINATED BY THE AQUATIC TEKU-MAZA, BUT THE WAKANDANS HAVE SINCE ENSLAVED THEM AND FORCED THEM TO
WORK IN THE VIBRANIUM MINES OF ZANJ AND OTHER SITES ACROSS THE GALAXY.

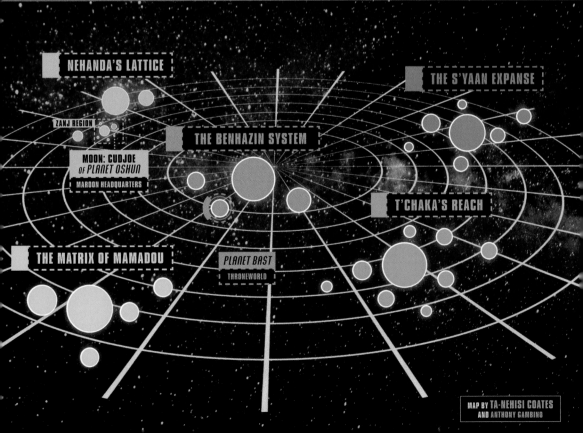

NEHANDA'S LATTICE

THE S'YAAN EXPANSE

ZANJ REGION

THE BENHAZIN SYSTEM

MOON: CUDJOE
of PLANET OSHUN
MAROON HEADQUARTERS

T'CHAKA'S REACH

THE MATRIX OF MAMADOU

PLANET BAST
THRONEWORLD

MAP BY TA-NEHISI COATES
AND ANTHONY GAMBINO

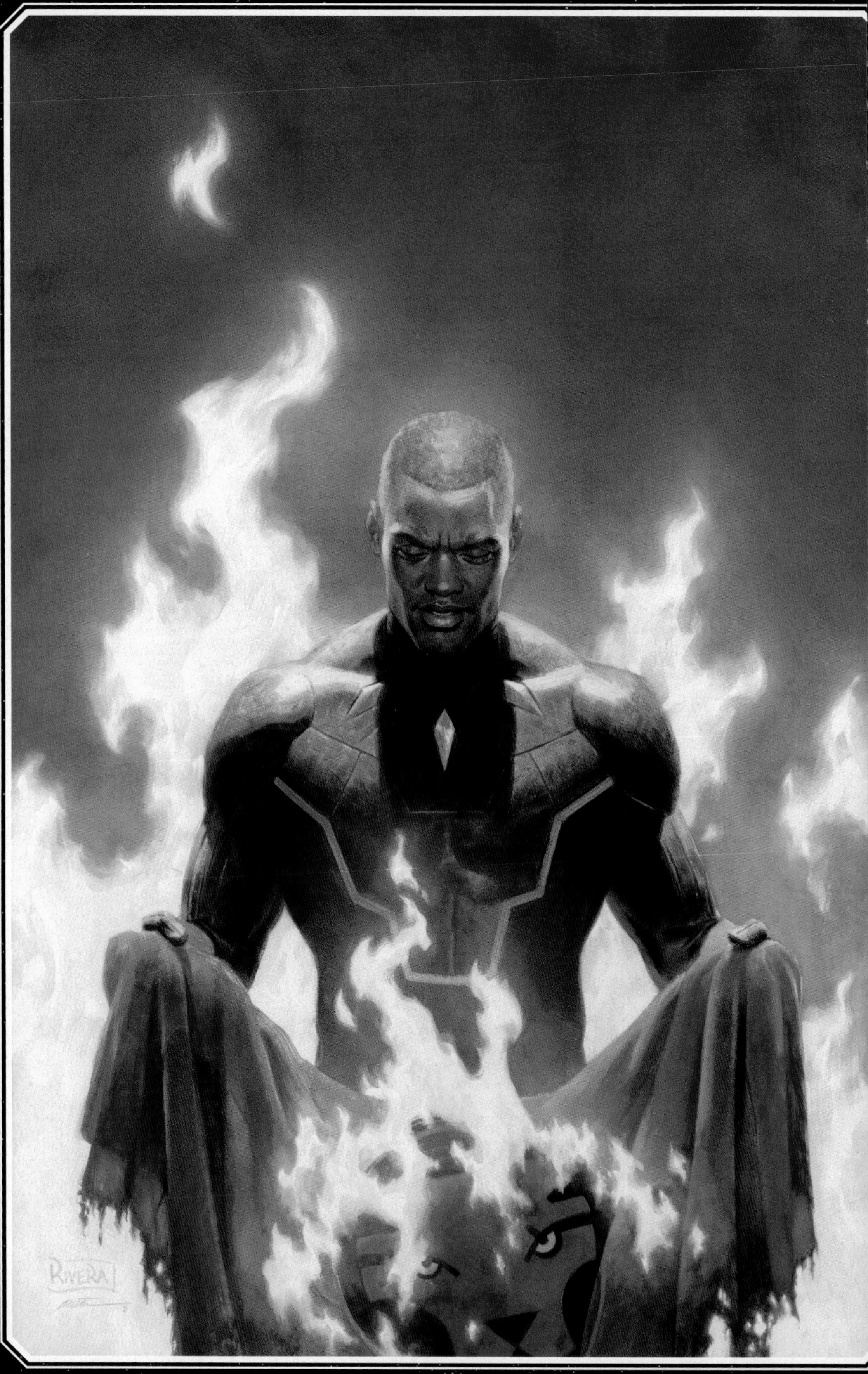
RIVERA

5

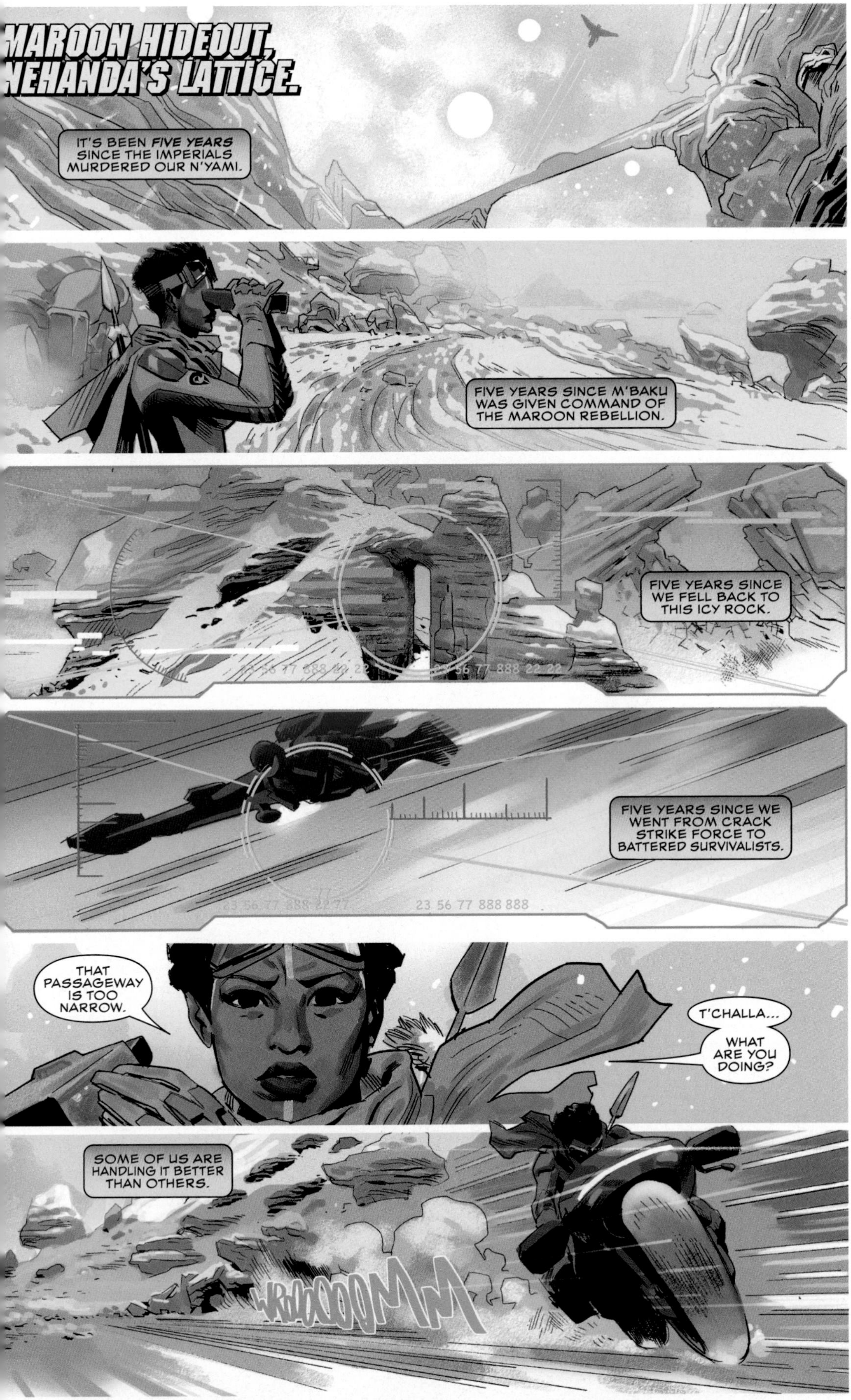

MAROON HIDEOUT, NEHANDA'S LATTICE.
IT'S BEEN FIVE YEARS SINCE THE IMPERIALS MURDERED OUR N'YAMI.
FIVE YEARS SINCE M'BAKU WAS GIVEN COMMAND OF THE MAROON REBELLION.
FIVE YEARS SINCE WE FELL BACK TO THIS ICY ROCK.
FIVE YEARS SINCE WE WENT FROM CRACK STRIKE FORCE TO BATTERED SURVIVALISTS.
23 56 77 888 22 77
23 56 77 888 888
THAT PASSAGEWAY IS TOO NARROW.
T'CHALLA...
WHAT ARE YOU DOING?
SOME OF US ARE HANDLING IT BETTER THAN OTHERS.
WRrOOOOMMM

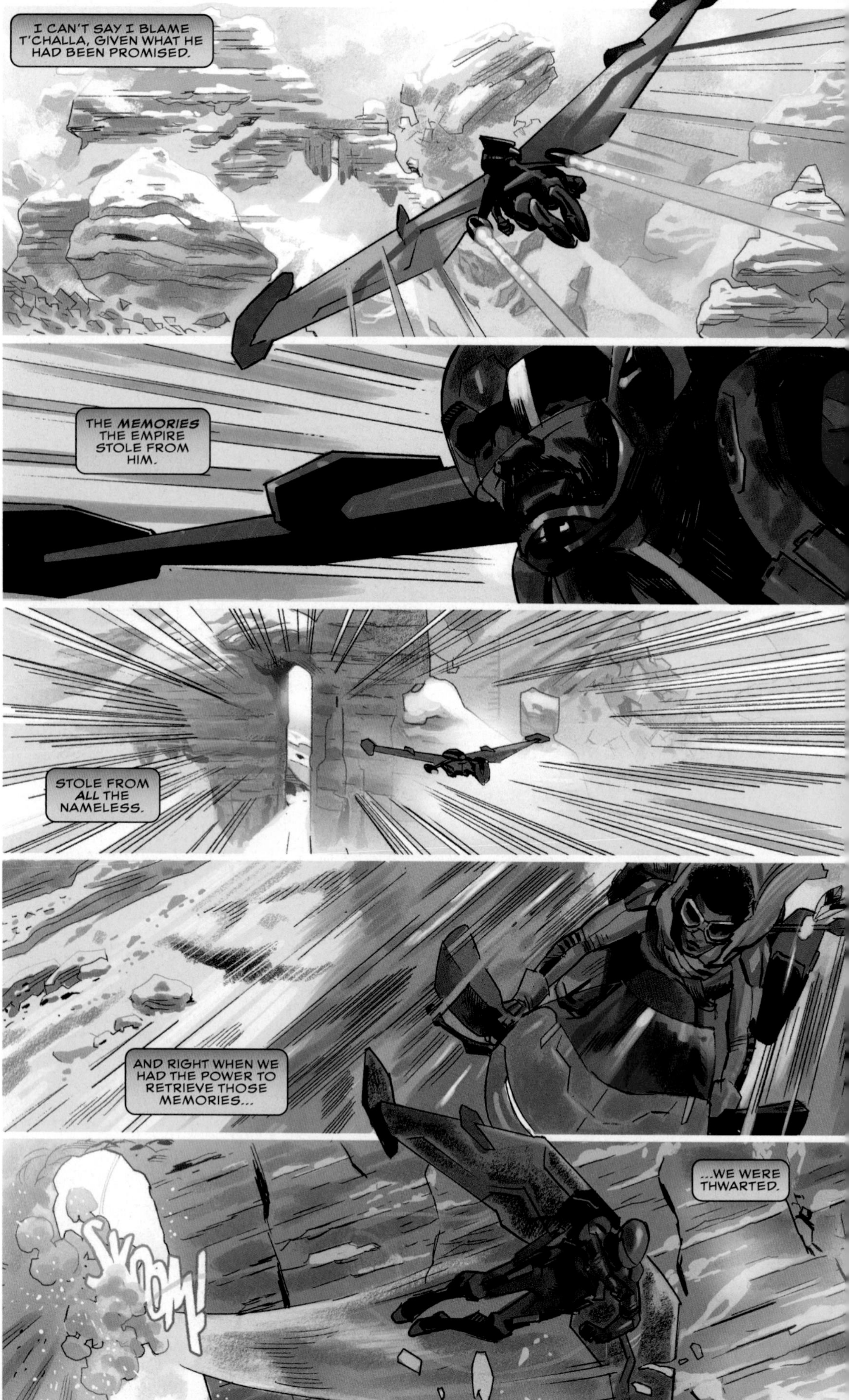
I CAN'T SAY I BLAME T'CHALLA, GIVEN WHAT HE HAD BEEN PROMISED.
THE *MEMORIES* THE EMPIRE STOLE FROM HIM.
STOLE FROM *ALL* THE NAMELESS.
AND RIGHT WHEN WE HAD THE POWER TO RETRIEVE THOSE MEMORIES...
...WE WERE THWARTED.
SWOOM!

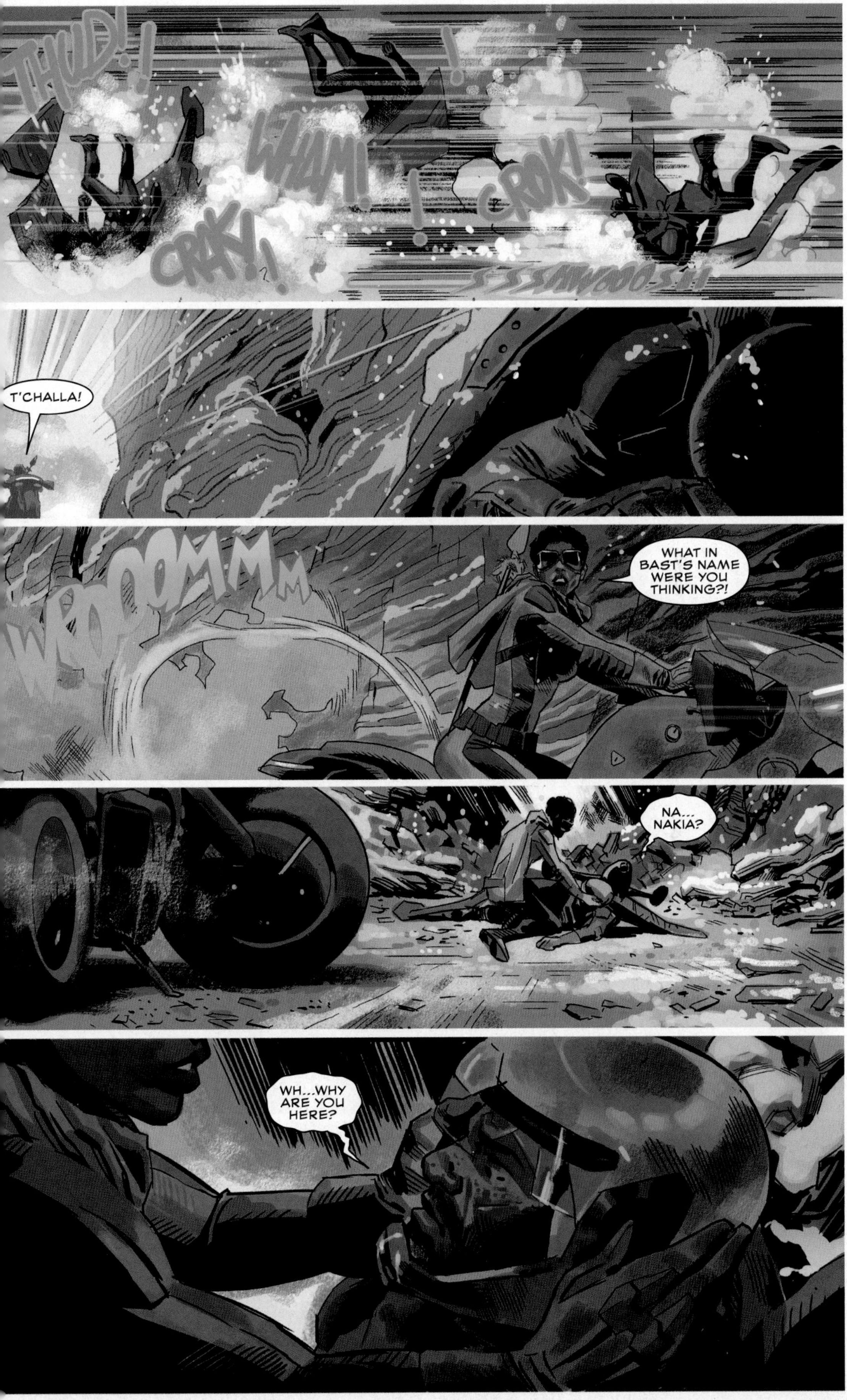
THUD!!
WHAM!!
CRAK!!
CRAK!
T'CHALLA!
WROOOMMMM
WHAT IN BAST'S NAME WERE YOU THINKING?!
NA... NAKIA?
WH...WHY ARE YOU HERE?

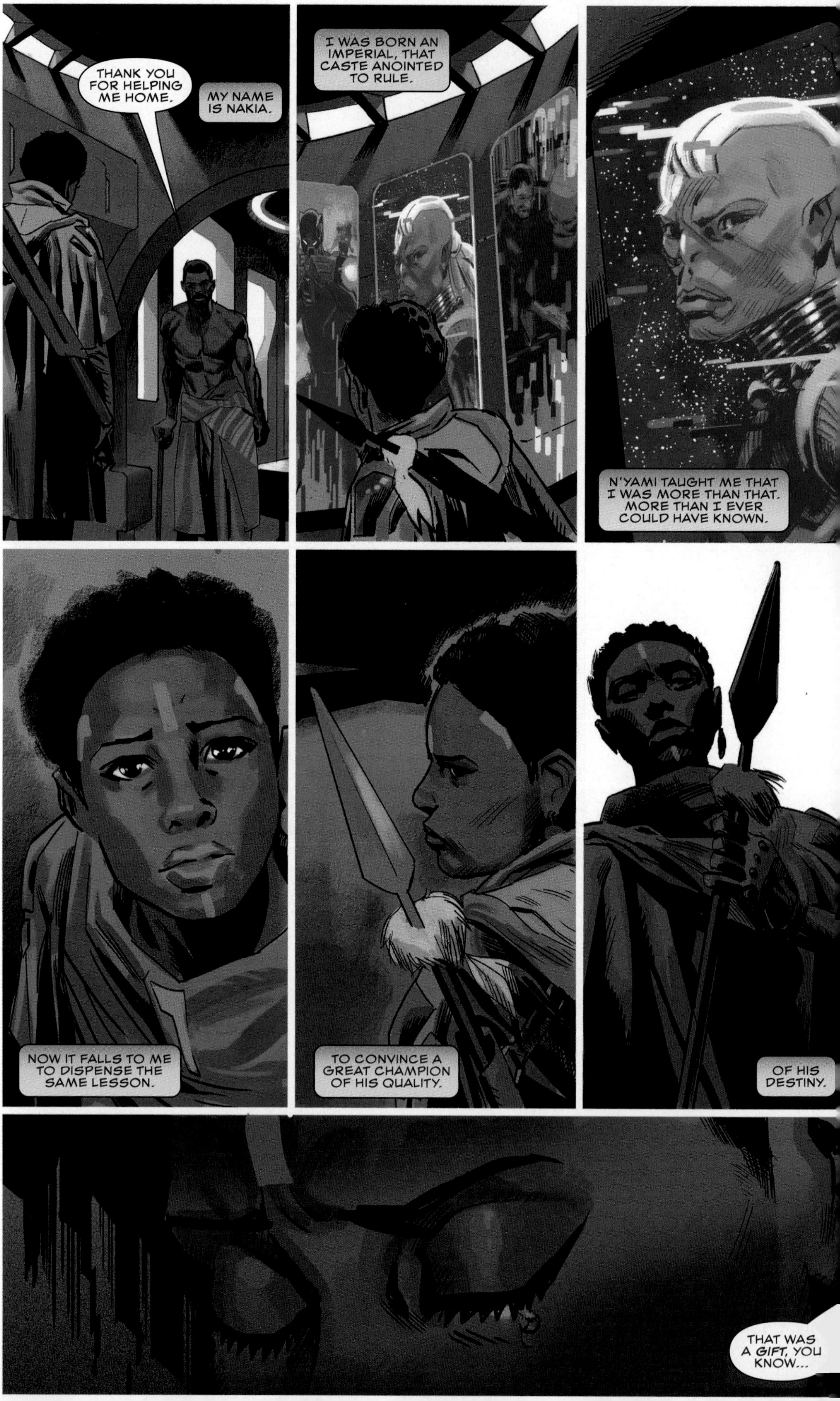
THANK YOU FOR HELPING ME HOME.
MY NAME IS NAKIA.
I WAS BORN AN IMPERIAL, THAT CASTE ANOINTED TO RULE.
N'YAMI TAUGHT ME THAT I WAS MORE THAN THAT. MORE THAN I EVER COULD HAVE KNOWN.
NOW IT FALLS TO ME TO DISPENSE THE SAME LESSON.
TO CONVINCE A GREAT CHAMPION OF HIS QUALITY.
OF HIS DESTINY.
THAT WAS A GIFT, YOU KNOW...

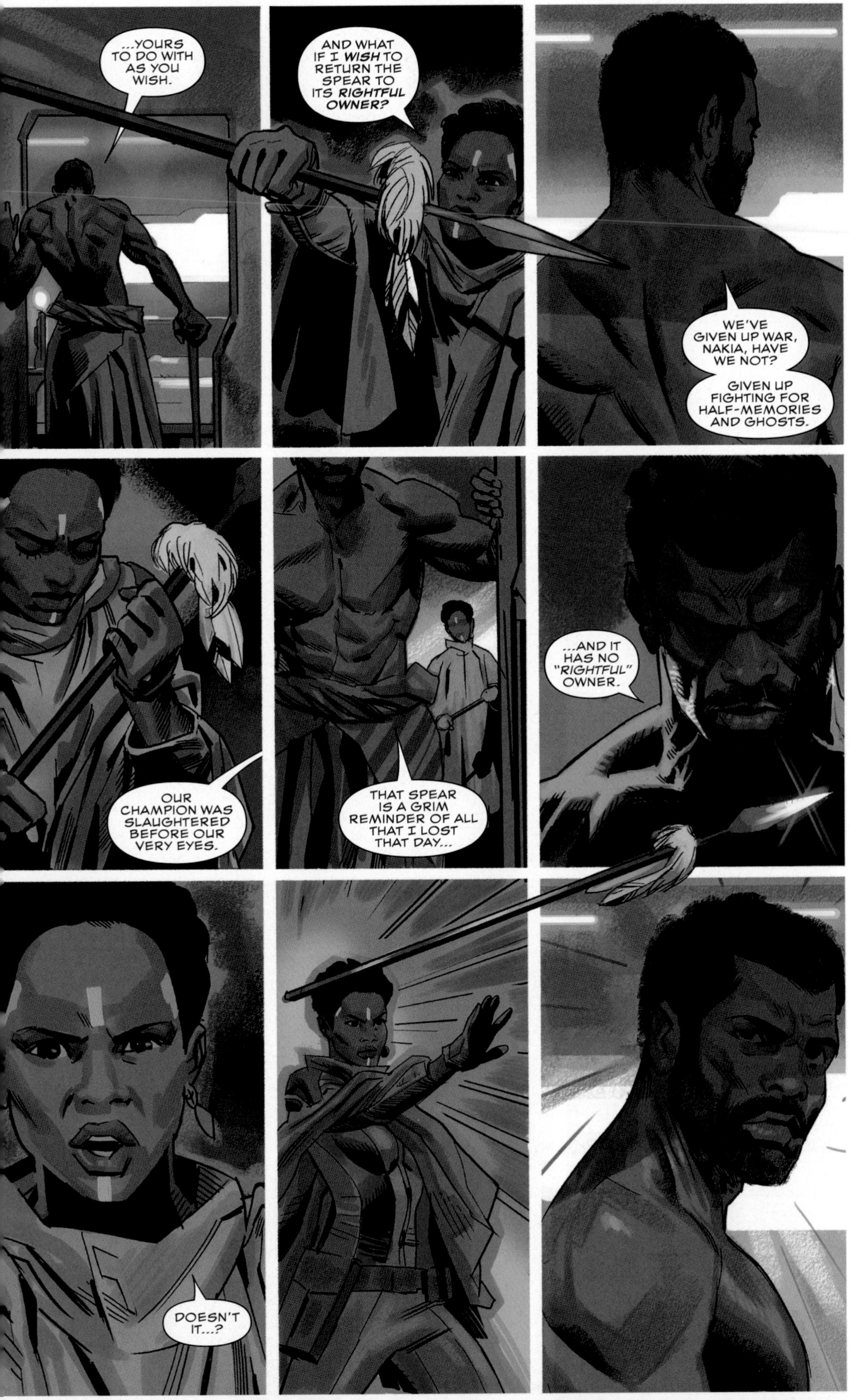
...YOURS TO DO WITH AS YOU WISH.
AND WHAT IF I *WISH* TO RETURN THE SPEAR TO ITS *RIGHTFUL* OWNER?
WE'VE GIVEN UP WAR, NAKIA, HAVE WE NOT?
GIVEN UP FIGHTING FOR HALF-MEMORIES AND GHOSTS.
OUR CHAMPION WAS SLAUGHTERED BEFORE OUR VERY EYES.
THAT SPEAR IS A GRIM REMINDER OF ALL THAT I LOST THAT DAY...
...AND IT HAS NO "*RIGHTFUL*" OWNER.
DOESN'T IT...?

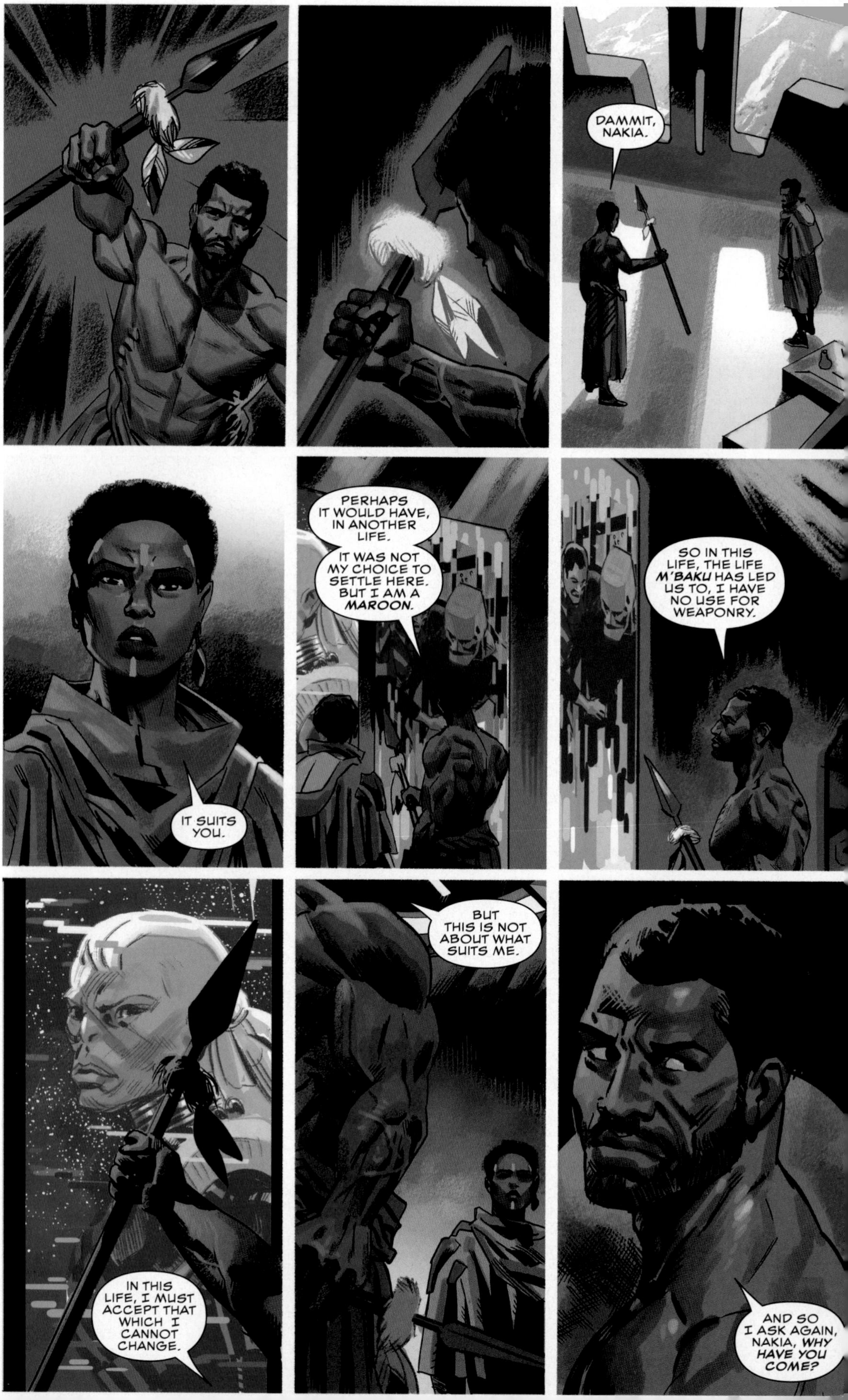
DAMMIT, NAKIA.
IT SUITS YOU.
PERHAPS IT WOULD HAVE, IN ANOTHER LIFE.
IT WAS NOT MY CHOICE TO SETTLE HERE. BUT I AM A *MAROON*.
SO IN THIS LIFE, THE LIFE *M'BAKU* HAS LED US TO, I HAVE NO USE FOR WEAPONRY.
IN THIS LIFE, I MUST ACCEPT THAT WHICH I CANNOT CHANGE.
BUT THIS IS NOT ABOUT WHAT SUITS ME.
AND SO I ASK AGAIN, NAKIA, *WHY HAVE YOU COME?*

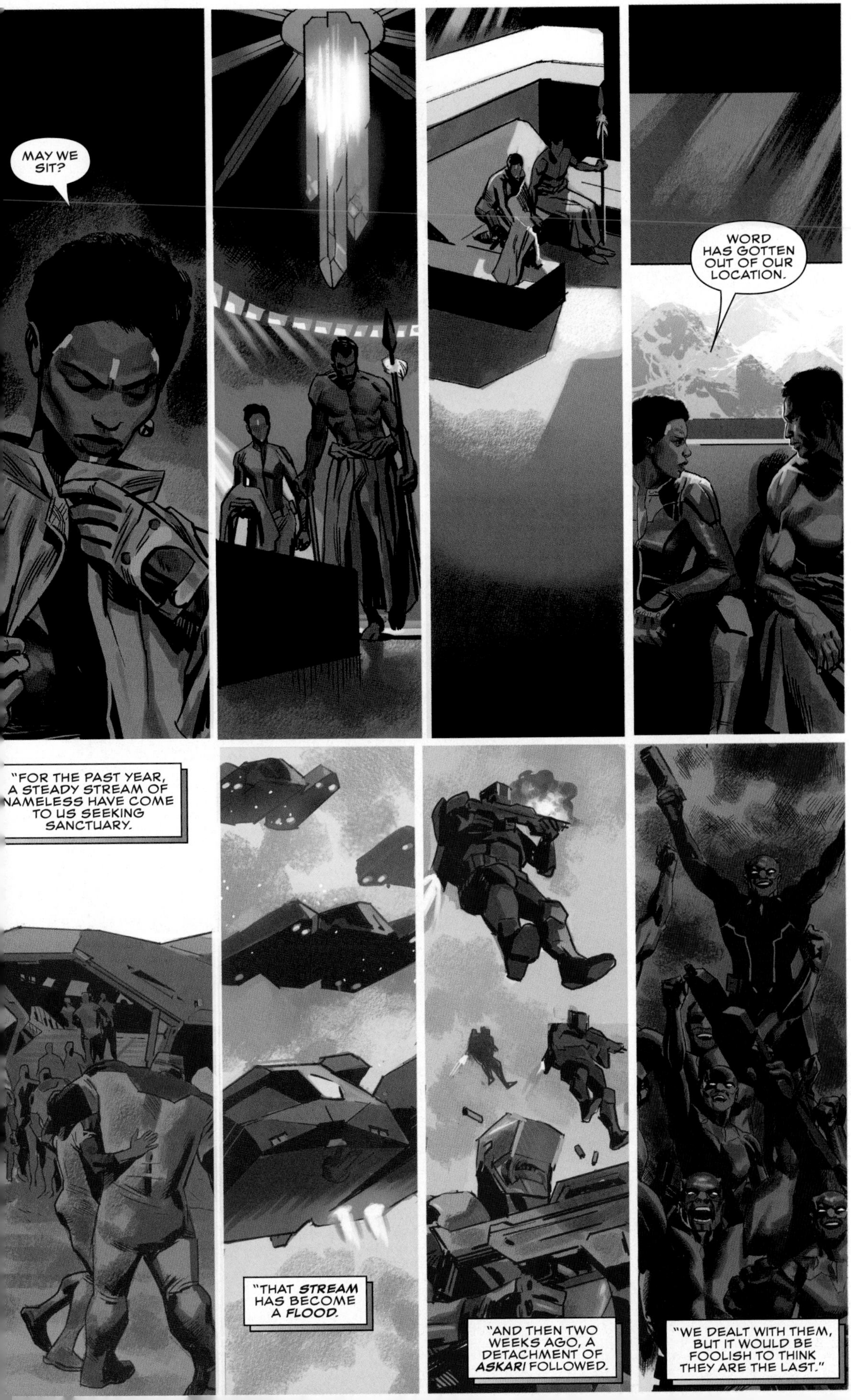
MAY WE SIT?
WORD HAS GOTTEN OUT OF OUR LOCATION.
"FOR THE PAST YEAR, A STEADY STREAM OF NAMELESS HAVE COME TO US SEEKING SANCTUARY.
"THAT STREAM HAS BECOME A FLOOD.
"AND THEN TWO WEEKS AGO, A DETACHMENT OF ASKARI FOLLOWED.
"WE DEALT WITH THEM, BUT IT WOULD BE FOOLISH TO THINK THEY ARE THE LAST."

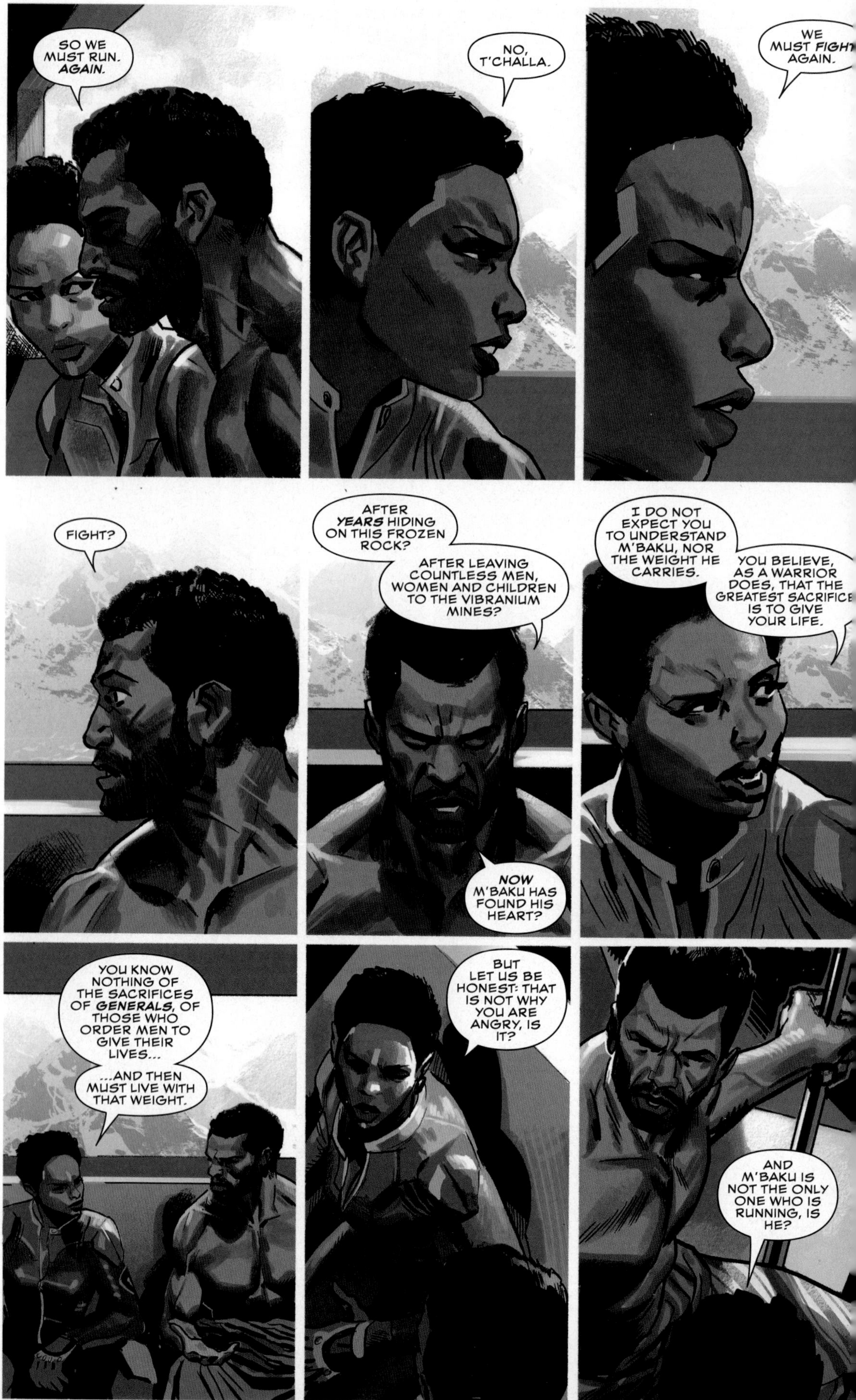
SO WE MUST RUN. AGAIN.
NO, T'CHALLA.
WE MUST FIGHT AGAIN.
FIGHT?
AFTER YEARS HIDING ON THIS FROZEN ROCK?
AFTER LEAVING COUNTLESS MEN, WOMEN AND CHILDREN TO THE VIBRANIUM MINES?
NOW M'BAKU HAS FOUND HIS HEART?
I DO NOT EXPECT YOU TO UNDERSTAND M'BAKU, NOR THE WEIGHT HE CARRIES.
YOU BELIEVE, AS A WARRIOR DOES, THAT THE GREATEST SACRIFICE IS TO GIVE YOUR LIFE.
YOU KNOW NOTHING OF THE SACRIFICES OF GENERALS, OF THOSE WHO ORDER MEN TO GIVE THEIR LIVES...
...AND THEN MUST LIVE WITH THAT WEIGHT.
BUT LET US BE HONEST: THAT IS NOT WHY YOU ARE ANGRY, IS IT?
AND M'BAKU IS NOT THE ONLY ONE WHO IS RUNNING, IS HE?

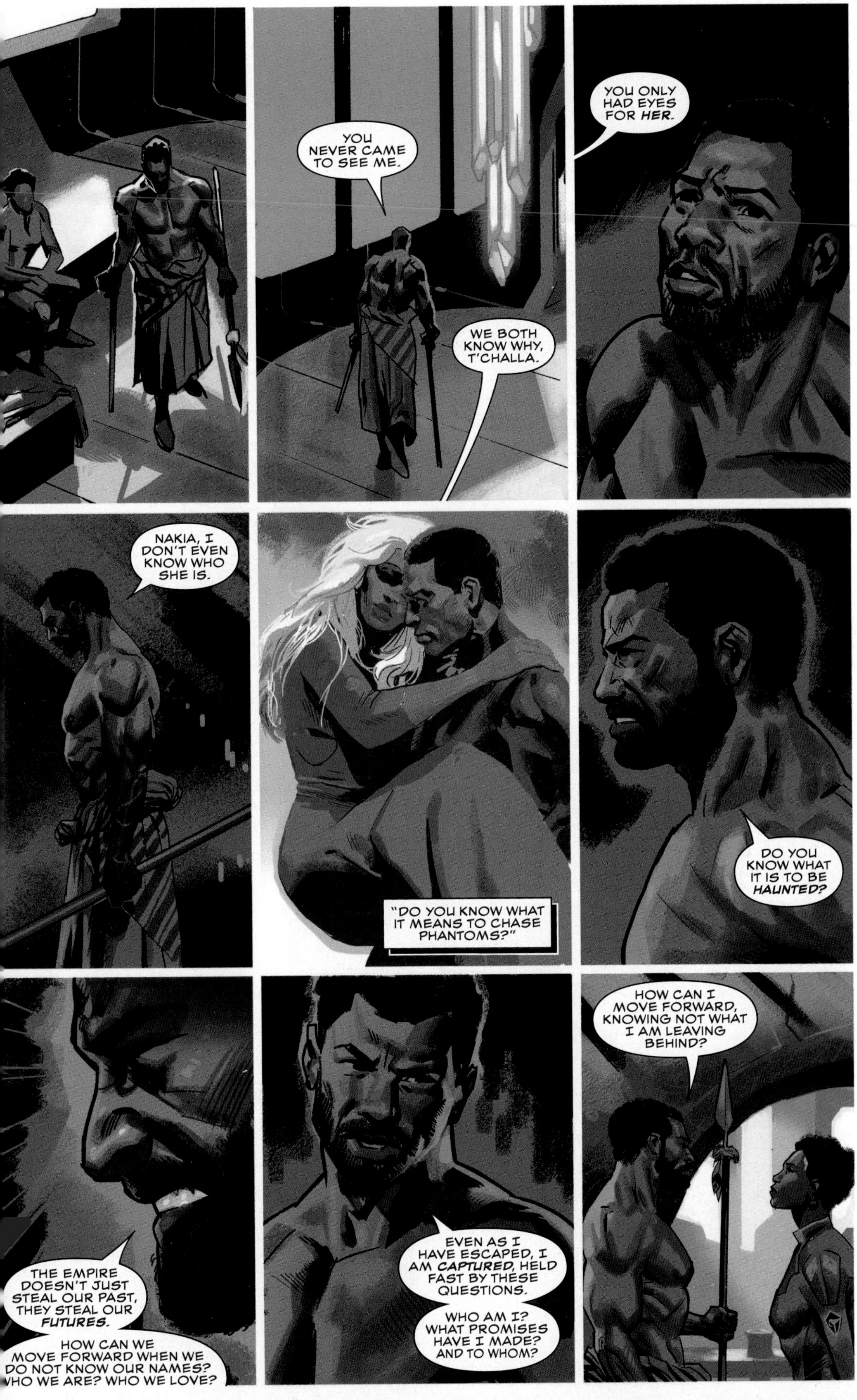
YOU NEVER CAME TO SEE ME.
WE BOTH KNOW WHY, T'CHALLA.
YOU ONLY HAD EYES FOR *HER*.
NAKIA, I DON'T EVEN KNOW WHO SHE IS.
"DO YOU KNOW WHAT IT MEANS TO CHASE PHANTOMS?"
DO YOU KNOW WHAT IT IS TO BE *HAUNTED?*
THE EMPIRE DOESN'T JUST STEAL OUR PAST, THEY STEAL OUR *FUTURES*.
HOW CAN WE MOVE FORWARD WHEN WE DO NOT KNOW OUR NAMES? WHO WE ARE? WHO WE LOVE?
EVEN AS I HAVE ESCAPED, I AM *CAPTURED*, HELD FAST BY THESE QUESTIONS.
WHO AM I? WHAT PROMISES HAVE I MADE? AND TO WHOM?
HOW CAN I MOVE FORWARD, KNOWING NOT WHAT I AM LEAVING BEHIND?

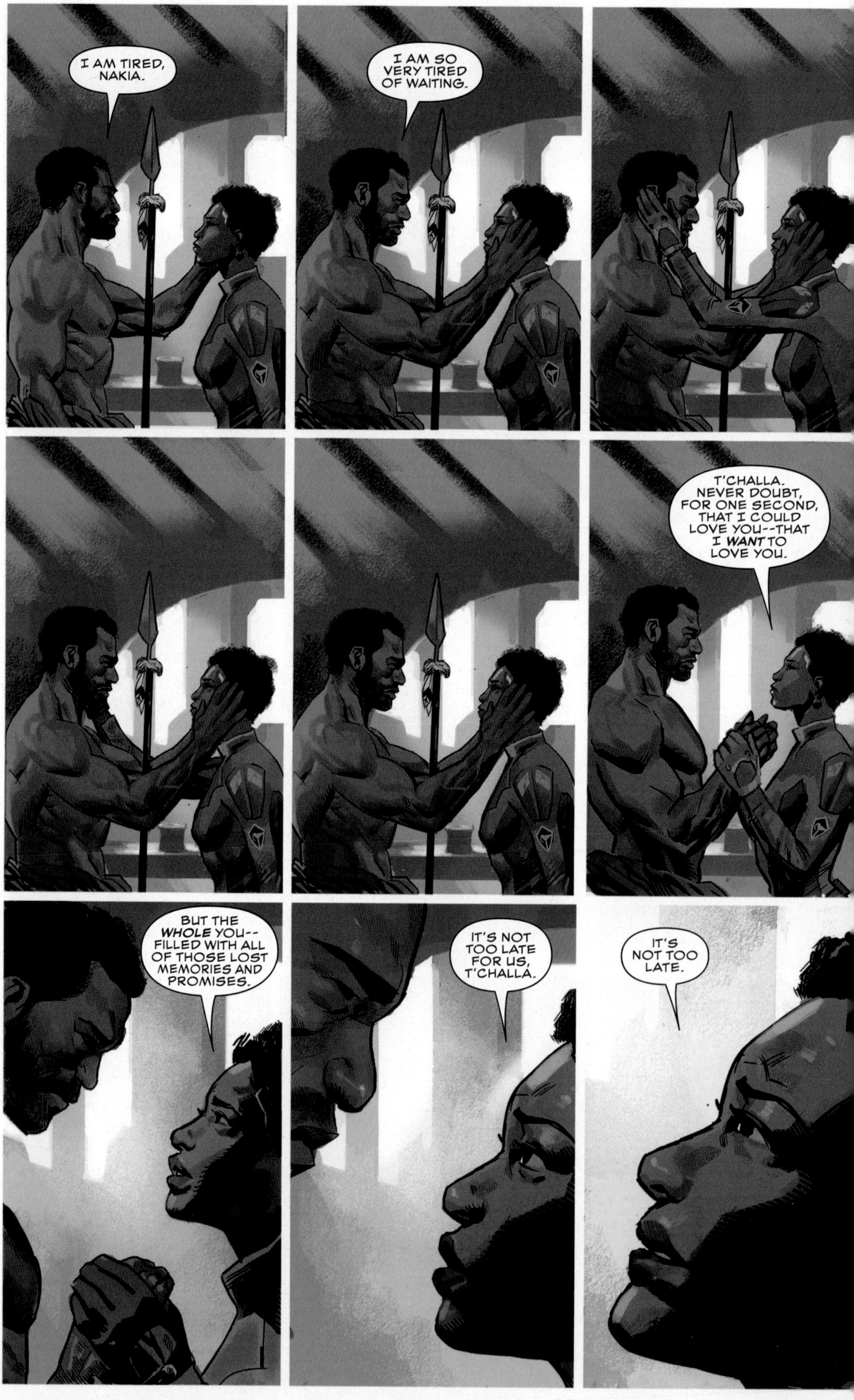
I AM TIRED, NAKIA.
I AM SO VERY TIRED OF WAITING.
T'CHALLA. NEVER DOUBT, FOR ONE SECOND, THAT I COULD LOVE YOU--THAT I *WANT* TO LOVE YOU.
BUT THE *WHOLE* YOU--FILLED WITH ALL OF THOSE LOST MEMORIES AND PROMISES.
IT'S NOT TOO LATE FOR US, T'CHALLA.
IT'S NOT TOO LATE.

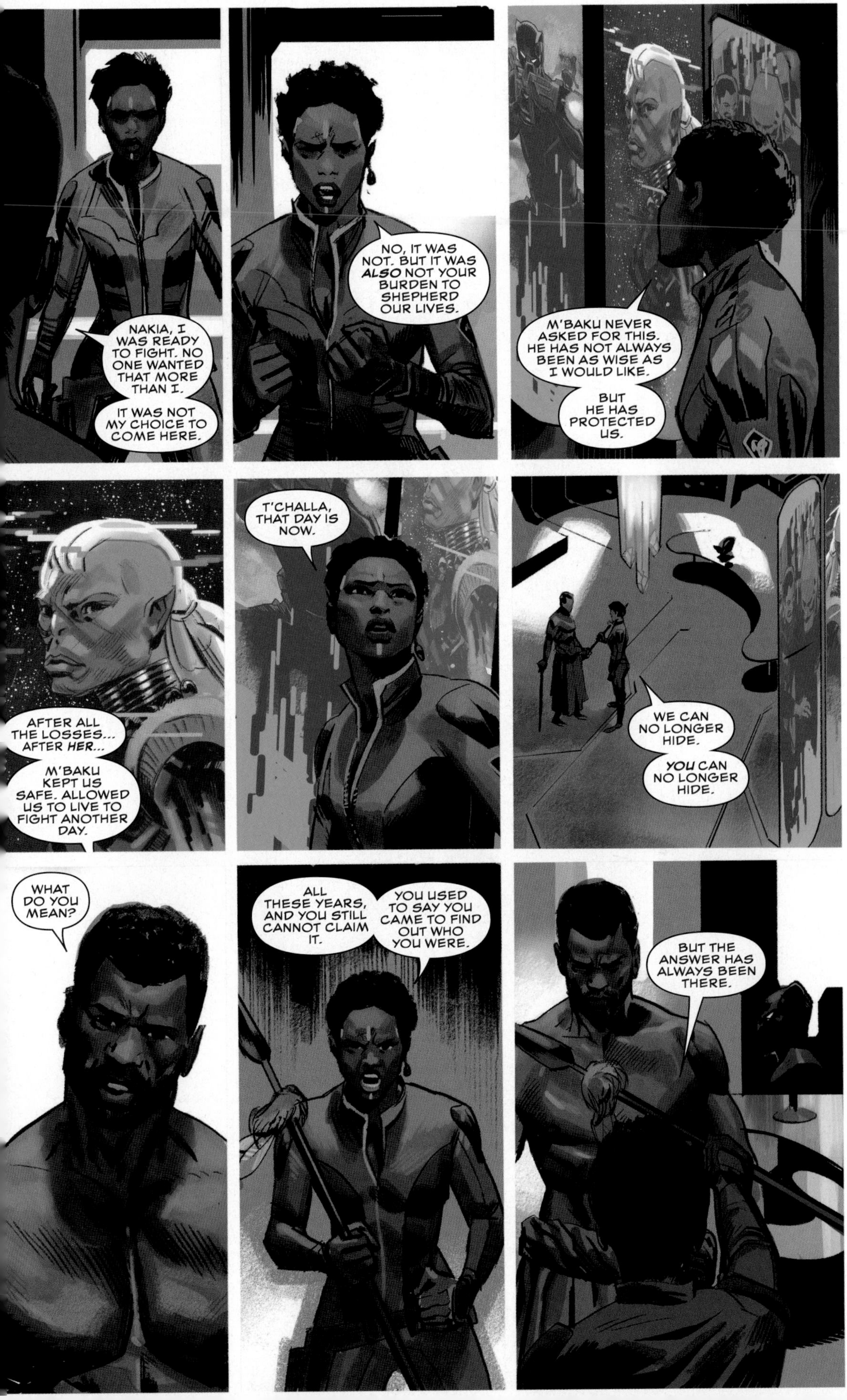
NAKIA, I WAS READY TO FIGHT. NO ONE WANTED THAT MORE THAN I.
IT WAS NOT MY CHOICE TO COME HERE.
NO, IT WAS NOT. BUT IT WAS *ALSO* NOT YOUR BURDEN TO SHEPHERD OUR LIVES.
M'BAKU NEVER ASKED FOR THIS. HE HAS NOT ALWAYS BEEN AS WISE AS I WOULD LIKE.
BUT HE HAS PROTECTED US.
AFTER ALL THE LOSSES... AFTER *HER*...
M'BAKU KEPT US SAFE. ALLOWED US TO LIVE TO FIGHT ANOTHER DAY.
T'CHALLA, THAT DAY IS NOW.
WE CAN NO LONGER HIDE.
YOU CAN NO LONGER HIDE.
WHAT DO YOU MEAN?
YOU USED TO SAY YOU CAME TO FIND OUT WHO YOU WERE.
ALL THESE YEARS, AND YOU STILL CANNOT CLAIM IT.
BUT THE ANSWER HAS ALWAYS BEEN THERE.

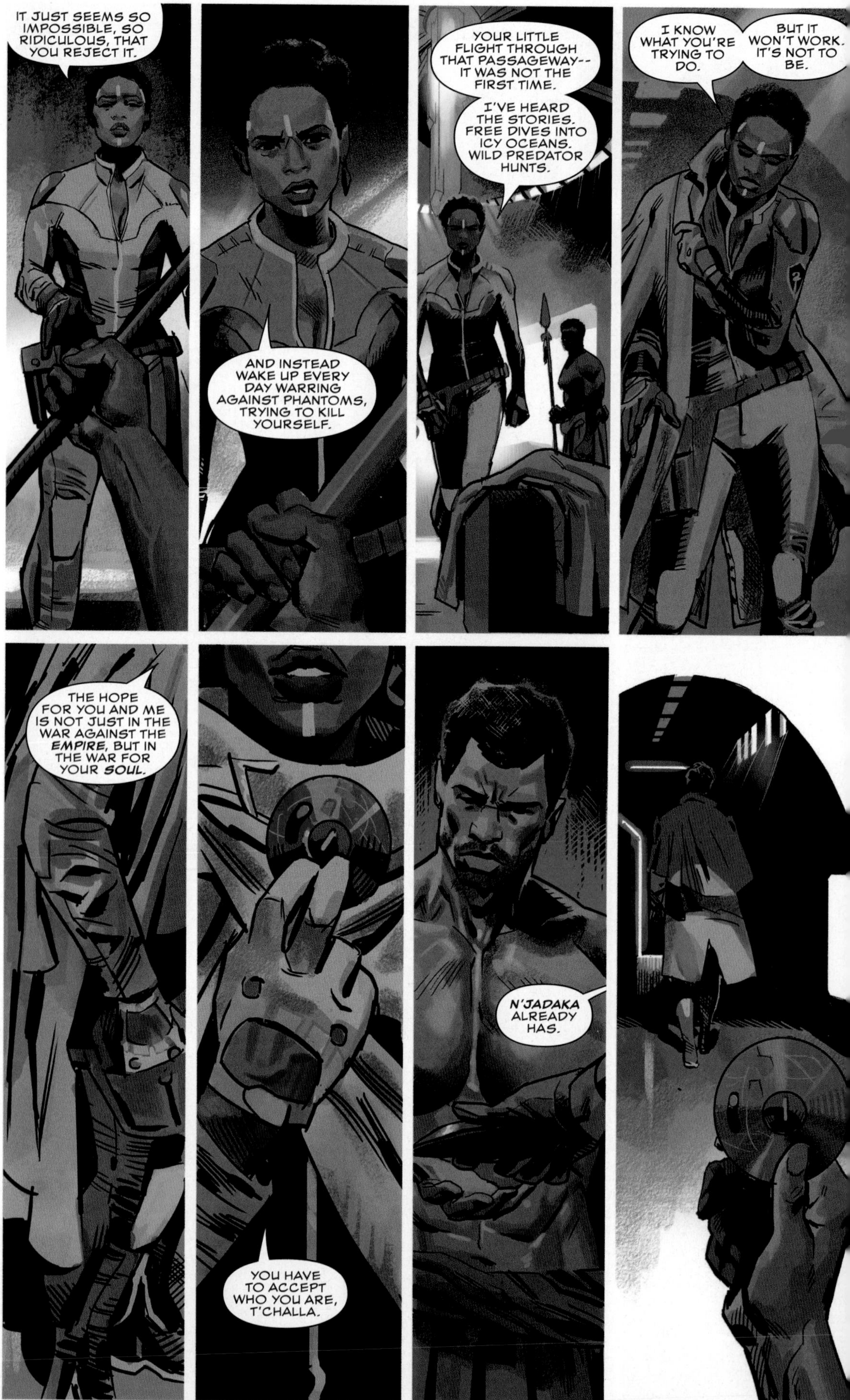
IT JUST SEEMS SO IMPOSSIBLE, SO RIDICULOUS, THAT YOU REJECT IT.
AND INSTEAD WAKE UP EVERY DAY WARRING AGAINST PHANTOMS, TRYING TO KILL YOURSELF.
YOUR LITTLE FLIGHT THROUGH THAT PASSAGEWAY--IT WAS NOT THE FIRST TIME.
I'VE HEARD THE STORIES. FREE DIVES INTO ICY OCEANS. WILD PREDATOR HUNTS.
I KNOW WHAT YOU'RE TRYING TO DO.
BUT IT WON'T WORK. IT'S NOT TO BE.
THE HOPE FOR YOU AND ME IS NOT JUST IN THE WAR AGAINST THE *EMPIRE*, BUT IN THE WAR FOR YOUR *SOUL*.
YOU HAVE TO ACCEPT WHO YOU ARE, T'CHALLA.
N'JADAKA ALREADY HAS.

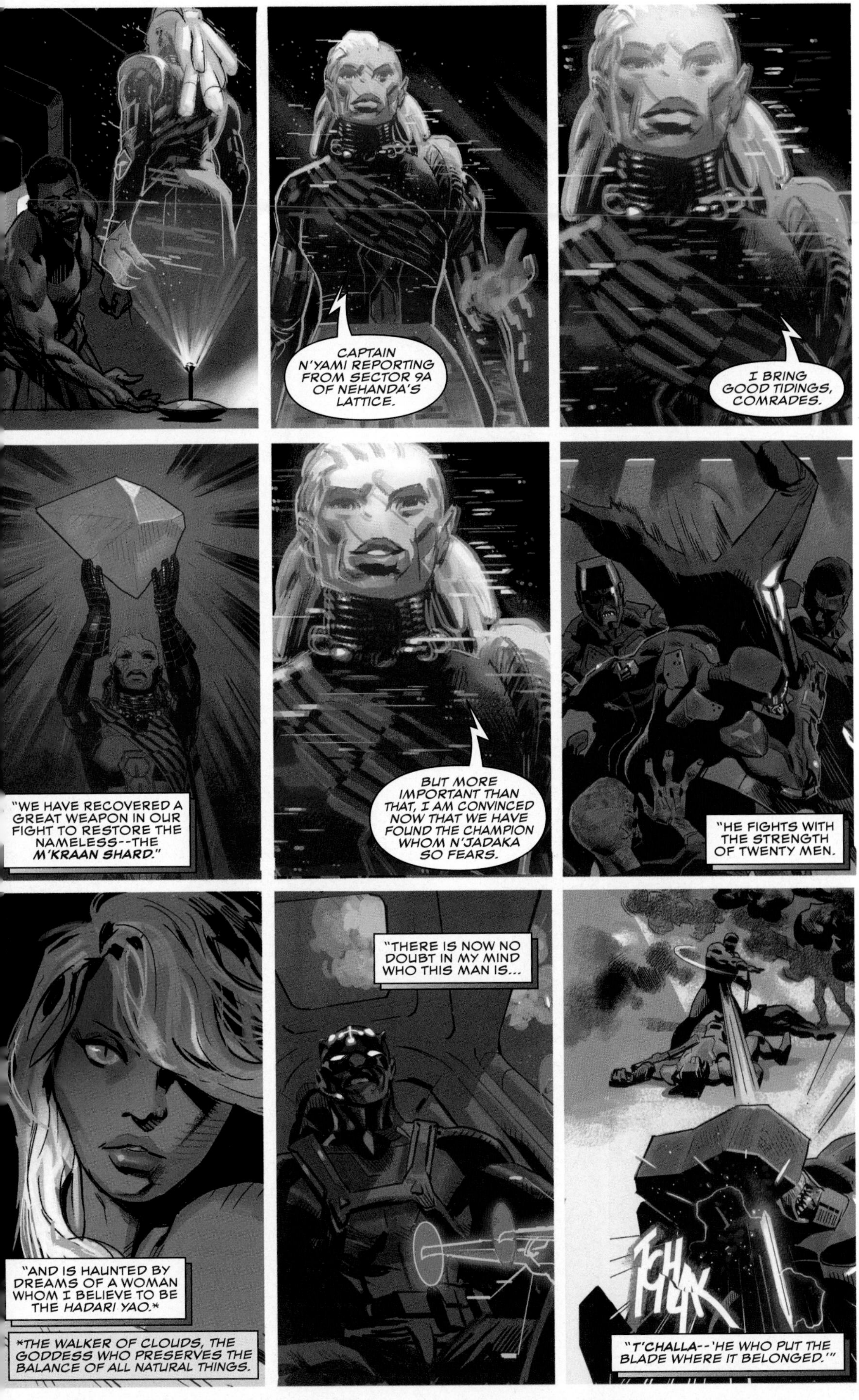
CAPTAIN N'YAMI REPORTING FROM SECTOR 9A OF NEHANDA'S LATTICE.
I BRING GOOD TIDINGS, COMRADES.
"WE HAVE RECOVERED A GREAT WEAPON IN OUR FIGHT TO RESTORE THE NAMELESS--THE M'KRAAN SHARD."
BUT MORE IMPORTANT THAN THAT, I AM CONVINCED NOW THAT WE HAVE FOUND THE CHAMPION WHOM N'JADAKA SO FEARS.
"HE FIGHTS WITH THE STRENGTH OF TWENTY MEN.
"AND IS HAUNTED BY DREAMS OF A WOMAN WHOM I BELIEVE TO BE THE HADARI YAO.*
*THE WALKER OF CLOUDS, THE GODDESS WHO PRESERVES THE BALANCE OF ALL NATURAL THINGS.
"THERE IS NOW NO DOUBT IN MY MIND WHO THIS MAN IS...
TCHUK
"T'CHALLA--'HE WHO PUT THE BLADE WHERE IT BELONGED.'"

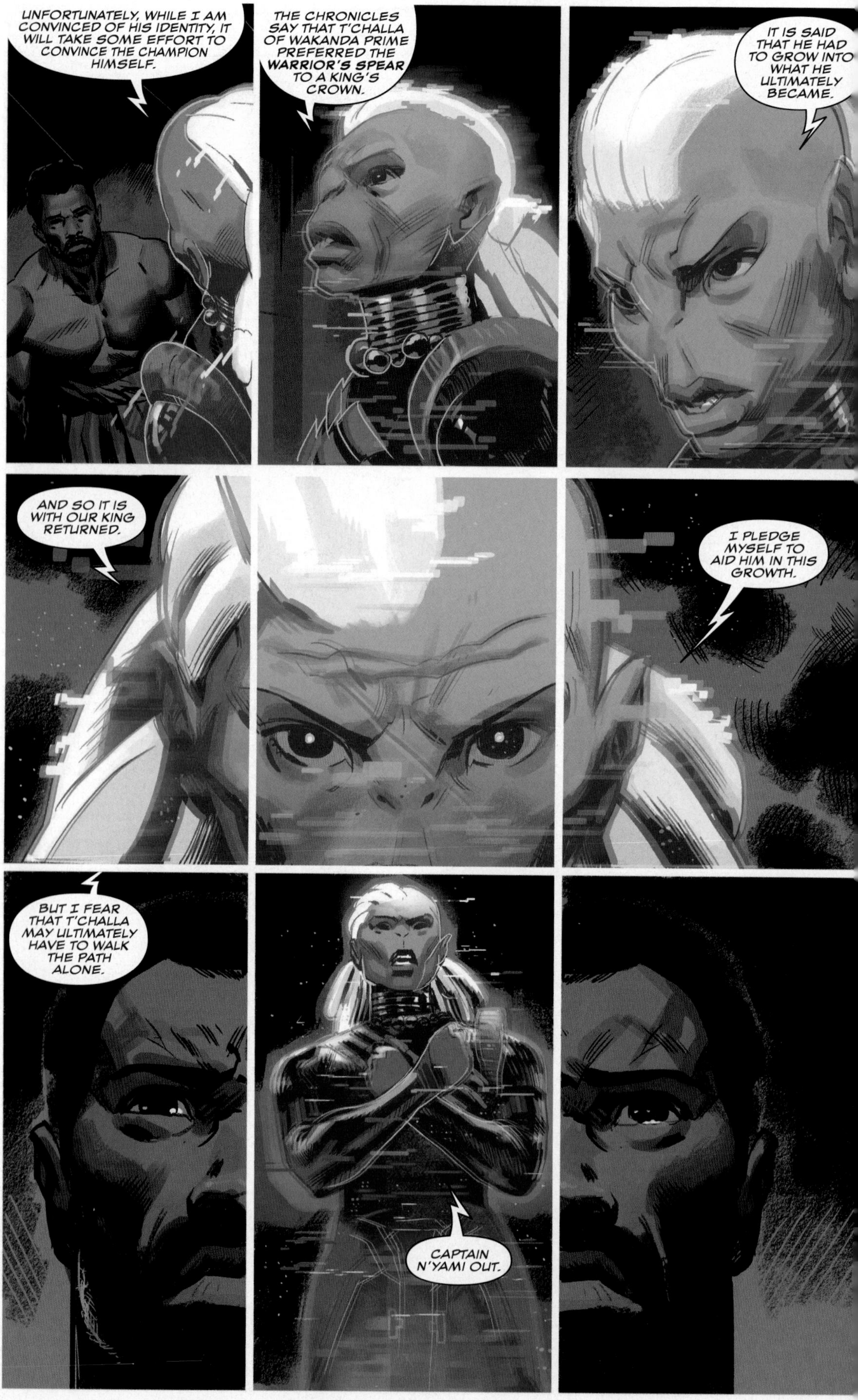
UNFORTUNATELY, WHILE I AM CONVINCED OF HIS IDENTITY, IT WILL TAKE SOME EFFORT TO CONVINCE THE CHAMPION HIMSELF.
THE CHRONICLES SAY THAT T'CHALLA OF WAKANDA PRIME PREFERRED THE **WARRIOR'S SPEAR** TO A KING'S CROWN.
IT IS SAID THAT HE HAD TO GROW INTO WHAT HE ULTIMATELY BECAME.
AND SO IT IS WITH OUR KING RETURNED.
I PLEDGE MYSELF TO AID HIM IN THIS GROWTH.
BUT I FEAR THAT T'CHALLA MAY ULTIMATELY HAVE TO WALK THE PATH ALONE.
CAPTAIN N'YAMI OUT.

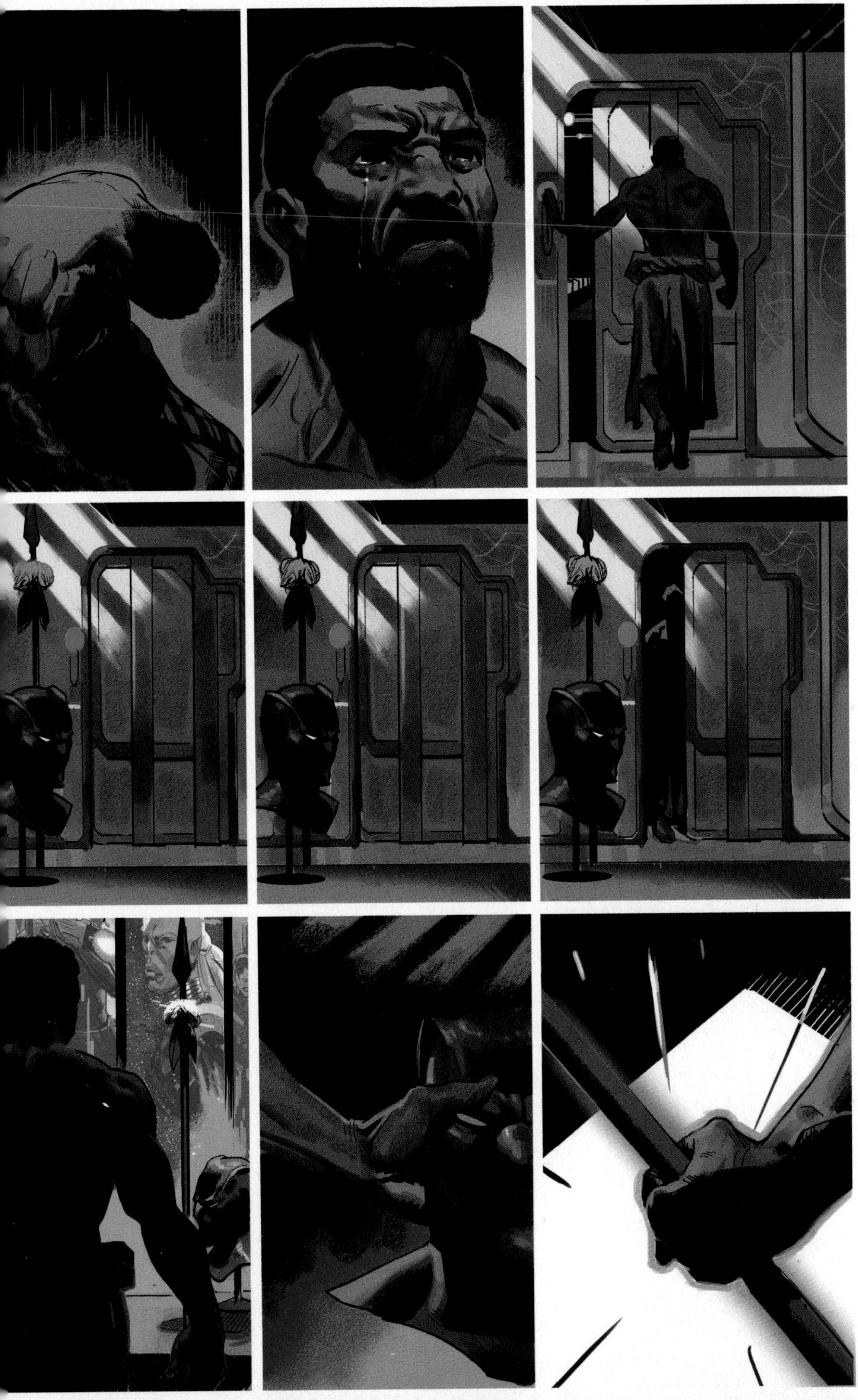

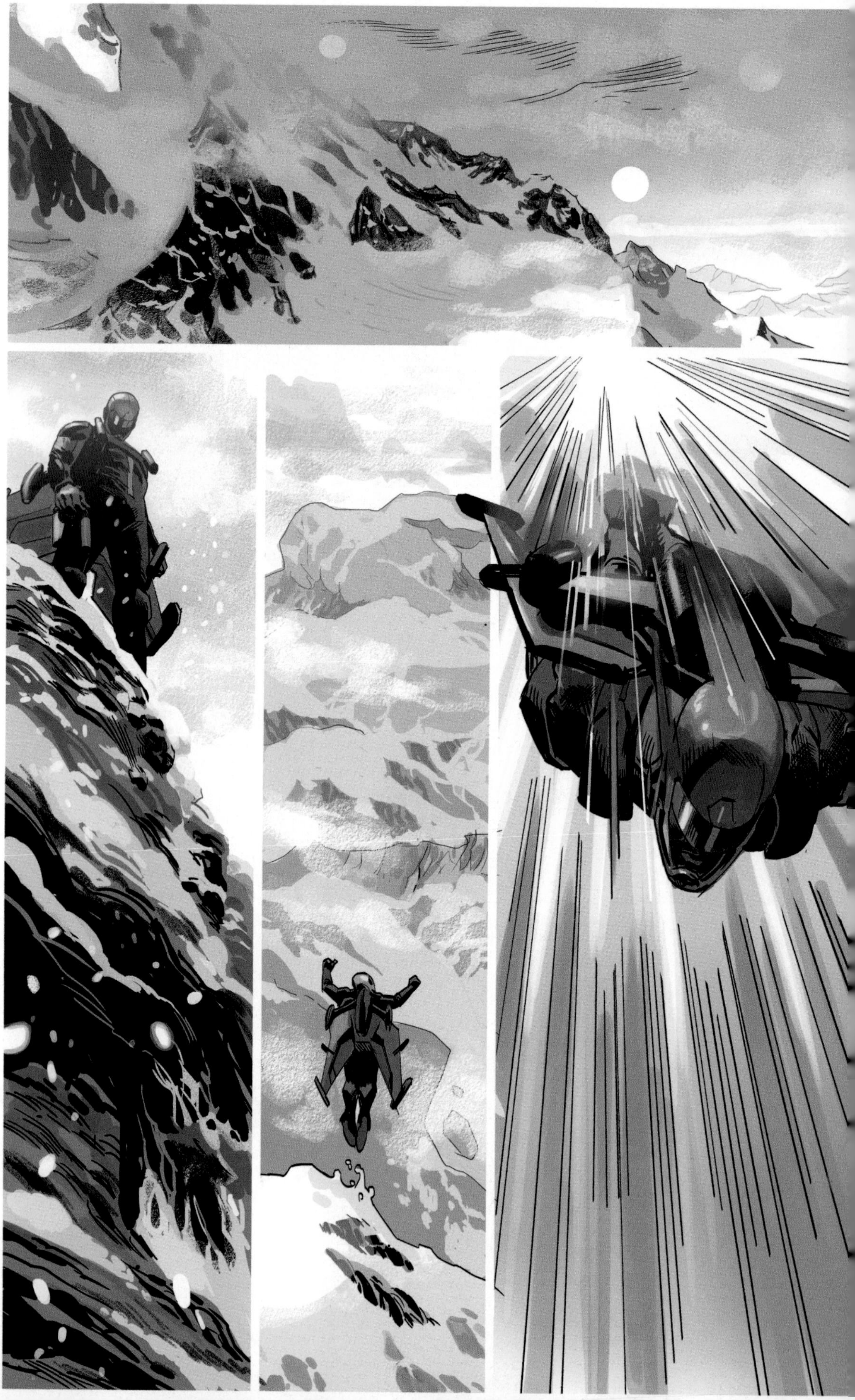

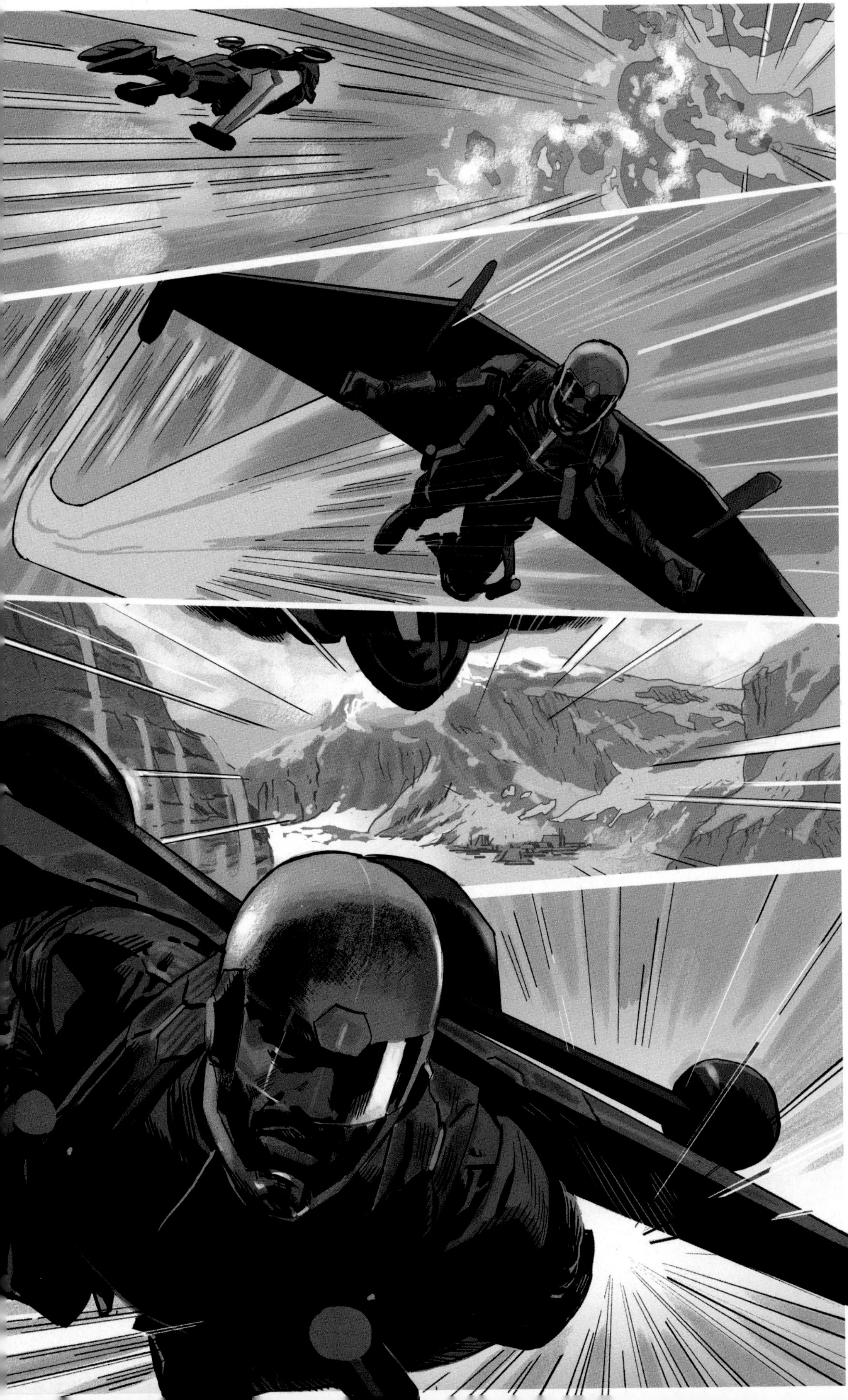

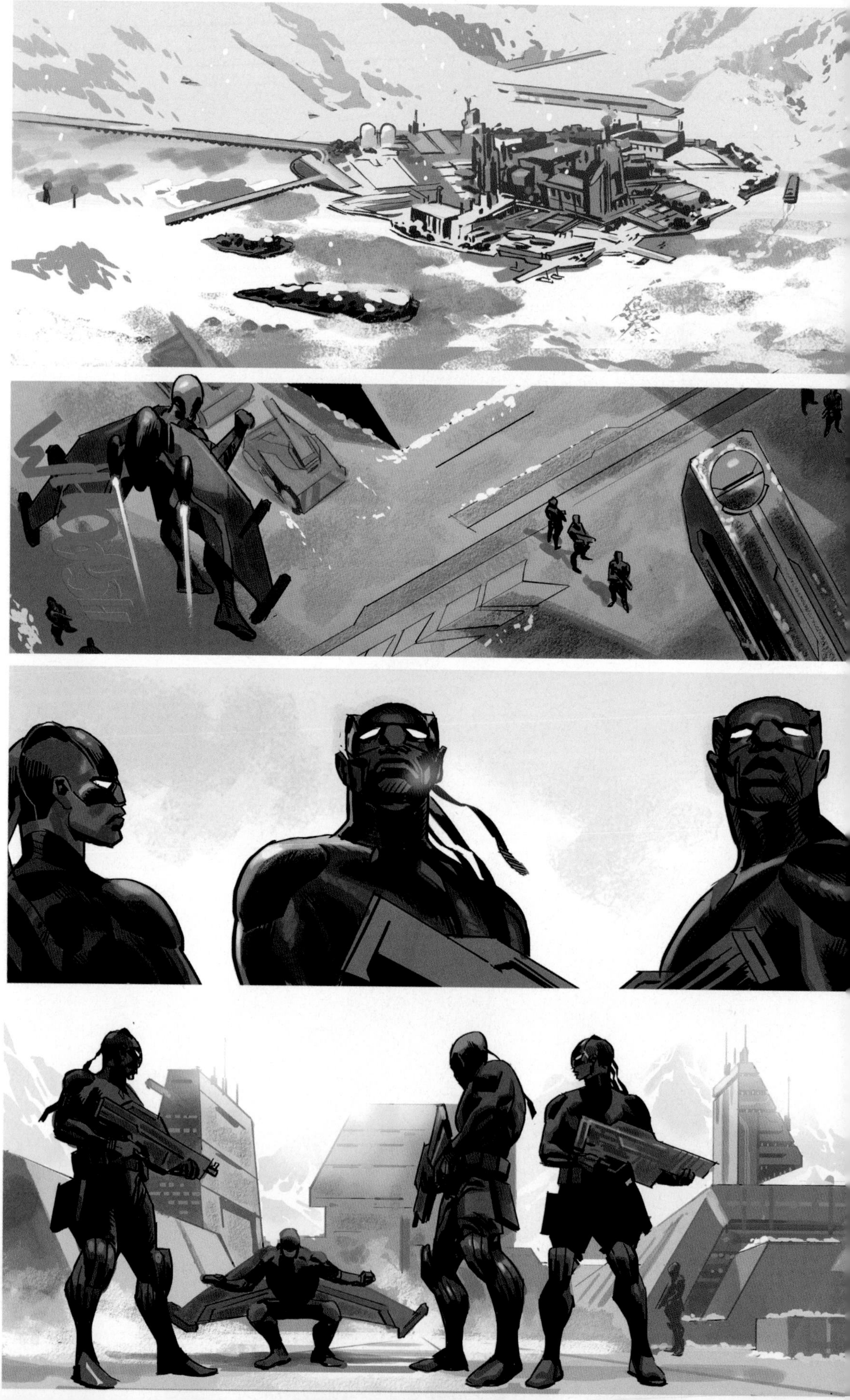
WHOOSH

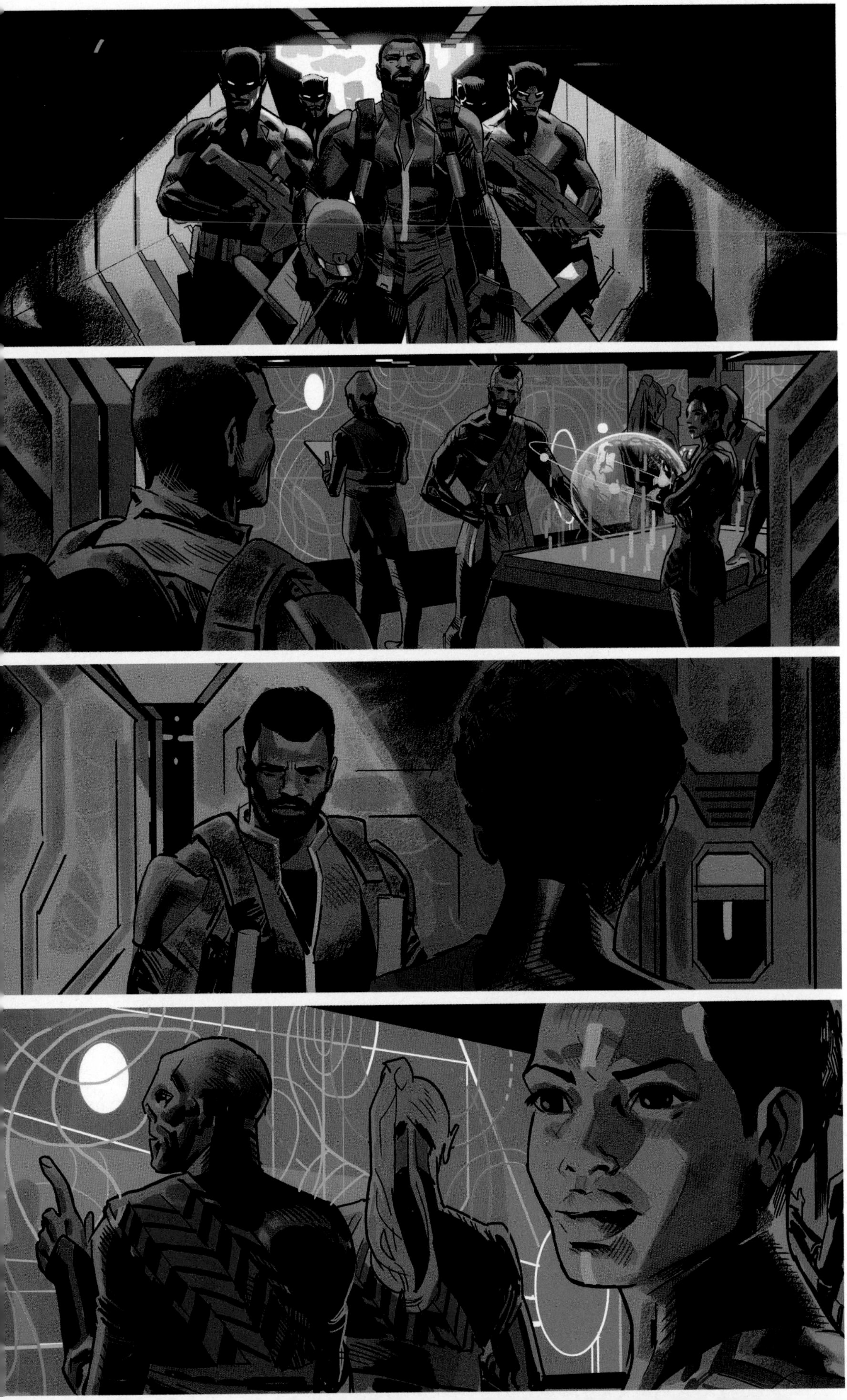

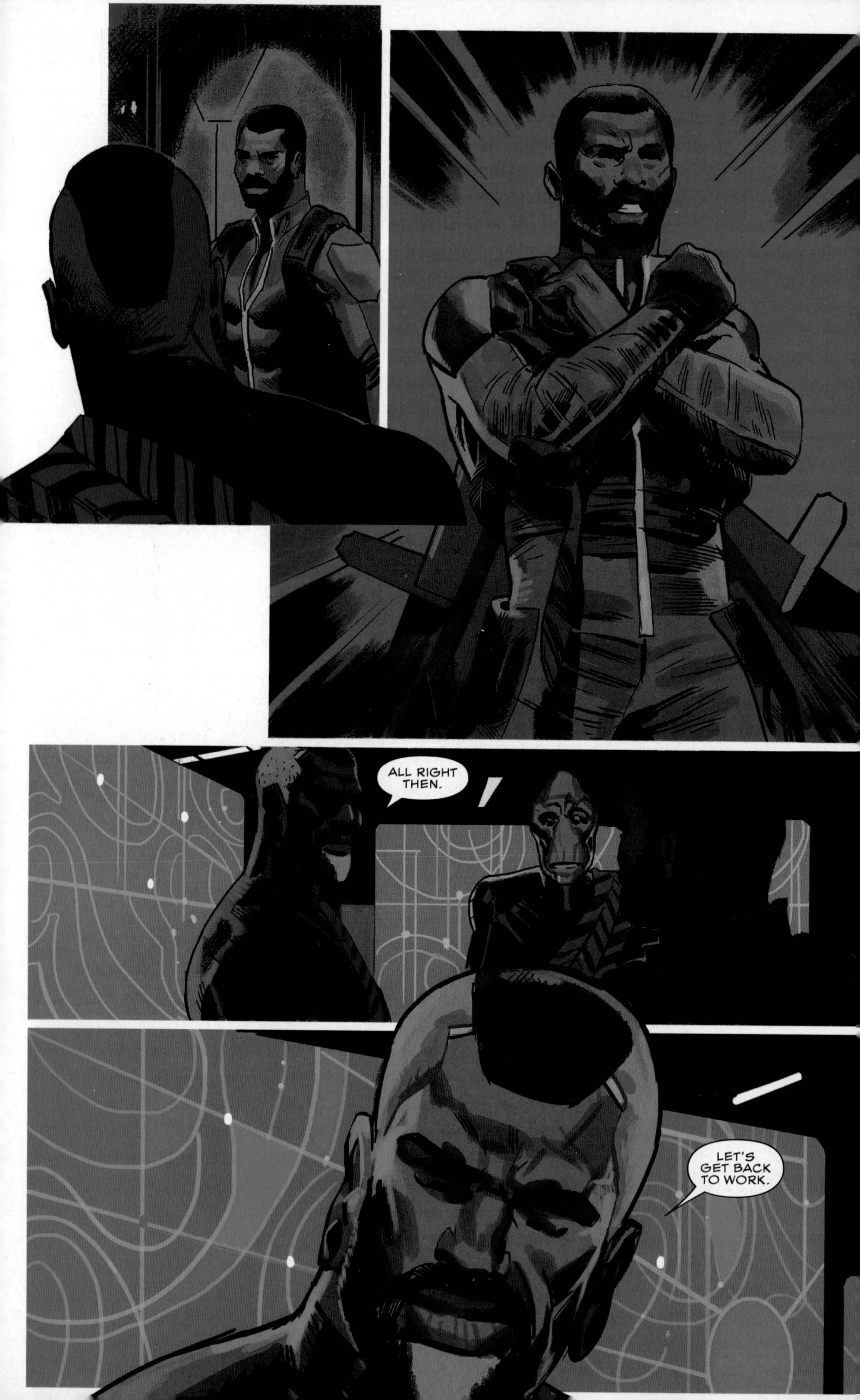
ALL RIGHT THEN.
LET'S GET BACK TO WORK.

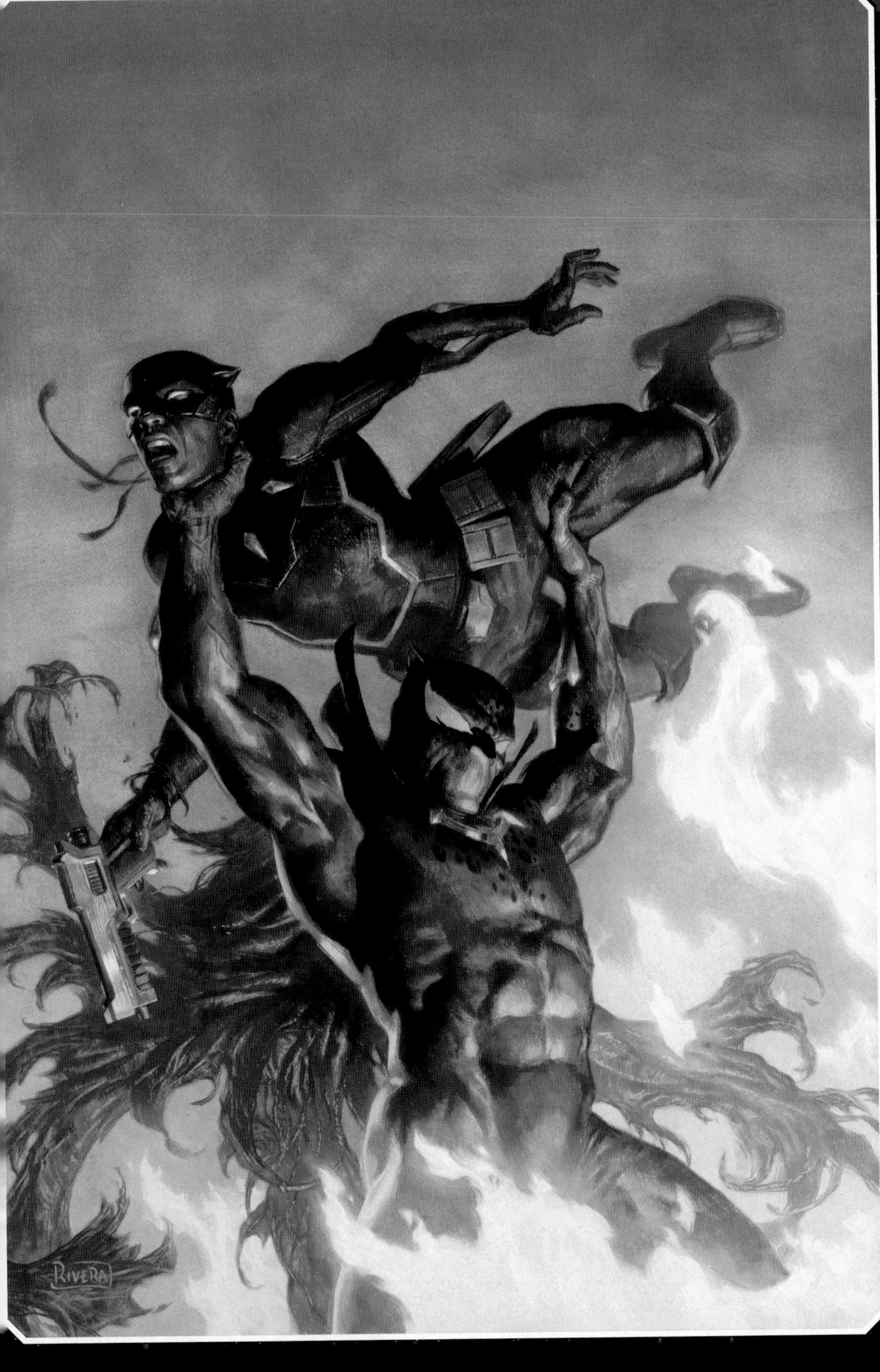
RIVERA

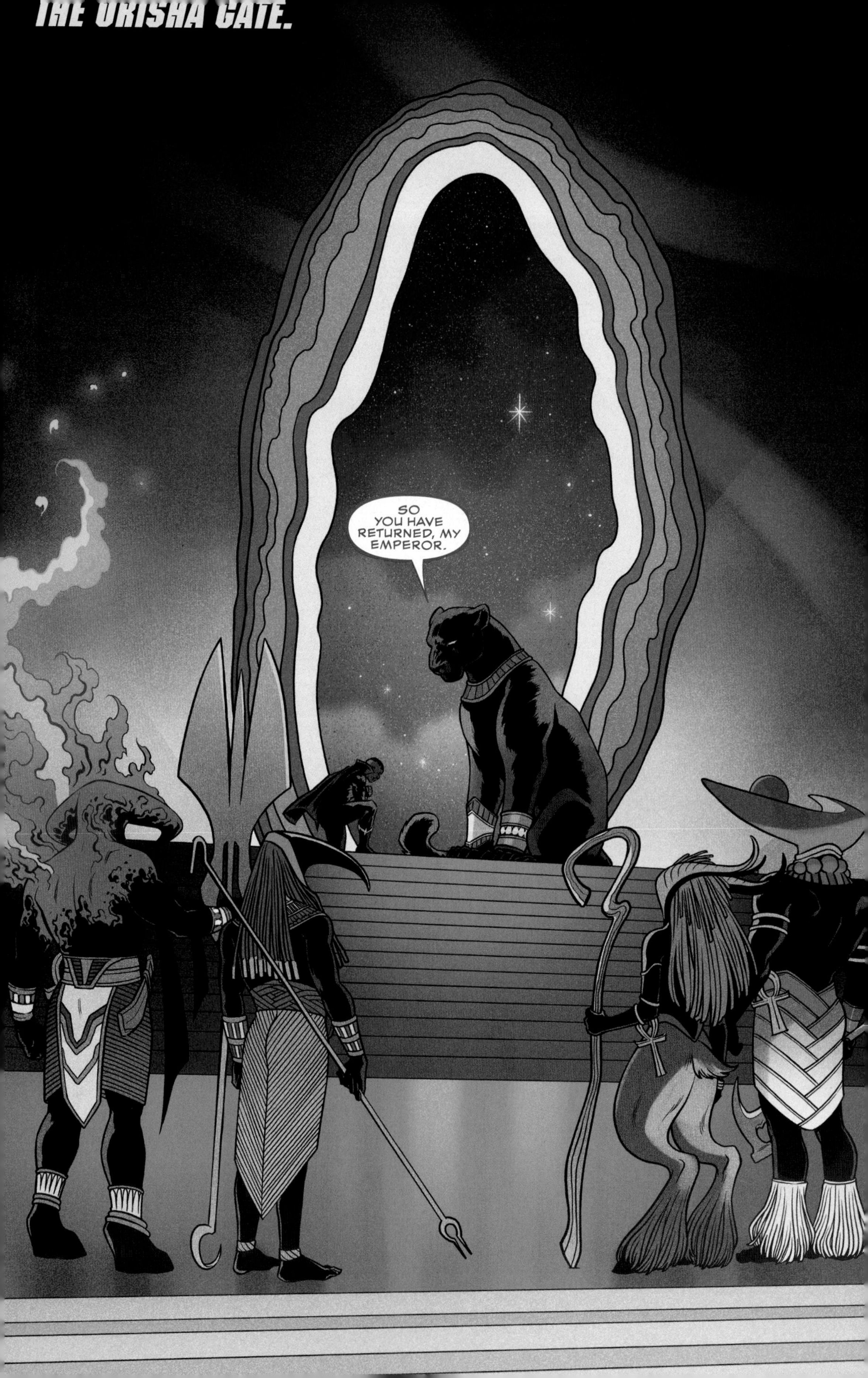
THE ORISHA GATE.
SO YOU HAVE RETURNED, MY EMPEROR.

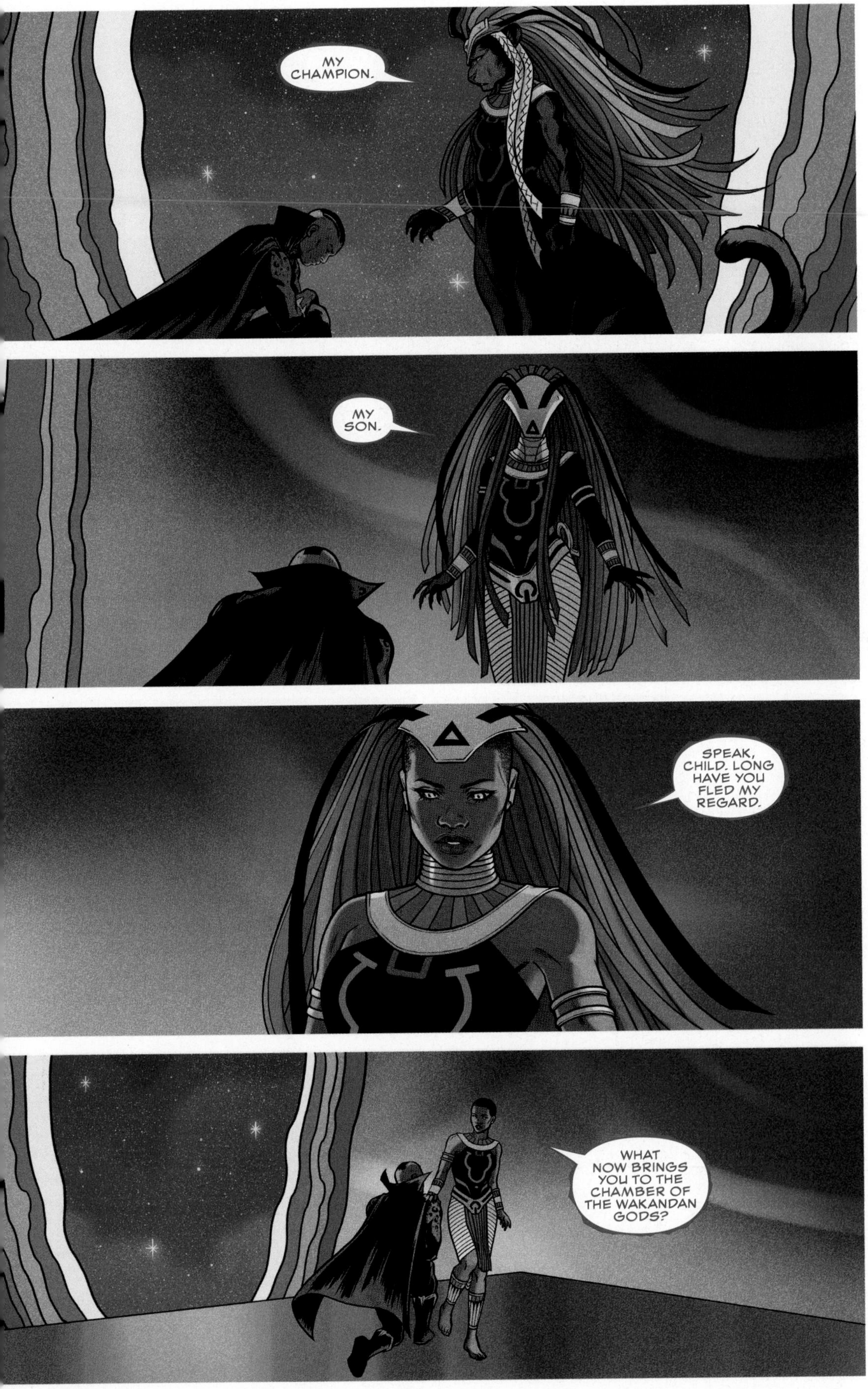
MY CHAMPION.
MY SON.
SPEAK, CHILD. LONG HAVE YOU FLED MY REGARD.
WHAT NOW BRINGS YOU TO THE CHAMBER OF THE WAKANDAN GODS?

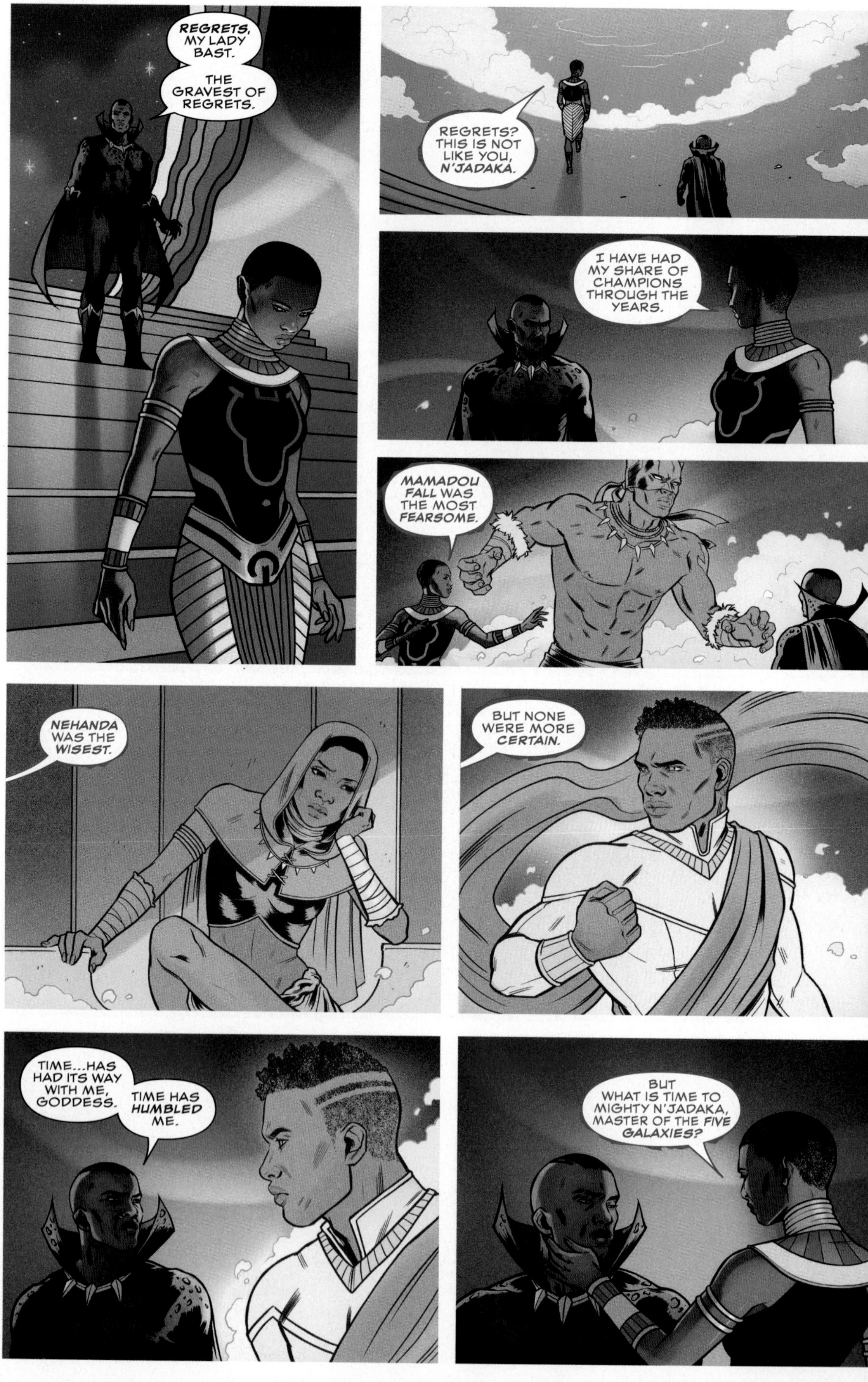
REGRETS, MY LADY BAST.
THE GRAVEST OF REGRETS.
REGRETS? THIS IS NOT LIKE YOU, N'JADAKA.
I HAVE HAD MY SHARE OF CHAMPIONS THROUGH THE YEARS.
MAMADOU FALL WAS THE MOST FEARSOME.
NEHANDA WAS THE WISEST.
BUT NONE WERE MORE CERTAIN.
TIME...HAS HAD ITS WAY WITH ME, GODDESS.
TIME HAS HUMBLED ME.
BUT WHAT IS TIME TO MIGHTY N'JADAKA, MASTER OF THE FIVE GALAXIES?

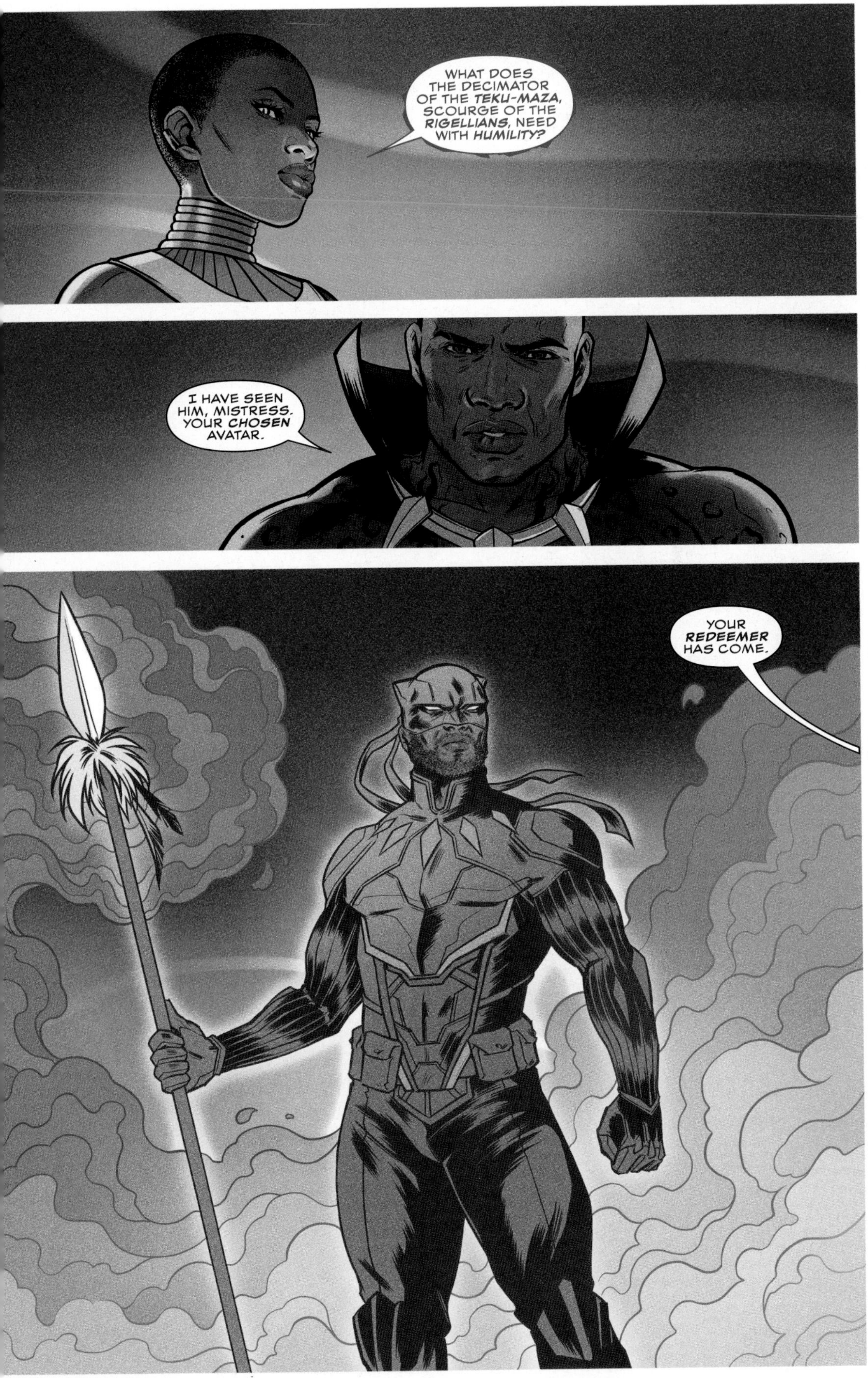
WHAT DOES THE DECIMATOR OF THE TEKU-MAZA, SCOURGE OF THE RIGELLIANS, NEED WITH HUMILITY?
I HAVE SEEN HIM, MISTRESS. YOUR CHOSEN AVATAR.
YOUR REDEEMER HAS COME.

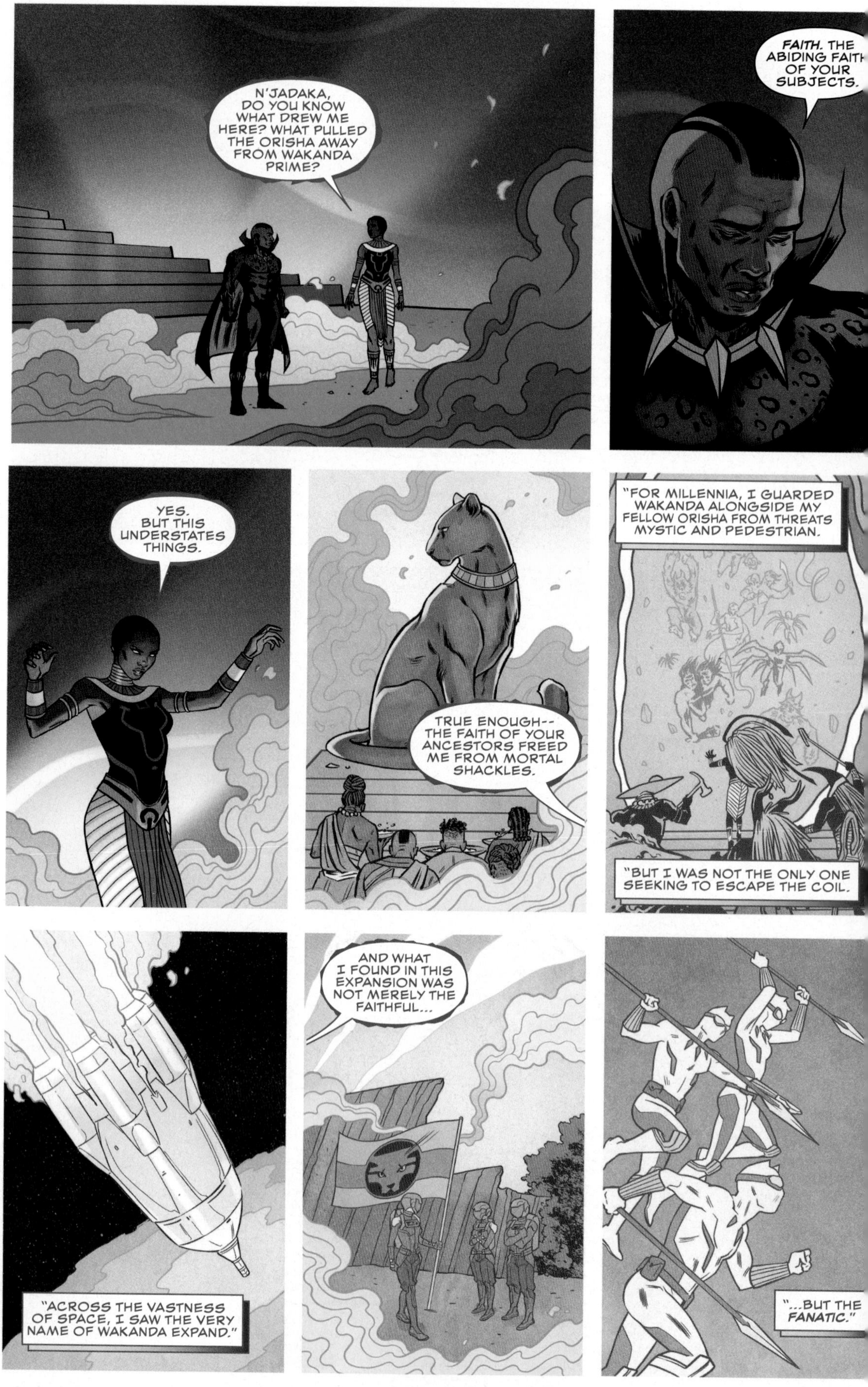
N'JADAKA, DO YOU KNOW WHAT DREW ME HERE? WHAT PULLED THE ORISHA AWAY FROM WAKANDA PRIME?
FAITH. THE ABIDING FAITH OF YOUR SUBJECTS.
YES. BUT THIS UNDERSTATES THINGS.
TRUE ENOUGH--THE FAITH OF YOUR ANCESTORS FREED ME FROM MORTAL SHACKLES.
"FOR MILLENNIA, I GUARDED WAKANDA ALONGSIDE MY FELLOW ORISHA FROM THREATS MYSTIC AND PEDESTRIAN.
"BUT I WAS NOT THE ONLY ONE SEEKING TO ESCAPE THE COIL.
"ACROSS THE VASTNESS OF SPACE, I SAW THE VERY NAME OF WAKANDA EXPAND."
AND WHAT I FOUND IN THIS EXPANSION WAS NOT MERELY THE FAITHFUL...
"...BUT THE *FANATIC.*"

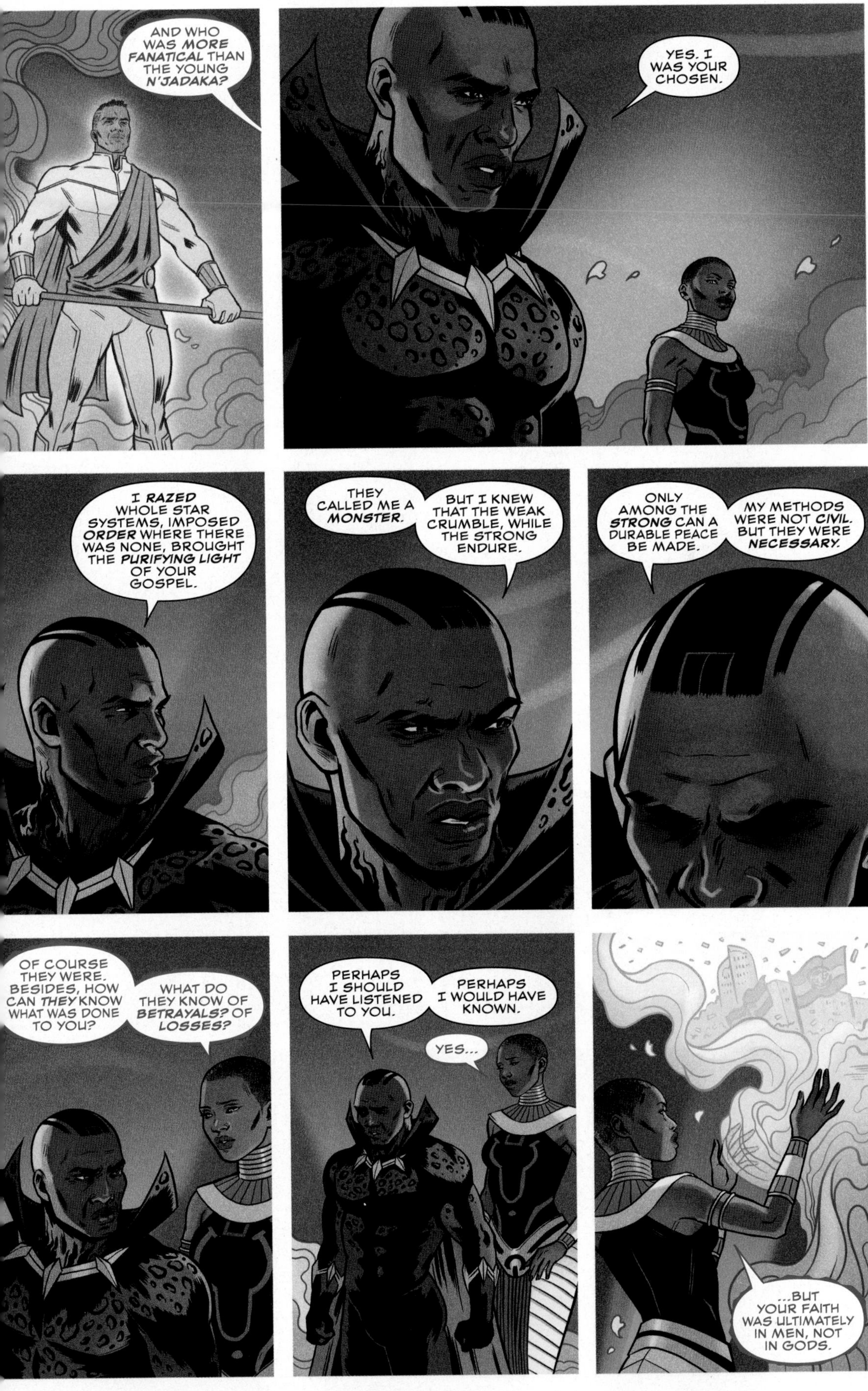
AND WHO WAS MORE FANATICAL THAN THE YOUNG N'JADAKA?
YES. I WAS YOUR CHOSEN.
I RAZED WHOLE STAR SYSTEMS, IMPOSED ORDER WHERE THERE WAS NONE, BROUGHT THE PURIFYING LIGHT OF YOUR GOSPEL.
THEY CALLED ME A MONSTER.
BUT I KNEW THAT THE WEAK CRUMBLE, WHILE THE STRONG ENDURE.
ONLY AMONG THE STRONG CAN A DURABLE PEACE BE MADE.
MY METHODS WERE NOT CIVIL. BUT THEY WERE NECESSARY.
OF COURSE THEY WERE. BESIDES, HOW CAN THEY KNOW WHAT WAS DONE TO YOU?
WHAT DO THEY KNOW OF BETRAYALS? OF LOSSES?
PERHAPS I SHOULD HAVE LISTENED TO YOU.
PERHAPS I WOULD HAVE KNOWN.
YES...
...BUT YOUR FAITH WAS ULTIMATELY IN MEN, NOT IN GODS.

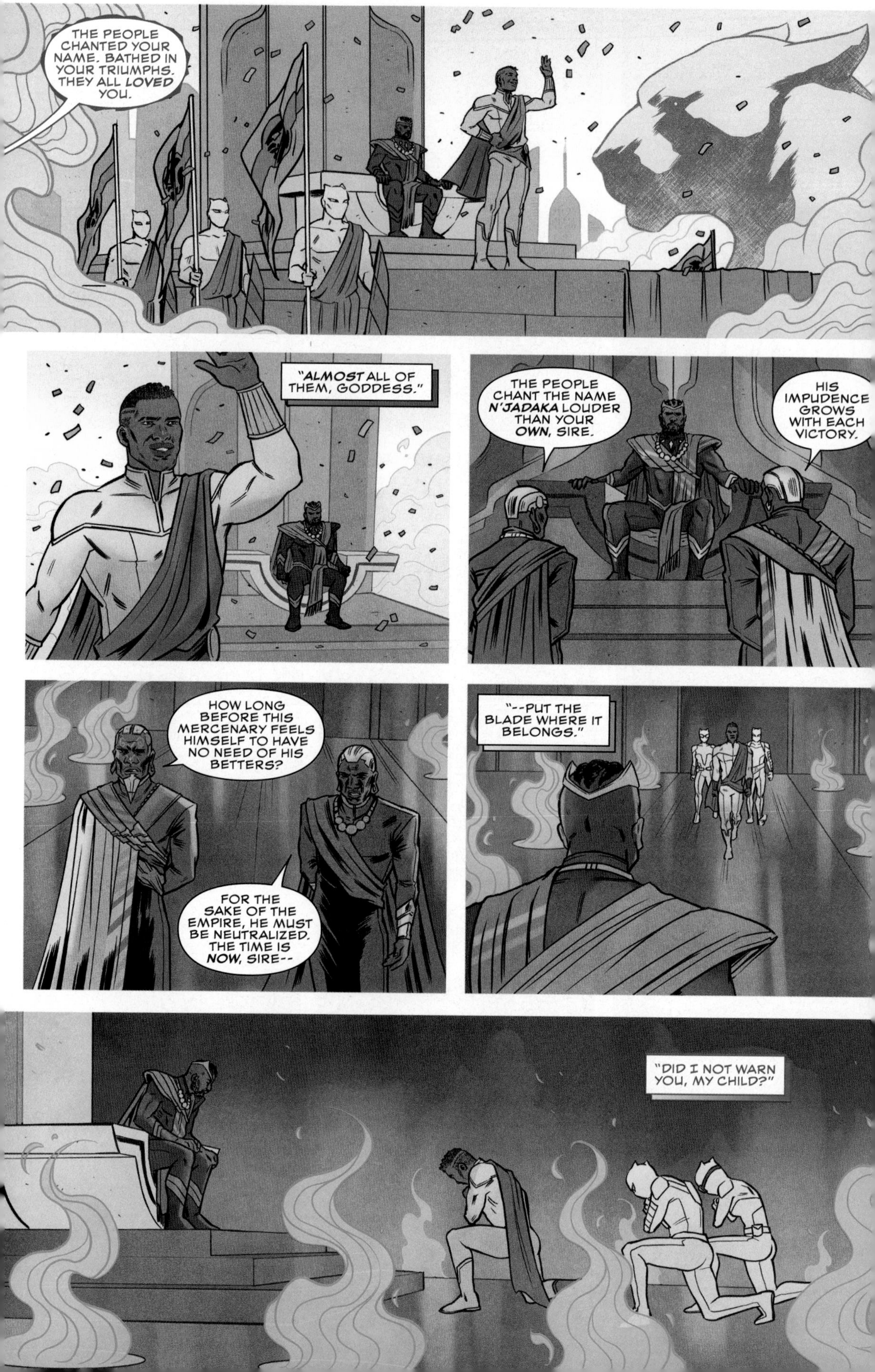
THE PEOPLE CHANTED YOUR NAME. BATHED IN YOUR TRIUMPHS. THEY ALL LOVED YOU.
"ALMOST ALL OF THEM, GODDESS."
THE PEOPLE CHANT THE NAME N'JADAKA LOUDER THAN YOUR OWN, SIRE.
HIS IMPUDENCE GROWS WITH EACH VICTORY.
HOW LONG BEFORE THIS MERCENARY FEELS HIMSELF TO HAVE NO NEED OF HIS BETTERS?
FOR THE SAKE OF THE EMPIRE, HE MUST BE NEUTRALIZED. THE TIME IS NOW, SIRE--
"--PUT THE BLADE WHERE IT BELONGS."
"DID I NOT WARN YOU, MY CHILD?"

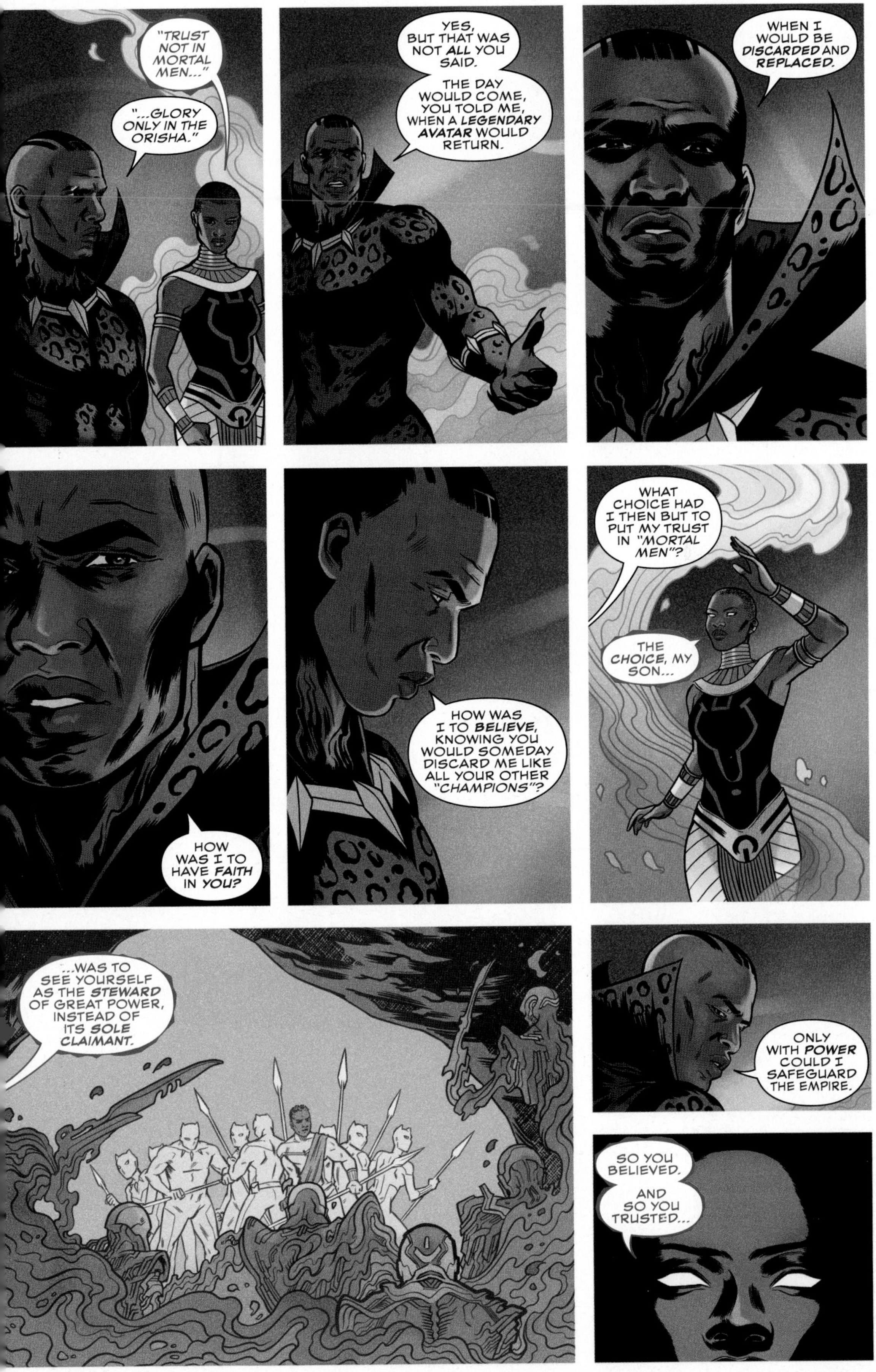
"TRUST NOT IN MORTAL MEN..."
"...GLORY ONLY IN THE ORISHA."
YES, BUT THAT WAS NOT ALL YOU SAID.
THE DAY WOULD COME, YOU TOLD ME, WHEN A LEGENDARY AVATAR WOULD RETURN.
WHEN I WOULD BE DISCARDED AND REPLACED.
HOW WAS I TO HAVE FAITH IN YOU?
HOW WAS I TO BELIEVE, KNOWING YOU WOULD SOMEDAY DISCARD ME LIKE ALL YOUR OTHER "CHAMPIONS"?
WHAT CHOICE HAD I THEN BUT TO PUT MY TRUST IN "MORTAL MEN"?
THE CHOICE, MY SON...
...WAS TO SEE YOURSELF AS THE STEWARD OF GREAT POWER, INSTEAD OF ITS SOLE CLAIMANT.
ONLY WITH POWER COULD I SAFEGUARD THE EMPIRE.
SO YOU BELIEVED.
AND SO YOU TRUSTED...

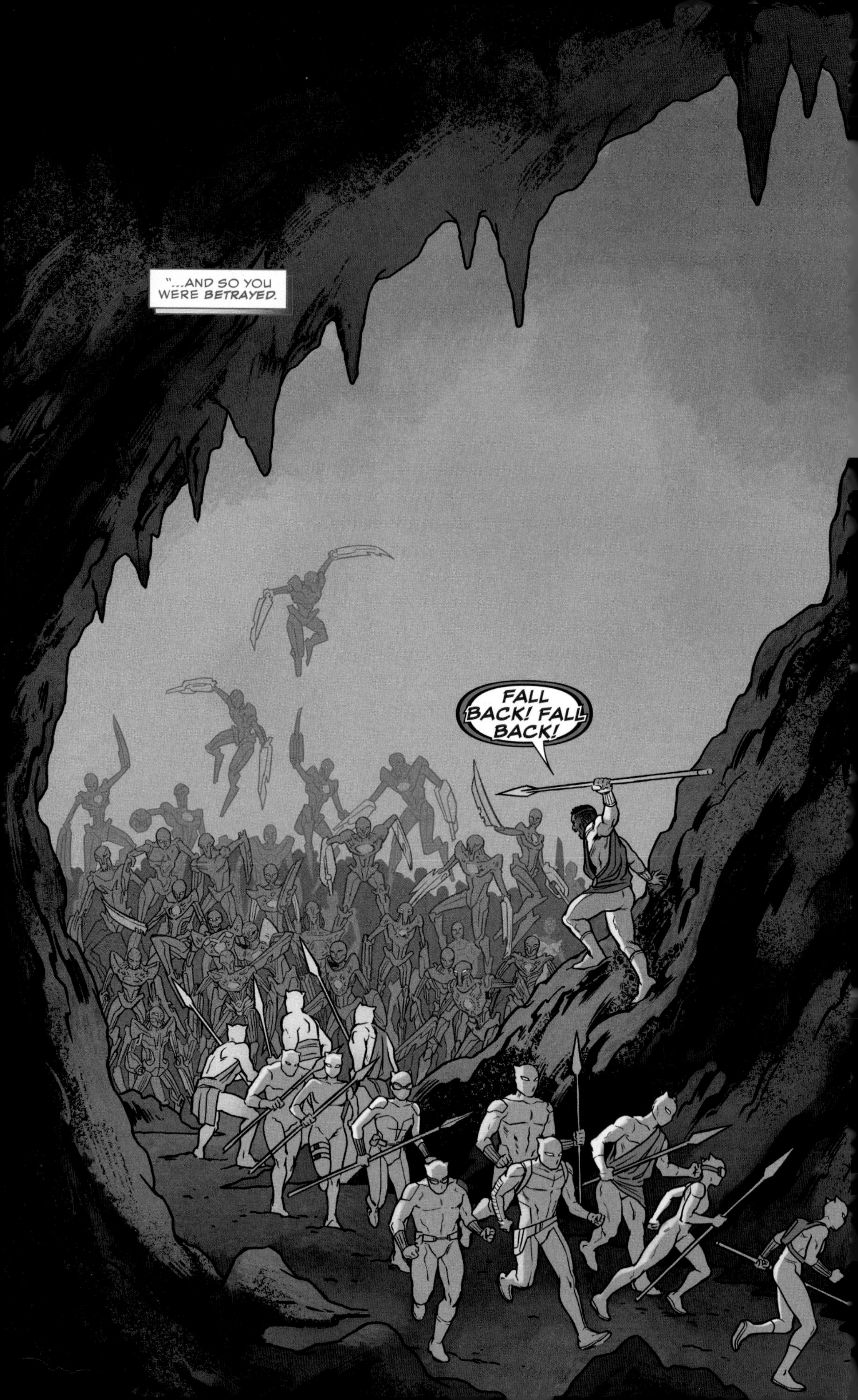
"...AND SO YOU WERE BETRAYED.
FALL BACK! FALL BACK!

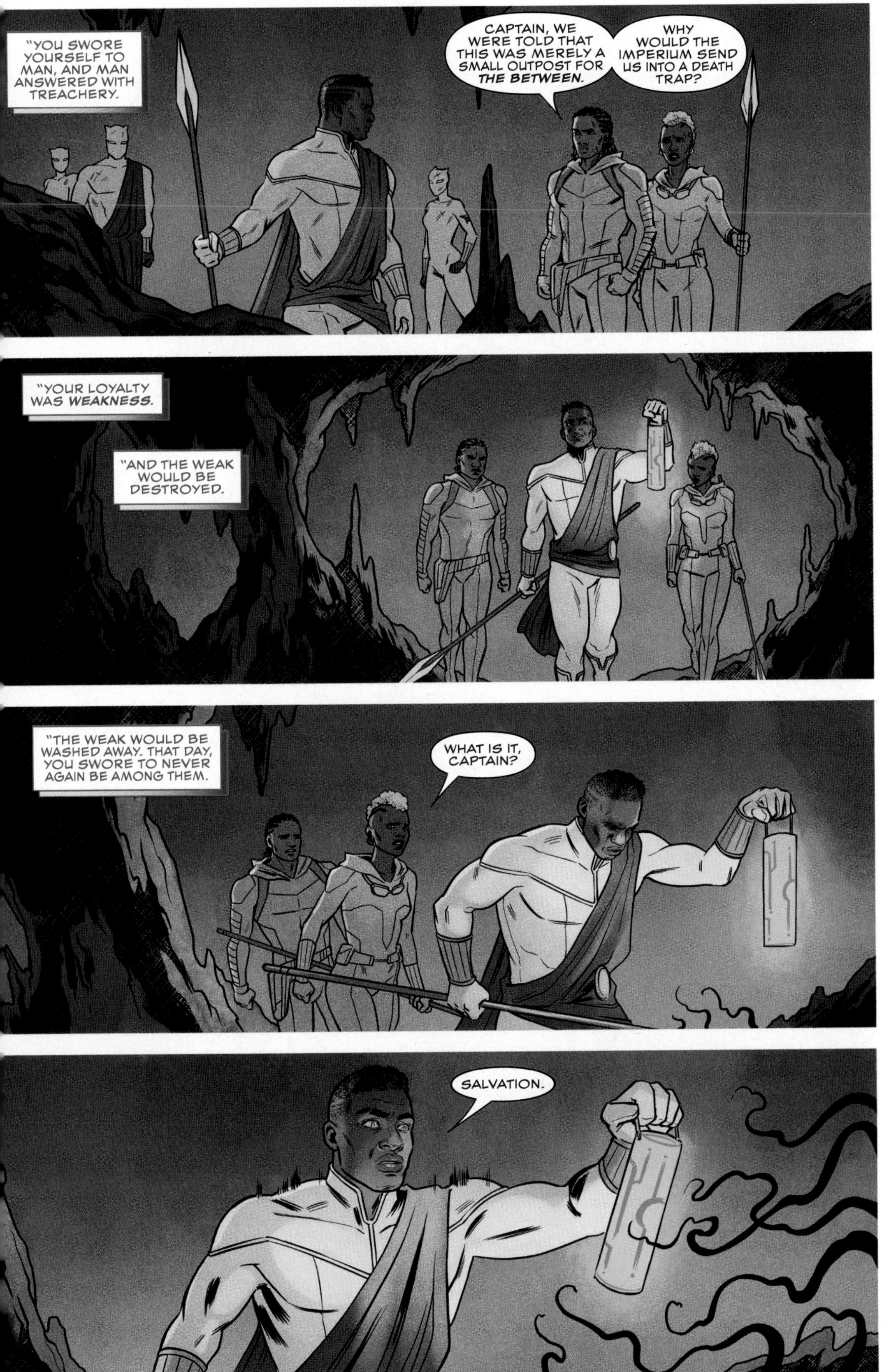
"YOU SWORE YOURSELF TO MAN, AND MAN ANSWERED WITH TREACHERY.
CAPTAIN, WE WERE TOLD THAT THIS WAS MERELY A SMALL OUTPOST FOR *THE BETWEEN.*
WHY WOULD THE IMPERIUM SEND US INTO A DEATH TRAP?
"YOUR LOYALTY WAS *WEAKNESS.*
"AND THE WEAK WOULD BE DESTROYED.
"THE WEAK WOULD BE WASHED AWAY. THAT DAY, YOU SWORE TO NEVER AGAIN BE AMONG THEM.
WHAT IS IT, CAPTAIN?
SALVATION.

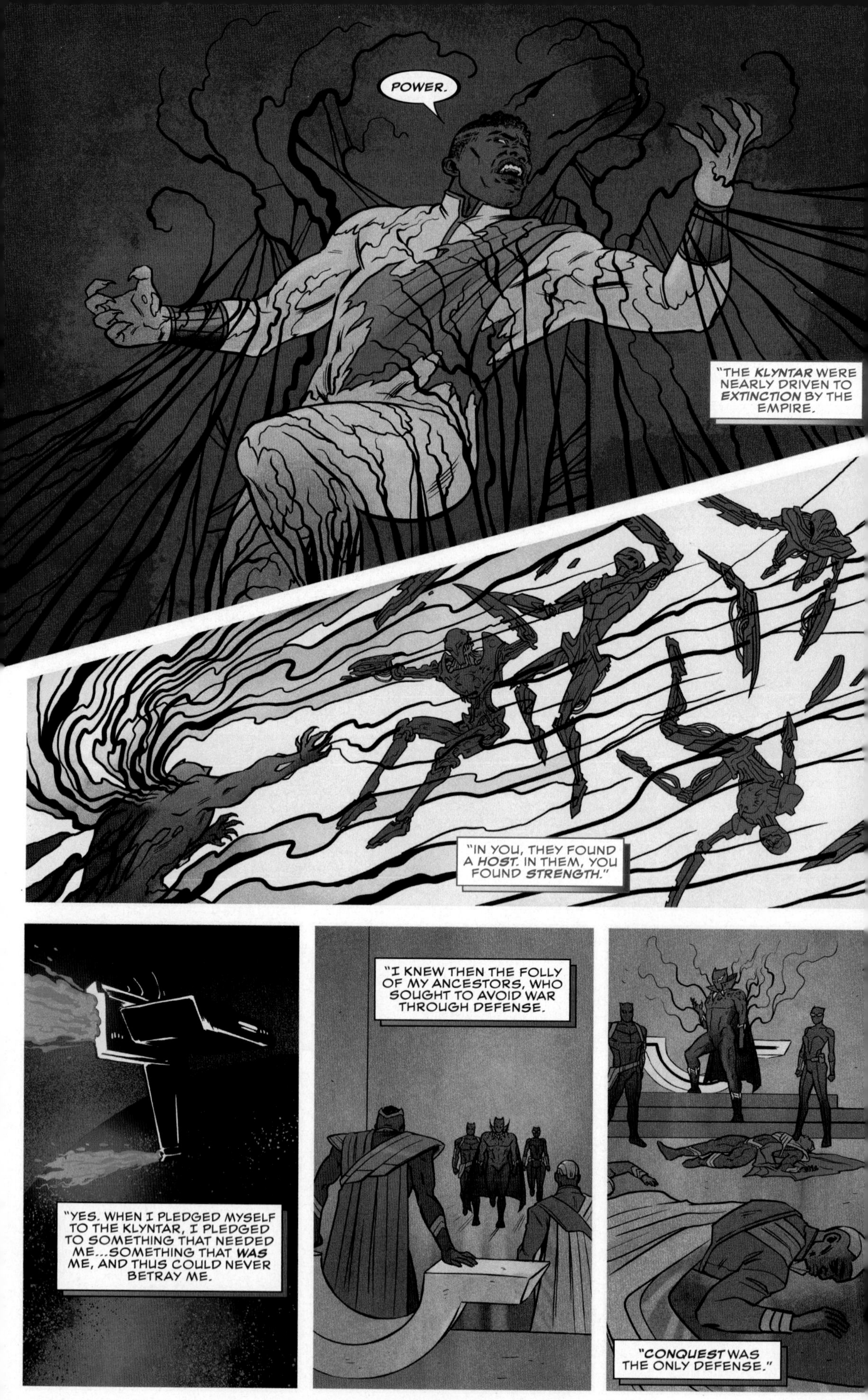
POWER.
"THE *KLYNTAR* WERE NEARLY DRIVEN TO *EXTINCTION* BY THE EMPIRE.
"IN YOU, THEY FOUND A *HOST.* IN THEM, YOU FOUND *STRENGTH.*"
"YES. WHEN I PLEDGED MYSELF TO THE KLYNTAR, I PLEDGED TO SOMETHING THAT NEEDED ME...SOMETHING THAT *WAS* ME, AND THUS COULD NEVER BETRAY ME.
"I KNEW THEN THE FOLLY OF MY ANCESTORS, WHO SOUGHT TO AVOID WAR THROUGH DEFENSE.
"*CONQUEST* WAS THE ONLY DEFENSE."

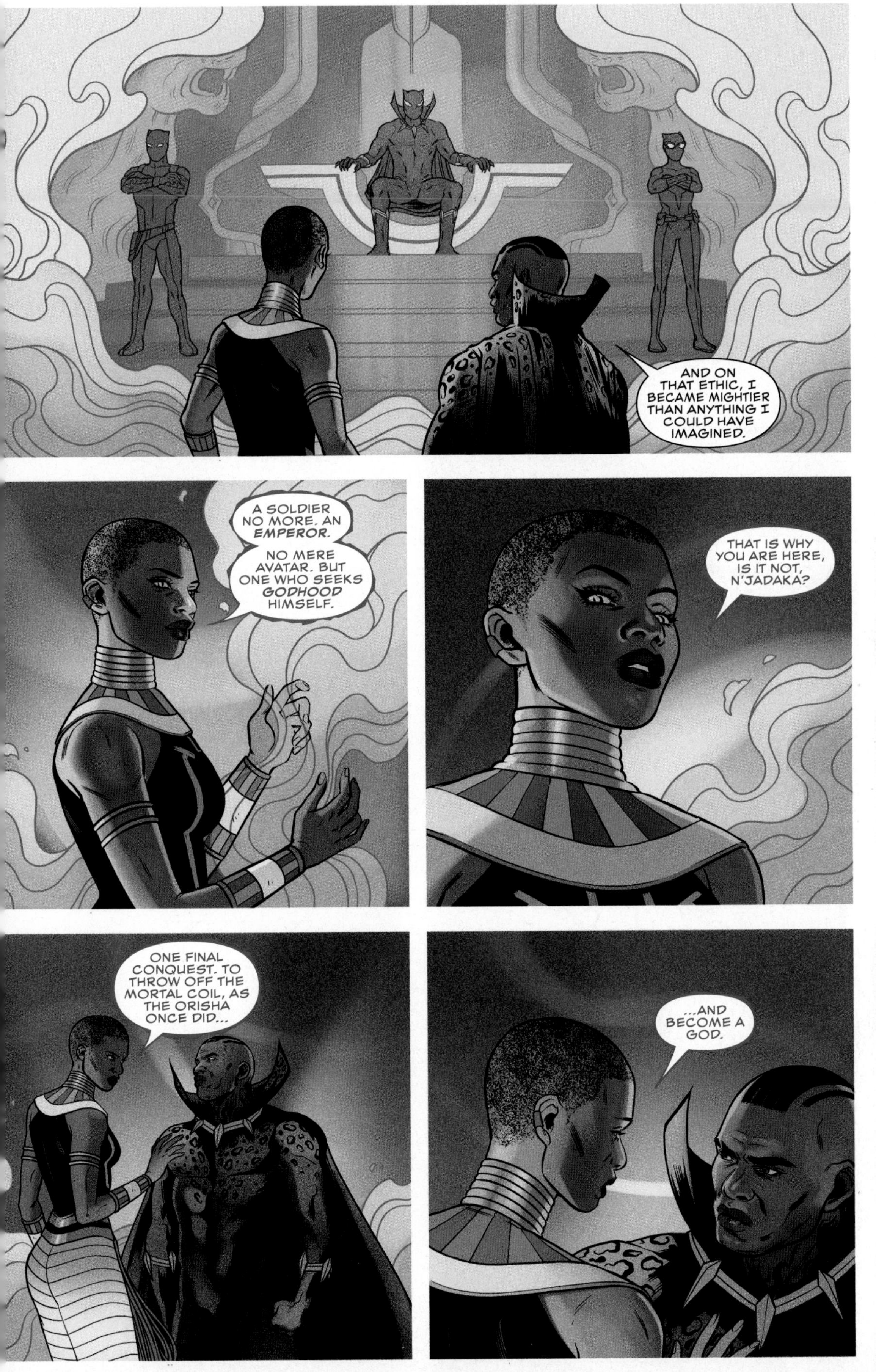
AND ON THAT ETHIC, I BECAME MIGHTIER THAN ANYTHING I COULD HAVE IMAGINED.
A SOLDIER NO MORE. AN *EMPEROR*.
NO MERE AVATAR. BUT ONE WHO SEEKS *GODHOOD* HIMSELF.
THAT IS WHY YOU ARE HERE, IS IT NOT, N'JADAKA?
ONE FINAL CONQUEST. TO THROW OFF THE MORTAL COIL, AS THE ORISHA ONCE DID...
...AND BECOME A GOD.

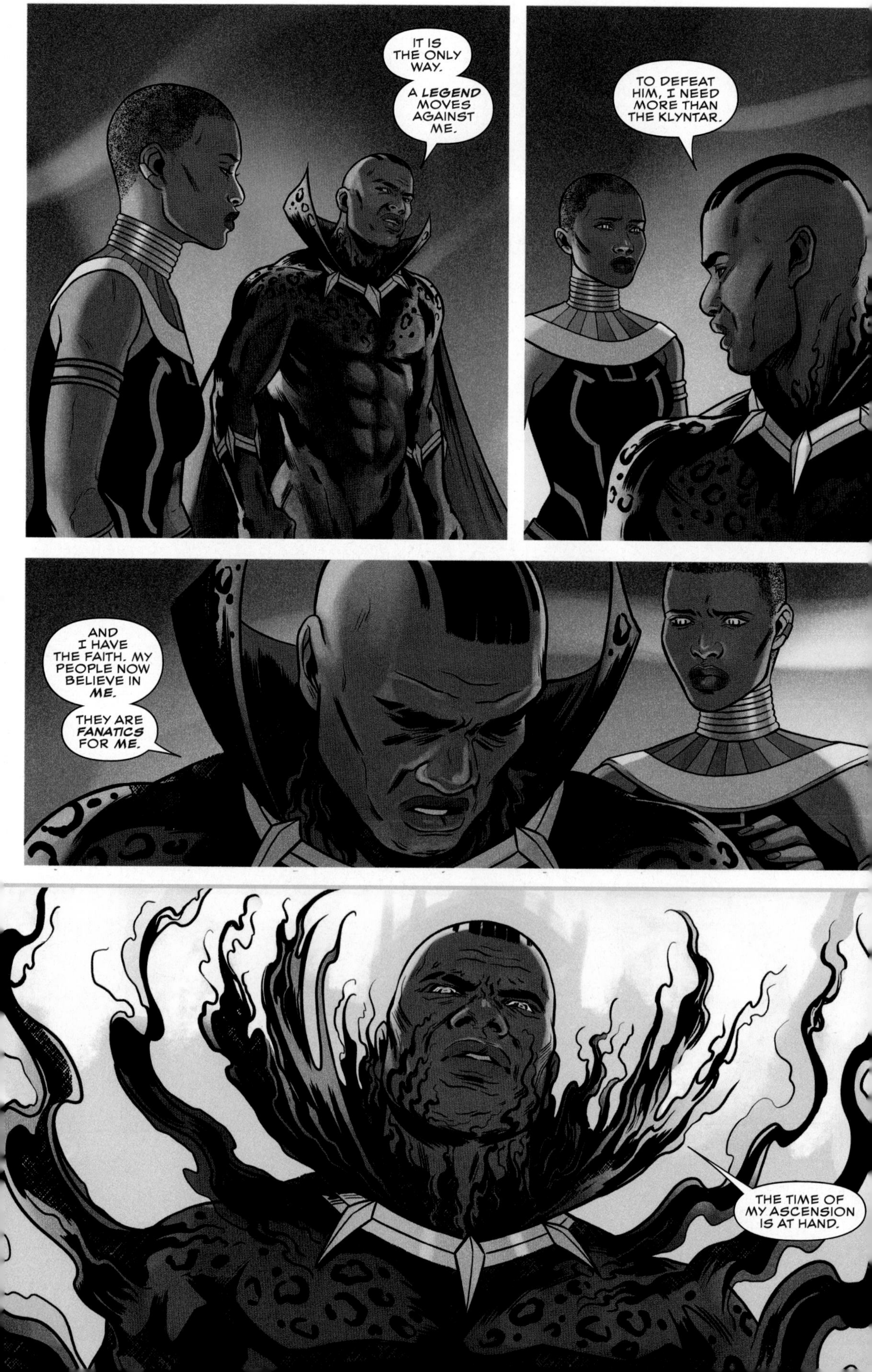
IT IS THE ONLY WAY.
A LEGEND MOVES AGAINST ME.
TO DEFEAT HIM, I NEED MORE THAN THE KLYNTAR.
AND I HAVE THE FAITH. MY PEOPLE NOW BELIEVE IN ME.
THEY ARE FANATICS FOR ME.
THE TIME OF MY ASCENSION IS AT HAND.

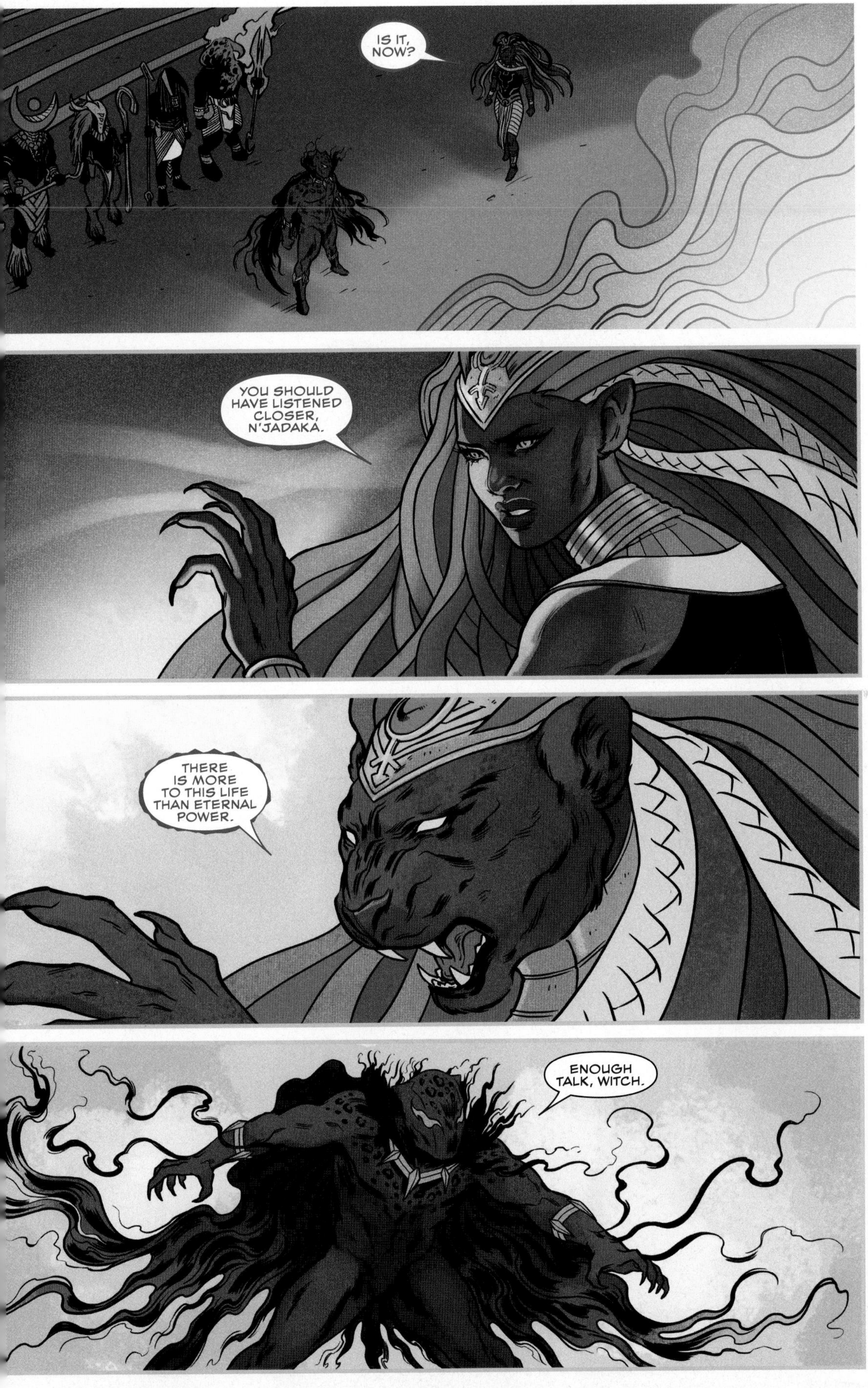
IS IT, NOW?
YOU SHOULD HAVE LISTENED CLOSER, N'JADAKA.
THERE IS MORE TO THIS LIFE THAN ETERNAL POWER.
ENOUGH TALK, WITCH.

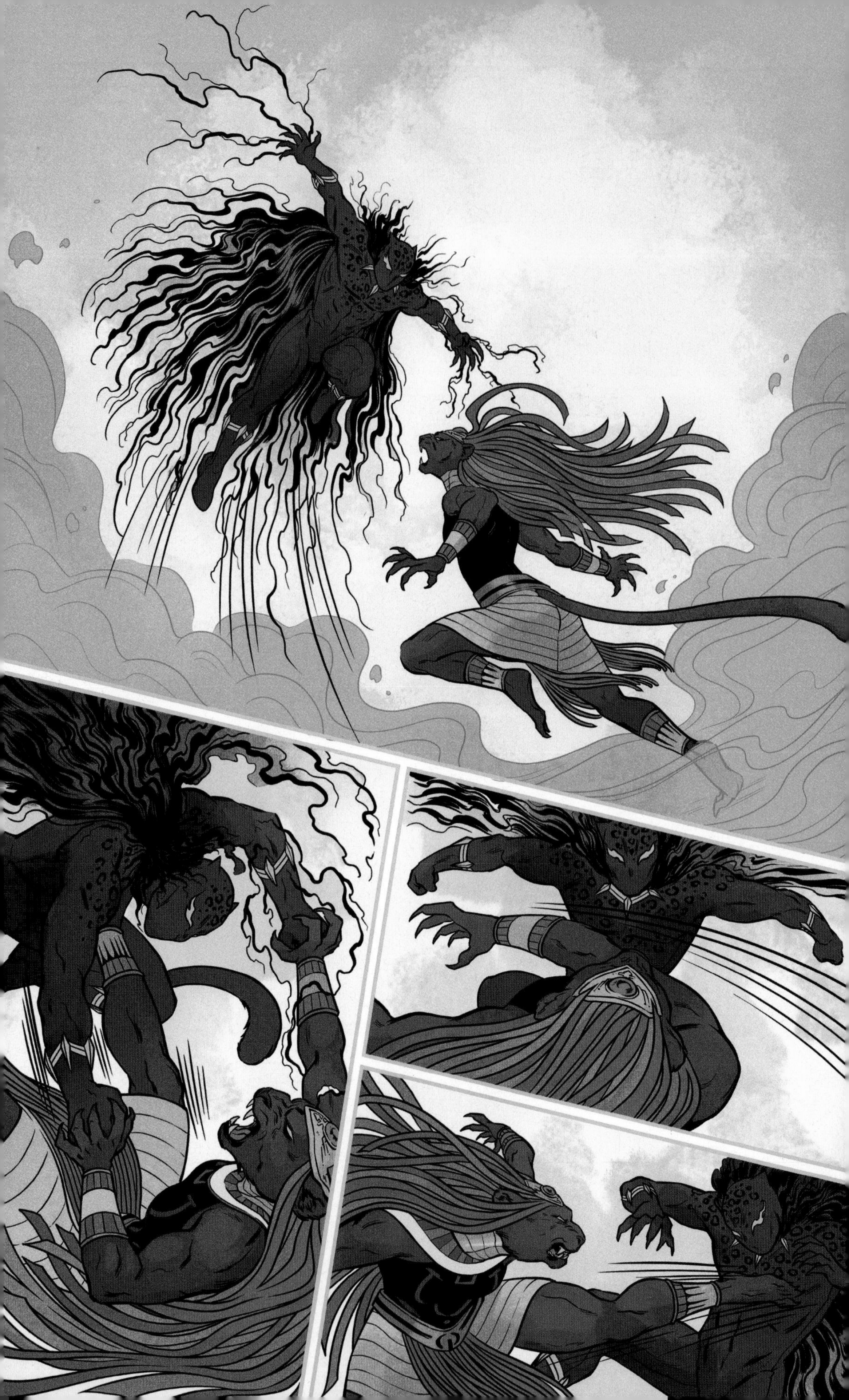

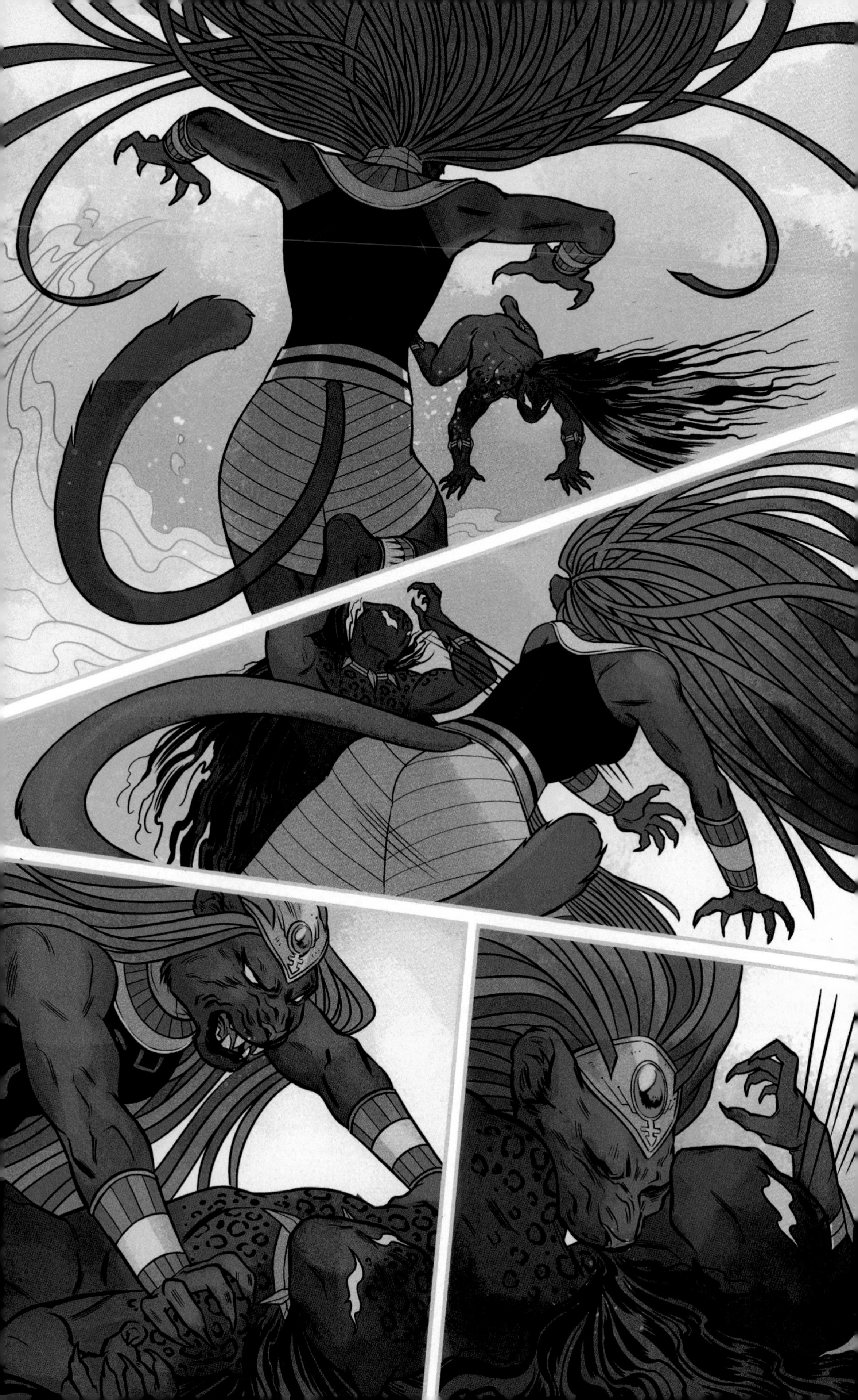

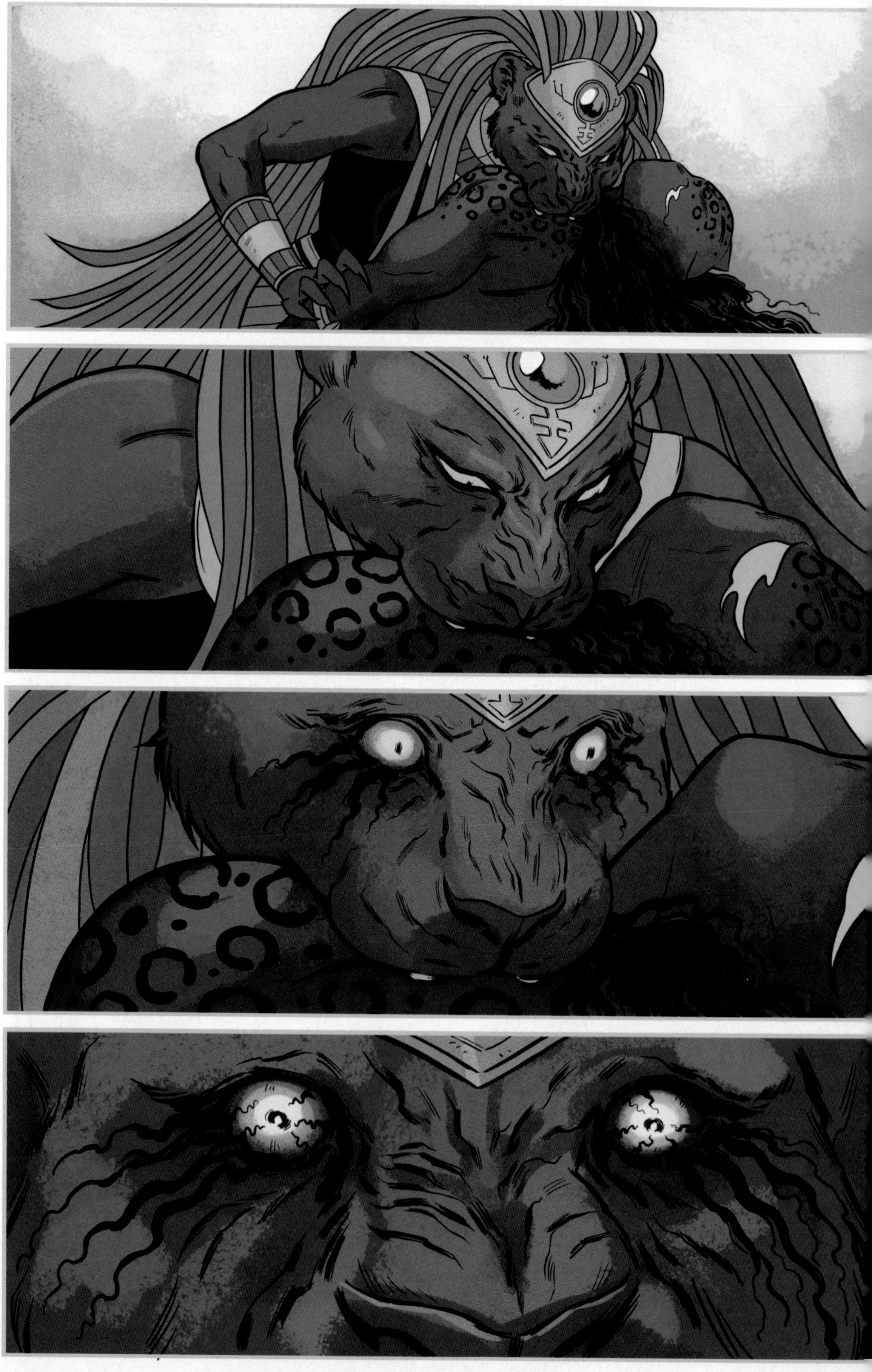

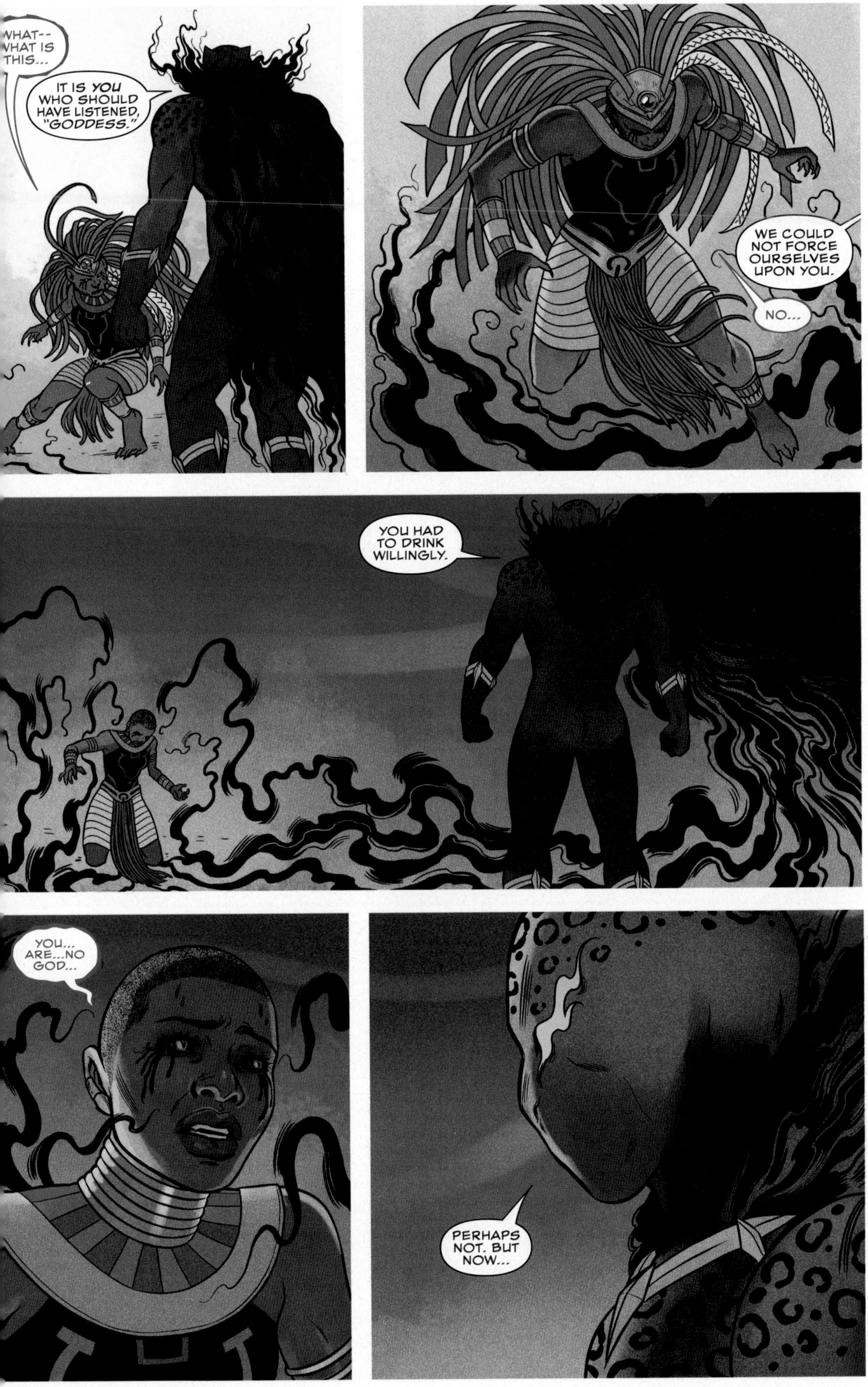
WHAT--
WHAT IS THIS...
IT IS *YOU* WHO SHOULD HAVE LISTENED, "GODDESS."
WE COULD NOT FORCE OURSELVES UPON YOU.
NO...
YOU HAD TO DRINK WILLINGLY.
YOU... ARE...NO GOD...
PERHAPS NOT. BUT NOW...

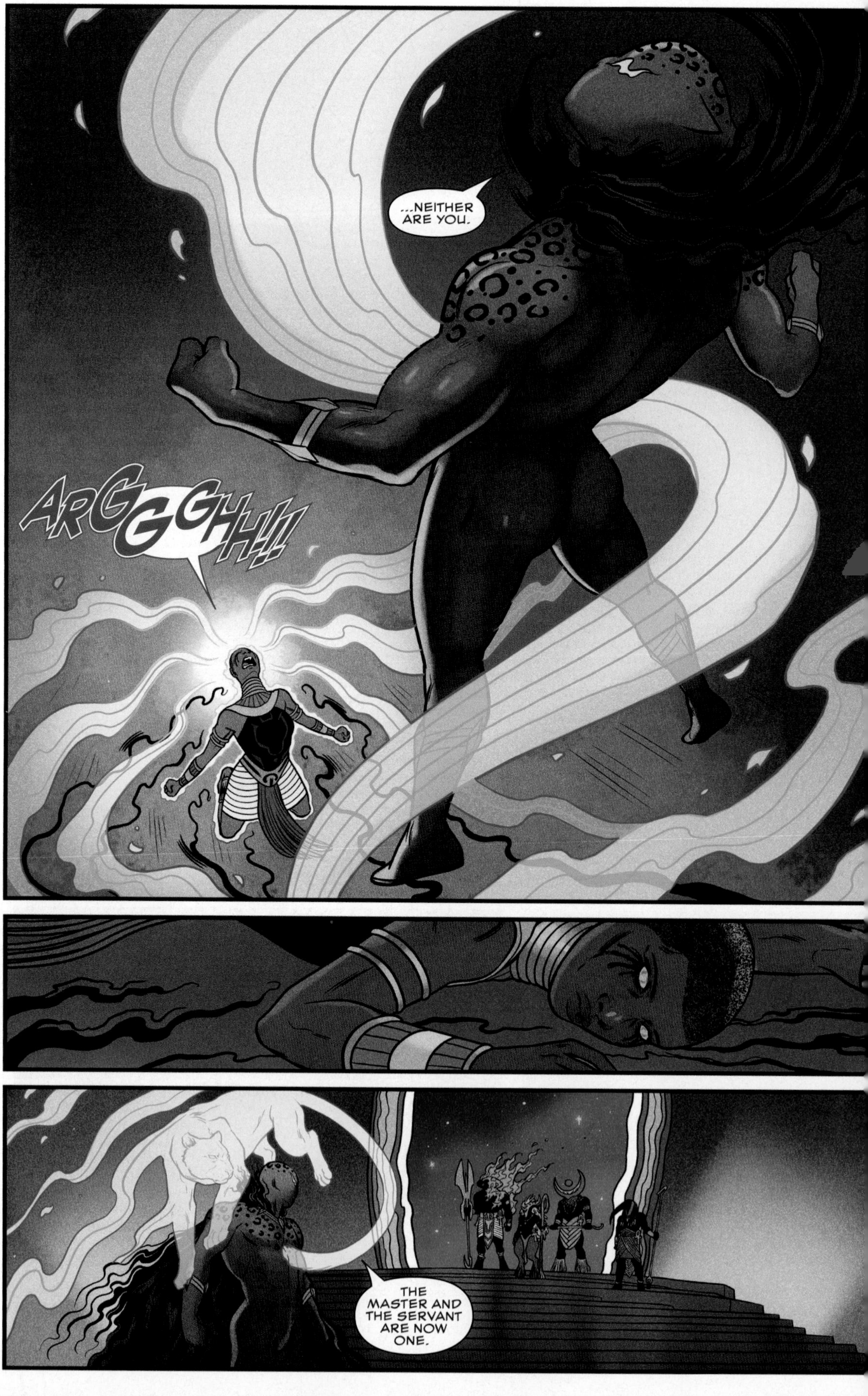
...NEITHER ARE YOU.
ARGGGHH!!!
THE MASTER AND THE SERVANT ARE NOW ONE.

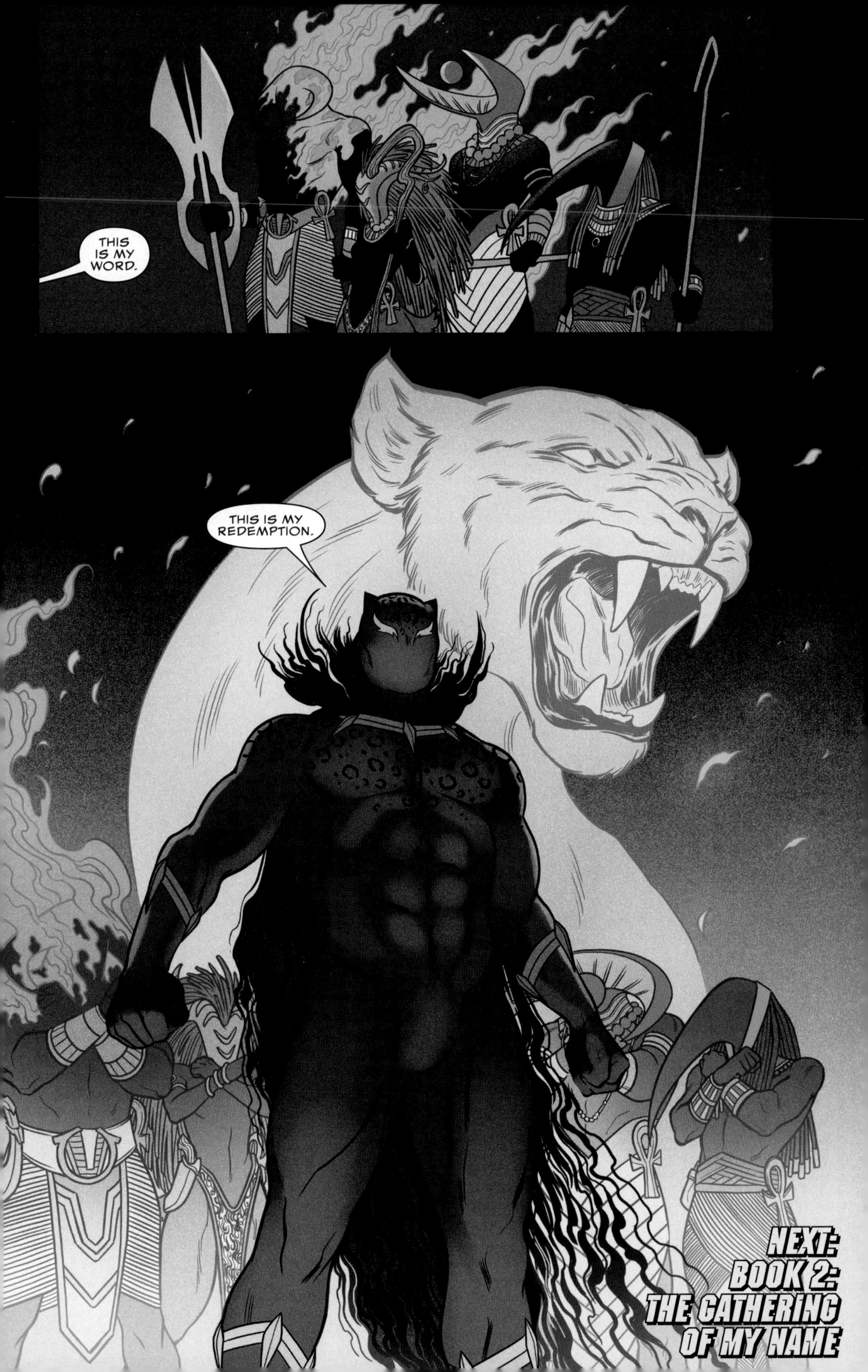
THIS IS MY WORD.
THIS IS MY REDEMPTION.
NEXT: BOOK 2: THE GATHERING OF MY NAME

OCCUPYING THE FAR REACHES OF THE UNIVERSE, THE INTERGALACTIC EMPIRE OF WAKANDA IS A SPRAWLING IMPERIU
MADE UP OF FIVE STAR CLUSTERS.

THE EARLY WAKANDAN SETTLERS OF THE BENHAZIN SYSTEM WERE INITIALLY PEACEFUL, PREFERRING TO REMAIN AMON THEIR OWN, AS WAS THE WAY OF THEIR FOREFATHERS. BUT A SERIES OF ATTEMPTED INVASIONS CONVINCED THE SETTLE THAT SELF-DEFENSE WOULD NOT BE ENOUGH FOR THIS BARBARIC PORTION OF SPACE — PREVENTIVE STRIKES MUST BE MA THEN, AFTER THE WAKANDANS MASTERED THE TECHNOLOGY OF DEEP-SPACE PASSAGE, THOSE PREVENTIVE STRIKES BECA PREVENTIVE OCCUPATION AND FINALLY PREVENTIVE CONQUEST.

ARMED WITH SUPERIOR TECHNOLOGY AND A TYPICAL WAKANDAN FEROCITY IN BATTLE, THE CONQUERORS QUICKLY BECAME MASTERS OF THEIR CORNER OF THE UNIVERSE — AND THERE IS NO REASON TO BELIEVE THEY WILL SIMPLY SETTLE FOR THAT CORN

AS THE WAKANDANS CHANGED THEIR CORNER OF THE UNIVERSE, SO IT CHANGED THEM.
UNTIL SOME...WERE BARELY WAKANDAN AT ALL.

EARLY IN IMPERIAL HISTORY, WAKANDANS MASTERED GENE THERAPY, ALLOWING WAKANDANS TO BE EXTREMELY LONG-LIVED. NOW ALL SUBJECTS OF THE EMPIRE UNDERGO THIS PROCESS AND NOT ONLY LIV LONGER, BUT REMAIN IN THEIR PRIME FOR MOST OF THEIR LIVES. BUT ONE SECT OF IMPERIAL WAKANDAN DID NOT THINK THIS PRACTICE WENT FAR ENOUGH. THIS SECT EMBRACED THE FORBIDDEN PRACTICE OF TRANSCORPREALISM — THE TRANSMISSION OF THE "SELF" OUT OF THE FLESH AND INTO MACHINES. IMPERI WAKANDANS BELIEVED THIS PRACTICE TO OFFEND THE ORISHA AND THUS SCORNED THE BETWEEN.

THE BETWEEN APPEAR AS VAGUELY HUMANOID BUT WITH COLD DEAD EYES. THEIR SKIN IS DEEP SILVER, AN THEIR BODIES ARE MADE OF A KIND OF MUTATED VIBRANIUM THAT ALLOWS THEIR LIMBS TO BE REFORME INTO VARIOUS TOOLS — OR WEAPONS.

TAKE A LOOK AT DESIGNS FOR THE BETWEEN BY KEV WALKER, THE ARTIST OF OUR NEXT ARC. AND ST TUNED FOR MORE ABOUT N'JADAKA AND HIS TAKEOVER OF THE EMPIRE — NEXT MONTH WILL BE FU OF REVELATIONS!

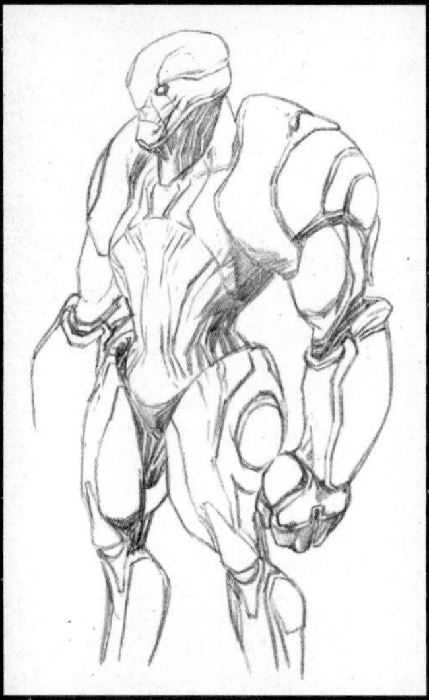

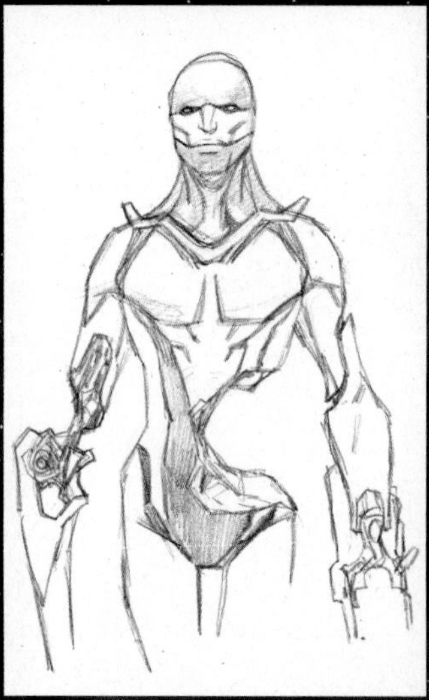

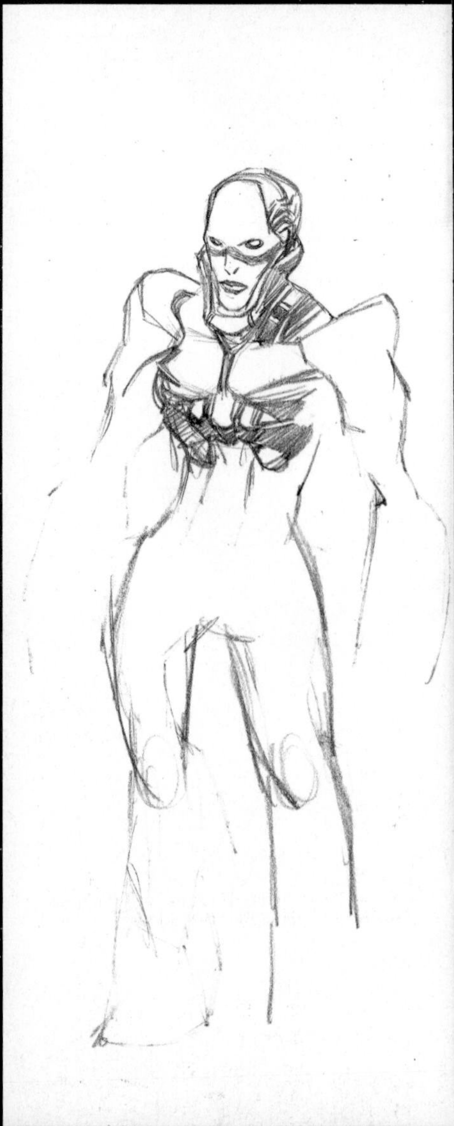

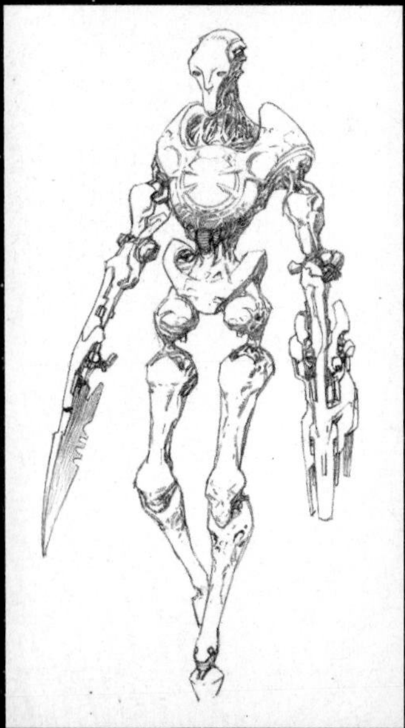

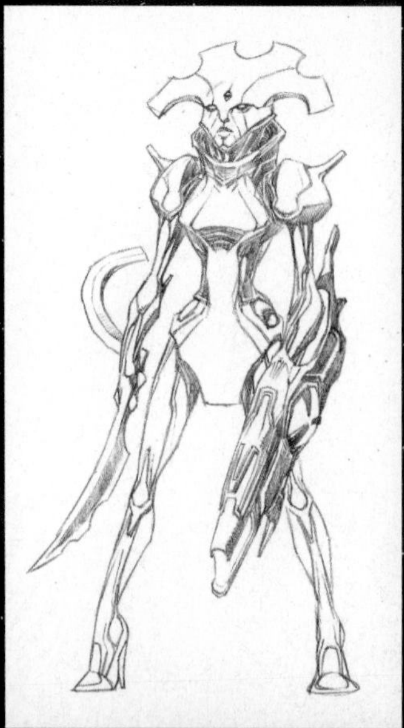

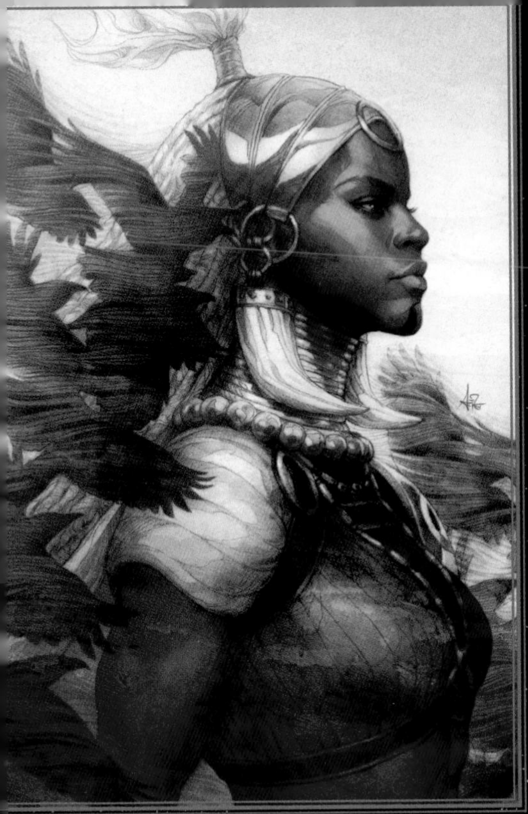

Artgerm
1 VARIANT

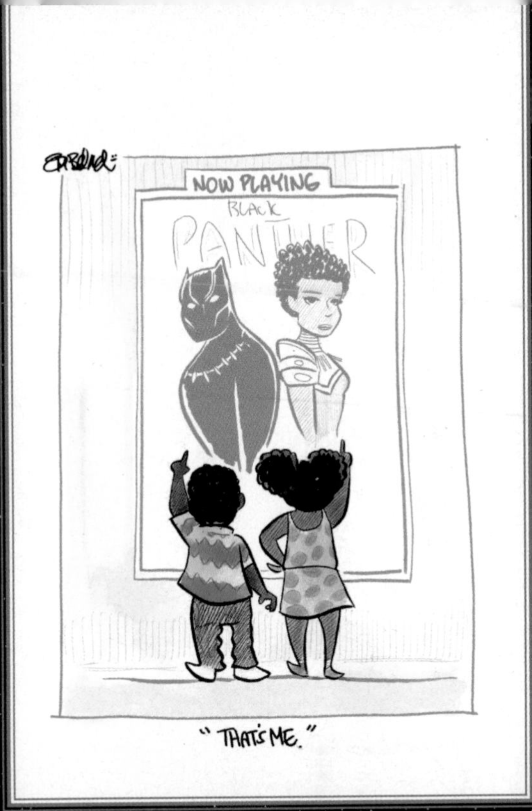
NOW PLAYING
BLACK
PANTHER
"THAT'S ME."

Tom Beland & Jordie Bellaire
1 VARIANT

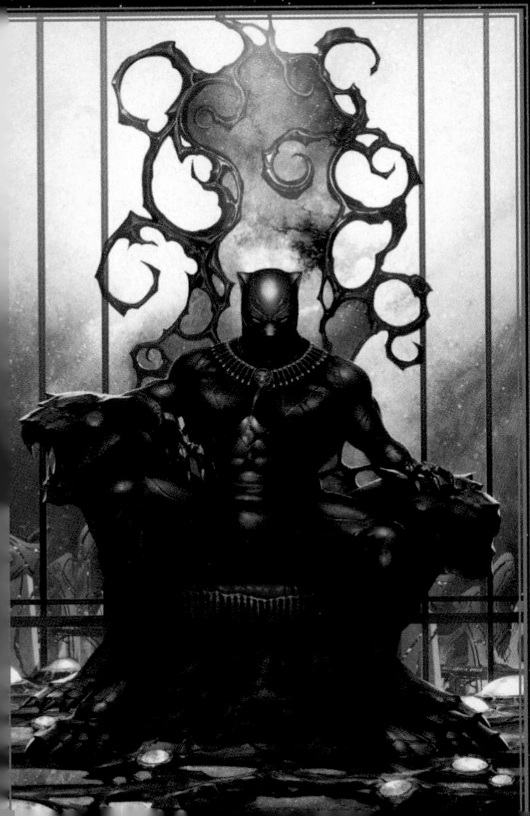

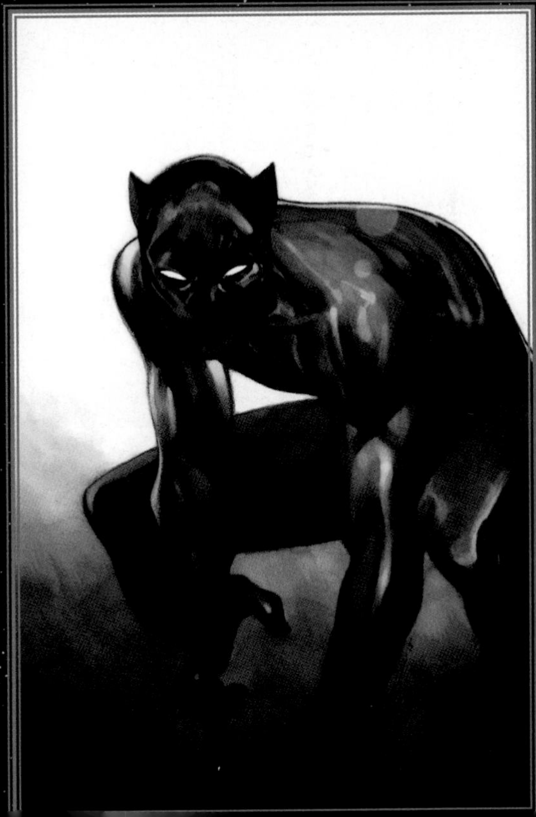

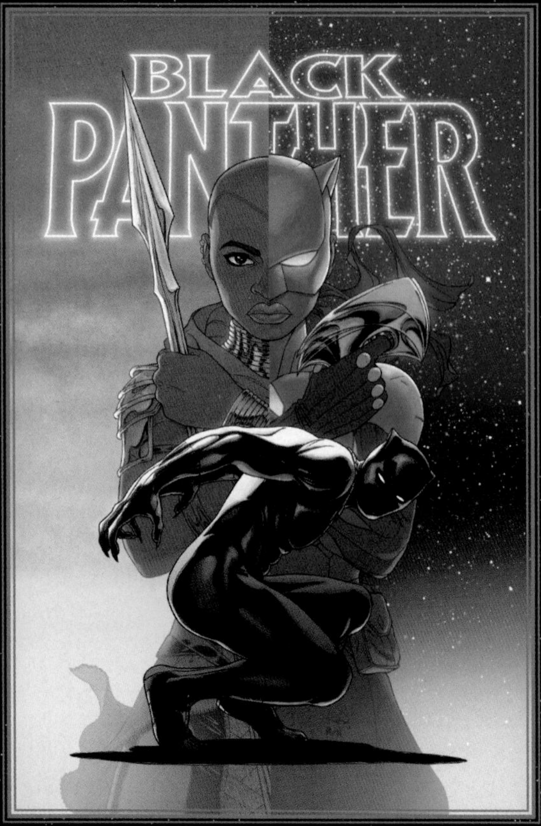
BLACK
PANTHER

Russell Dauterman & Matthew Wilson
2 VARIANT

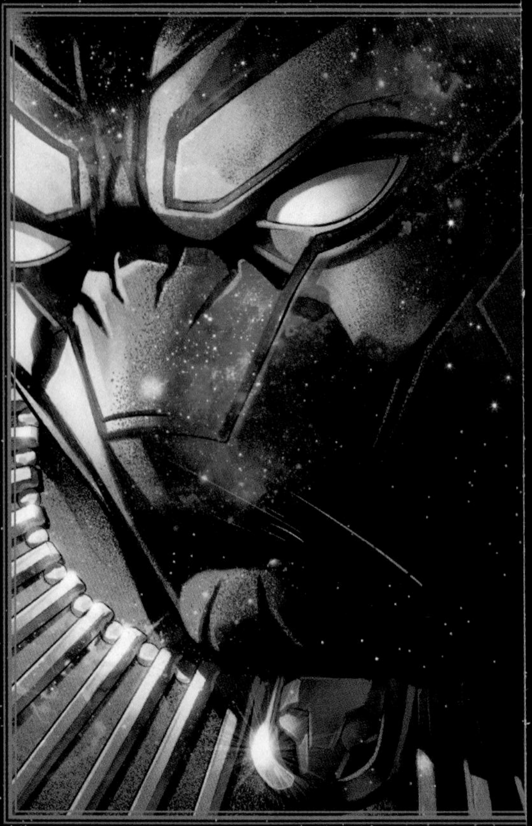

Jamal Campbell
3 VARIANT

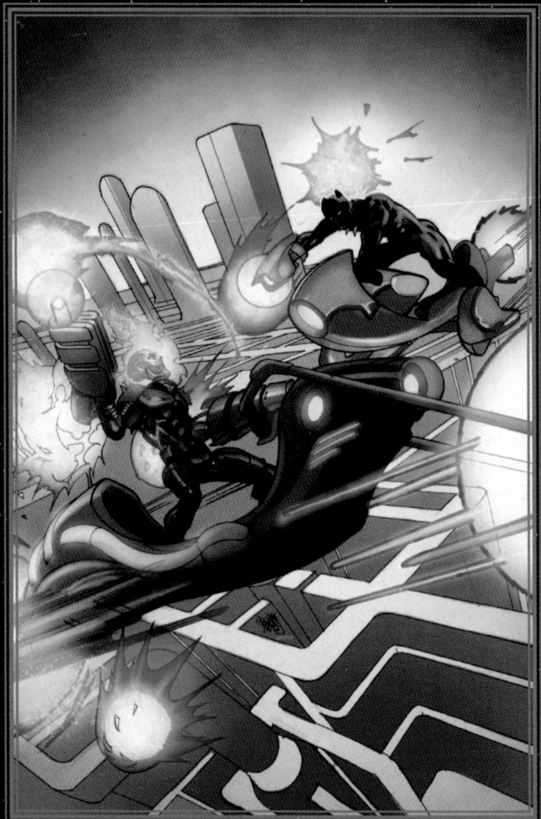

Pasqual Ferry & Chris Sotomayor
4 VS. COMIC GHOST RIDER VARIANT

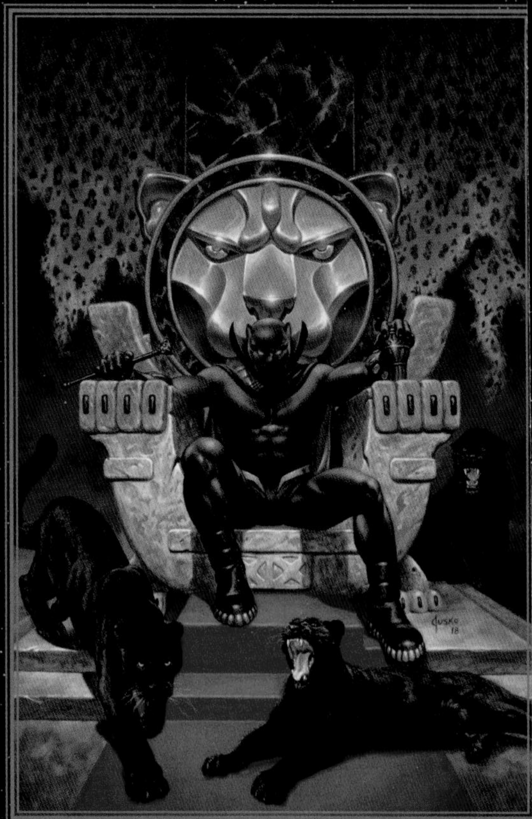

Joe Jusko
5 MARVEL KNIGHTS 20TH ANNIVERSARY VARIANT